ADVANCE PRAISE FOR **A Long Way to Go**

"Darrell Cleveland's *A Long Way to Go* is a timely and thought-provoking collection of readings that places a much-needed focus on the experiences of African Americans in higher education. The chapters capture the struggles and accomplishments of African American graduate students and faculty and speak to contemporary issues that affect this group at a critical time for African Americans in higher education. As African American graduate students and faculty continue to bring their gifts and talents to academia, this book will serve as a 'beacon of light' on resilience, survival, and excellence."

Linda C. Tillman, Associate Professor,
Wayne State University, Detroit, Michigan

"*A Long Way to Go: Conversations About Race by African American Faculty and Graduate Students* proposes topics of discussion that are critical to higher education. The subtopics proposed for the book are very enlightening, and the authors are individuals who are not only knowledgeable on the subtopics but who have experienced what they are writing about. The book would be educational for everyone and very helpful for African Americans aspiring to become college students and faculty members. A book on this topic would be very powerful and of deep interest to many."

Carol L. Patitu, Associate Professor
Buffalo State University, Buffalo, New York

A Long Way to Go

Higher Ed

Questions about the Purpose(s) of Colleges & Universities

Norm Denzin, Josef Progler, Joe L. Kincheloe, Shirley R. Steinberg

General Editors

Vol. 14

PETER LANG
New York • Washington, D.C./Baltimore • Bern
Frankfurt am Main • Berlin • Brussels • Vienna • Oxford

A Long Way to Go

Conversations about
Race by African American
Faculty and Graduate Students

EDITED BY
Darrell Cleveland

PETER LANG
New York • Washington, D.C./Baltimore • Bern
Frankfurt am Main • Berlin • Brussels • Vienna • Oxford

Library of Congress Cataloging-in-Publication Data

A long way to go: conversations about race by African American faculty
and graduate students / edited by Darrell Cleveland.
p. cm. — (Higher ed; v. 14)
Includes bibliographical references and index.
1. African American college teachers—Social conditions. 2. African
American graduate students—Social conditions. 3. African Americans—
Education (Graduate) 4. African Americans—Race identity.
I. Cleveland, Darrell. II. Series.
LC2781.5.B74   378.1'2'08996073—dc21   2002156039
ISBN 0-8204-6366-3
ISSN 1523-9551

Bibliographic information published by Die Deutsche Bibliothek.
Die Deutsche Bibliothek lists this publication in the "Deutsche
Nationalbibliografie"; detailed bibliographic data is available
on the Internet at http://dnb.ddb.de/.

Cover design by Lisa Barfield

The paper in this book meets the guidelines for permanence and durability
of the Committee on Production Guidelines for Book Longevity
of the Council of Library Resources.

Printed in the United States of America

CONTENTS

PART II
What Is It Like to Be an African American Faculty Member?

Lee Jones

FOREWORD

As I reflect on the espoused mission and goals of the academy, I am reminded of the countless people—seen and unseen, heard and unheard—who have impacted my life. I often tell my students of various races and backgrounds, "Be careful in selecting your careers because there will be times when you will question your sanity about why you selected that particular profession."

I also tell them, "You should never work in an environment if you do not feel good about getting out of bed and coming to work." I have held to this credo for nearly twenty years; but one of the things I did not understand when I decided to live by this creed was that the academy can be a plethora of contradictions. On the one hand, it takes the stance that it is one of the most liberal and democratic of organizational enterprises. On the other hand, it rarely accepts the challenge of looking at its practices and seeing the constant injustices it inflicts upon African American and other underrepresented groups.

The high-profile public debate surrounding our mentor, scholar, and statesman Cornel West gives cause to reflect on how far we have actually *not* come in the academy. Whether one agrees with his ideology or not, the mere fact that Harvard University challenged him not only to examine how he spends his time but also to conform to the status quo is mind-boggling and extremely discouraging. Such a situation makes it very difficult to encourage aspiring African American graduate students to choose higher education as a profession. It's discouraging because Cornel West represents the true essence of a scholar. What he postulates is sound; his work truly presents opportunities for critical dialogue among scholars in the many fields his work bridges. Additionally, his work has consistently been well regarded and critically analyzed by some of the most renowned intellectuals in higher education.

Furthermore, this debate over his work is discouraging because it is being attacked by those who not only refuse to see their own arrogance but also refuse to broaden their limited definitions of scholarship. Such conservatism leaves little hope for developing scholars like those whose work appear in this important book to find a place in the monolithic culture of higher education.

As I travel around the country, African American and Latino students often ask me, "Why should I choose to pursue an advanced degree and teach at the collegiate level when I won't be free to teach and produce scholarship that reflects my own experiences?" I have very few satisfying responses to this question, but my response is always fraught with hope that one day our persistent efforts to transform higher education into a true community of scholars will be realized!

I would be remiss if I did not acknowledge the diligence and hard work of Black, Brown, and White scholars, who have helped us to this point. I truly believe that we have made significant progress in opening the doors to higher education. Institutions like Florida State University, University of Michigan, University of Wisconsin, and a few others have been on the forefront of transforming higher education. I hasten to add, however, that although we have come so far, we still have far to go. It would be nice to dedicate oneself to a profession in higher education where one's day would be occupied by such activities as teaching, research, and service, as our White counterparts do. However, the truth of the matter is that, regardless of whether African Americans choose to ignore the challenges or roll up their sleeves and actively participate to help to change the culture, we must continue to serve multiple roles. These multifarious duties include, but are not limited to, serving as mentors for many African American students and as an experiential group for many White students who, through their own isolation, have never been taught by an African American professor. Not only are we African Americans asked to participate in an academic setting whose ethos we have not helped to develop, but we are also asked to be the constant experts on African American issues.

This plethora of contradictions first manifests itself when we are told, whether subtly and blatantly, that our research interests (passions) are slanted toward "minority issues" and therefore do not fit a predetermined, narrow view of "authentic" scholarship. Not only are we forced to reevaluate our research agenda, but we are also forced to struggle with philosophical, spiritual, and psychological internal debates. The issues that confront African American men in the academy are not unlike issues that women and many underrepresented groups confront. What makes African American issues more pronounced are the very low numbers of Black Ph.D. holders, and what the noted international scholar Na'im Akbar calls the "stimulus value" placed upon us. I am sure that our views on equity and equality in the academy are as diverse as we are as individuals.

This important and timely book, *A Long Way to Go: Conversations about Race by African American Faculty and Graduate Students,* is not only timely and necessary, but it is also badly needed during a time when we are addressing a crisis of morale and motivation within higher education. Higher education continues to flounder. African Americans in higher education can have the feeling that we are participating in our own diversity demise as we attempt to open the doors for diversity even while the opportunities for people to truly express their own ideological perspectives are shutting down.

Within this book, you will find an exploration of issues by current African American faculty and/or graduate students aspiring to enter the ranks of the professorate. Each chapter details interconnecting phenomena of similar themes that build on decades of exploration documented in the growing literature on faculty diversity.

I applaud the efforts of the scholars and developing scholars who desire to keep these issues on the forefront of the higher education agenda. I commend Darrell Cleveland for assembling these essays, as they will surely continue to inform us all. After all, higher education has yet to realize that the bottom line is results, and anything else is rhetoric!

INTRODUCTION

When I decided to pursue my Ph.D. in education, I had no idea what I was getting into. I mean, I knew that I would take the necessary coursework, write a dissertation, successfully defend the dissertation, and graduate. I assumed that because I was entering a doctoral program at a well-respected predominantly White institution (PWI) that I would be well received by faculty, administrators, and other graduate students. Within two weeks of beginning my program, I realized that this was not the case and that I was treading in unsafe space.

As an African American male graduate student at a PWI, I expected to challenge and to be challenged by the status quo in higher education, a microcosm of society (Jones, 2000). Knowing this, I realized and accepted the fact that I was entering an environment that would attempt to resocialize me by inventing and reinventing the social White identity presented by the curriculum. Because I have been socialized to form my personal identity and my social identity through my own life experiences, I chose to accept the role of a student in search of knowledge by allowing myself to become resocialized—in essence, giving up my social identity to achieve status while maintaining my caste position.

Like our enslaved ancestors, we accept the master's terms for surviving on the plantation, settling for crumbs instead of the whole meal. In the end, we're still alive, but our souls die a little every day, just so we can stay alive to make it better for those who follow us. This hope gives us the strength to go on; but, admittedly, pessimism gnaws our hearts and we struggle against the weight of the institutional silence imposed on us.

As a minority born into a "lower" caste, I was/am subjected to laws and expectations that do not necessarily serve my best interest, therefore minimizing my human agency. As a result, my acquisition of knowledge was regulated by written and unwritten rules set forth by instructors, the school of education, and the university as a whole. After realizing that I was not being taken seriously and that I was being judged primarily on my skin color rather than my merits, I began to rethink my position as an African American graduate student at a PWI. As an assertive, confident, and sometimes outspoken individual, I shared my thoughts, feelings, and beliefs about the inequities in education (public and higher) and society with the rest of my cohort and instructors. By speaking and writing what I really felt and by not sugar-coating the issues, I deviated from what was perceived to be the norm in graduate school at a PWI. This, in turn, produced both necessary and unnecessary conflict. As a result of this conflict, tension mounted between me and my instructors, cohort members, and school of education. After careful self-evaluation or checking myself, I chose not to allow the academy or "plantation" to dictate my behavior and attempted to force others to treat me as an individual rather than as a statistic. In short, I was not going to let them shrug off the responsibility for their nonsupportive environments, naive assumptions, and inappropriate behavior. Thus the first half of the title of this book emerged—*A Long Way To Go*.

As a member of an "inferior" caste in American society, I was assigned readings that revealed contradictions about the classism, racism, sexism, and other oppressive dimensions that I lived with daily. However, the readings and assignments that documented these dimensions of oppression by disclosing the politics and special interests behind the language used the same language to promote oppressive dimensions within my doctoral program. As an up-and-coming scholar, I consequently felt that the assigned readings and assignments invalidated and devalued me because of my caste position in American society. As an African American student, I was moving up in social class and status, but I still belonged to the same social caste. Because society has placed me in an inferior caste, I did not feel emancipated by my schooling, even though the knowledge I acquired was supposed to empower me. This, I would argue, had everything to do with my skin color. Hence, these issues substantiate that in American higher education, we have a great need to break our silences.

Now in my first full-time position after completing my Ph.D., I still struggle with the racial dynamics at a PWI. As the only Black male professor at a small predominantly White Catholic liberal arts institution, I still inhabit an unsafe space. When I entered the classroom and met my students for the first time, their loud chatter instantly became silence and the shock on their faces was visible. Being Black is one thing, but being young, Black, and male is another. Immediately most students assumed that I was a student—a surprise for them in itself because most of them had attended parochial schools and had never taken classes with Black students or any minority for that matter. When I introduced myself as the professor of the class, I could see the various expressions of shock, amazement, disgust, surprise, and discomfort. Without planning to, I began to speak about my training, trying to convince the students and myself that I was qualified to be there. After the initial shock wore off, students then began to challenge me about my syllabus. "I don't see how we can possibly do all this work." "Can we drop one of the assignments?" "I don't know where I am going to get the time." Much to their dismay, the syllabus stayed the same. I later learned that students complained that I gave too much work. Fortunately, my department supported me. However, moving into the faculty role presented many obstacles because of my skin color.

A Long Way To Go: Conversations about Race by African American Faculty and Graduate Students highlights the experiences of graduate students pursuing Ph.D.'s and of faculty members across the country who successfully navigate in academic waters despite hostile environments and obstacles that cause many to leave the academy or never enter it at all. African American students contemplating terminal degrees are often advised to and/or have to settle for pursuing their degrees at PWIs. Many African American students earn their bachelors' degree at PWIs and are assimilated to the White culture, curricula, and teaching styles of higher learning (Taylor, 1989). However, because PWIs are tailored to White students, many African American graduate and potential graduate students see graduate school as unfriendly and frightening. In far too many cases, this appearance turns out to be reality.

To successfully negotiate graduate education at a PWI, individuals must meet "White" standards, even though these standards are inconsistent with the learning styles of African Americans. These standards include but are not limited to high GRE scores (or the desired measure for a particular discipline), high grade point averages, high writing standards, and in some cases a good "fit," meaning one is willing to assimilate (Delgado, 1998; Easley, 1993; Sedlacek, 1999; Suen, 1983). Individuals who do not meet these standards often struggle in graduate school at PWIs. Even for those who do, hostile environments, attitudes of indifference, ignorance, and other issues all emerge as challenges. This situation can breed intimidation, isolation, unnecessary stress, dread, and inferiority; eventually individuals find themselves silenced (Benton, 2001; Delpit, 1995). Although this book is not the first aimed at African American graduate students and faculty members, it offers concrete strategies for completing graduate school and succeeding in the academy.

A Long Way To Go: Conversations about Race by African American Faculty and Graduate Students is divided into four parts. Part I, "Journey to the Ivory Tower," highlights the experiences of African American students working toward terminal degrees at PWIs. Fred Bonner and Marchetta Evans launch this section with their discussion of the on-going struggle of African American students at PWIs to find their voice, comparing and contrasting the experiences of men and women and discussing factors that impact their matriculation: campus climate, academic integration and mentoring, social integration, identity development, self-perception, and family influence.

Current statistics reveal that a disproportionately low number of African

Americans are earning doctoral and professional degrees. Richard Milner considers four influences on this high attrition rate: the lack of value and respect, invalidating stereotypes, misconceptions of expertise, and alienation. Milner challenges faculty to mitigate these influences by making the implicit explicit, mentoring, and developing culturally appropriate advising. He calls for further conceptual and empirical research to further enhance the experiences of African American graduate students.

Increasing the representation of African Americans in the professoriate is of paramount importance. Joy Gaston speaks to this need by critically examining the experiences of African American graduate students, de-mything some of the unknowns about faculty life, and suggesting how to prepare for the professoriate.

Completing a Ph.D. can often be an experience that offers no clear trajectory of what is either ahead or behind. Research supports mentoring as a crucial key to navigating this maze, especially given that different phases of the program present different challenges. In Chapter 4, Cassandra Sligh DeWalt presents both personal experiences with mentoring and strategies for working through difficult situations.

In Chapter 5, Theodorea Regina Berry describes her struggles as an African American woman who was guided by White women feminists to the detriment of her Blackness. She notes the resemblances of but also the differences between feminist theory and critical race feminism. Into her explication of theory, she weaves autobiography and poetry in describing these encounters with White feminists.

As African American doctoral candidates at predominantly White institutions, we sometimes must construct identities for accommodating peers, instructors, and administrators. Sherick Hughes (Chapter 6) discusses the ethical dilemmas and challenges of this identity negotiation, especially regarding our obligation to help the communities that produced us and encouraged our education.

Part II queries, "What Is It Like to Be an African American Faculty Member?" Paul Bitting (Chapter 7) discusses the transition of up-and-coming Black professors into higher education by applying motivation and learning theory, evaluating the methods and systems of making the transition, examining who chooses the professoriate as a career, and probing justifications for the more painful aspects of educational advancement (Is it all a necessary part of learning to "think and act like a professor"?).

The minute increase in the number of African Americans who receive doctoral degrees and who consequently enter the professoriate is often attributed to the small "pool" of doctoral candidates. In Chapter 8, Robin Hughes explores what she identifies as "suburban legends" about the pool theory and especially how institutions use the flawed logic of these legends to justify nonhires. Issues of race are embedded in the hiring conversations, a backdrop against which to critically analyze historical and contemporary inequities that are often overlooked during the transition from doctoral student to professor.

In Chapter 9, Lisa D. Hobson-Horton addresses the life lesson that, despite diligent preparation, unforeseen factors will sometimes interfere with or prevent the individual from accomplishing the desired objective. Based on experiences from her first year in the professorate, she analyzes the microaggressions that novice minority faculty may encounter and offers suggestions for coping with the university environment without internalizing negative experiences.

Kimberly Lenease King and Ivan Watts address the influence of stereotypes about African American men and women that new faculty often inherit when they are hired. The first two African Americans in their department, they share the myriad ways that White colleagues constructed them and how they themselves responded.

Using her personal experience, Gloria Kersey-Matusiak challenges faculty of color to consider the positive difference they can make, despite their limited numbers, at small PWIs. She focuses on the pressures and conflicts that faculty of color face at these institutions, the barriers they must surmount, and the choices they must make to succeed in an institutional culture that rewards those who maintain the status quo.

Dia Sekayi concludes this section by addressing the challenges African American faculty face from students at PWIs who lack experience with Black faculty and often express disbelief that they are expected to accept his or her intellectual leadership of this individual, assumptions that the teacher is not truly qualified, and disrespect by constant challenges to the teacher's intellectual leadership. Dia Sekayi contrasts this experience with the affirmation and respect she receives from her graduate students at a historically Black institution.

In the third section, "Teaching Race in a Predominantly White University," the authors document obstacles to teaching when White students refuse to take African American faculty seriously or feel threatened by their personal approach to racial issues. James Osler illustrates seven factors that disrupt the collegiate teaching environment based on his own experience in the classroom and in discussions with colleagues. Cyrus Marcellus Ellis (Chapter 14) explores the difficulty of teaching race, culture, and ethnicity as an African American, while Denise Taliaferro Baszile (Chapter 15) revisits her family politics, not as a commitment to a certain political agenda, but rather as the struggle of African Americans to name themselves in a context of national, local, and school politics that work to reimagine and rearrange them. Using her family's politics as a springboard, she explains her pedagogical struggle for social justice and how teaching is a viable front in the struggle against oppression.

William A. Smith (Chapter 16) describes the phenomenon of racial priming, or the cumulative socialization process by which Whites systematically internalize racist attitudes, stereotypes, assumptions, fears, resentments, discourses, images, and fictitious racial scripts which fit into a dominant White worldview and rhetoric. As a result of encountering racially primed students, many Black professors and other professors of color experience a kind of battle fatigue. Unlike typical occupational stress, racial battle fatigue is a natural response to distressing mental/emotional work when facing consistent hostile classroom challenges and confrontations, potential threats or dangers under tough to violent and potentially life-threatening conditions. For professors of color, to chronically live and work in "no safe place," made unsafe by other people, has serious physiological and emotional consequences.

The final section, Part IV, "Where Do We Stand? How Can the Academy Serve African American Students and Faculty's Needs?" focuses on the experiences of senior African American faculty who, despite the odds, have persevered through graduate school, secured tenure and promotion, and succeeded in maintaining a research agenda and teaching style that are comfortable for them even though many feel that they are still not taken seriously by the academy or by society. Lemuel W. Watson (Chapter 17) identifies the effects of institutional fit, professional tasks, and environmental characteristics on the job satisfaction of African American faculty. This chapter also offers both an extensive review of the literature and a personal narrative.

In Chapter 18, Amiri Yasin Al-Hadid surveys the history of African Americans in higher education and the experiences of African Americans as they progress through graduate school, first job, promotion, and tenure. In Chapter 19, Jerlando F. L. Jackson addresses the access, retention, and advancement of African American administrators in PWIs, an understudied group. This chapter integrates the results of two Delphi studies to propose strategies for achieving these goals.

In Chapter 20, Ella Forbes presents a compressed autobiography of her challenges in achieving promotion and tenure in an PWI African American Studies department and offers thoughtful suggestions to others undergoing the same process. Student experiences in higher education run the gamut; however, exploring the experiences of African American graduate students engaged in doctoral studies reveals disturbing realities. In Chapter 21, Sibby Anderson-Thompkins, Marybeth Gasman, Cynthia Gerstl-Pepin, Kerry Lane Hathaway, and Lisa Rasheed return to battle imagery, contrasting students who feel like "casualties of war" with those who feel like "valued colleagues." Designed as a collaborative qualitative study using autobiographical methods, the researchers (two faculty members and three graduate students) also serve as research participants. Among their practical recommendations are self-reflection, creating a supportive classroom environment, and mentoring.

In the final chapter, Mark A. Williams addresses the situation in which some African American faculty and graduate students who have found academic success, refuse to help, mentor, or counsel other African American graduate students and junior faculty. He documents the damage, not only to individuals, but to the African American community as a whole.

The ideas and strategies presented by the contributing scholars are based on the actual experiences of African American graduate students and professors across the country. They form a testament of the struggles we as African Americans face in the academy but also offer both hope and help for successfully completing graduate school and transitioning into tenure track positions.

Acknowledgments

I would like to thank the many people who assisted me in this process. I first thank my mother, Goldie Mae Cleveland (7/1/1948– 11/26/02) who laid the foundation in my upbringing and socialization to bring me to this point in my life. Words cannot describe how indebted I am to her for her love, discipline, and nurturing, nor for the confidence and assertiveness she instilled in me. I know she is watching me as I continue to work hard to make her proud.

My beloved wife, Ann H. Cleveland, has supported me through my hectic times, and I will always appreciate that continued support. My grandmother, Pearl Scott, helped shape me into the man I am through her thoughts, prayers, nurturing, and discipline. My brother Maurice Cleveland merits my thanks for always being a brother in the best sense of the word and letting me also be a brother. My children, Darrell Cleveland Jr., Briana Cleveland, and Shavonna Reed, are the reason I fought hard to make it to this point in my life.

I also thank all the authors who invested their time in writing these chapters and who took the great risk of sharing their difficult experiences in higher education. I am deeply indebted to each of them for bringing to the fore such painful and challenging experiences. As the editor, I was amazed that so many members of the African American higher education community, many of whom I have never met personally, embraced this project and made such significant contributions out of the belief that people need to know what we as African Americans experience in the academy. I was also amazed at the generosity of spirit of these contributors and their willingness to help and encourage those who follow our footsteps into the academy.

I express special appreciation to Lee Jones, who wrote the foreword, and Etta Hollins, who wrote the epilogue. Both of them had to squeeze the time out of very busy schedules, and their contributions are invaluable.

Many other people should be acknowledged. Phyllis Korper embraced my idea and found others to support this project. George Noblit, my dissertation chair, supported me 100% during my doctoral studies, reviewed my original thoughts for this volume, and provided constructive feedback. Lavina Fielding Anderson copyedited and indexed this book. Ella Forbes, in addition to her contribution to this book, mentored and influenced me in more ways than she will ever know. I owe deepest thanks to the other members of my dissertation committee: Alan Tom, Paul Bitting, Dwight Rogers, and Dorothy Mebane. The lack of adequate mentoring is a frequently expressed concern in this book; and I also confess to feeling a lack of support from my own graduate school of education as a whole. But I could not have had a more supportive committee, and the continuation of opportunities, friendship, and professional encouragement are deeply appreciated.

I owe many thanks to my Kappa Alpha Psi fraternity brothers. I have met and continue to meet brothers who achieve through every field of human endeavor. I also owe much gratitude to Brothers of the Academy (BOTA) and Sisters of the Academy (SOTA). During a particularly tough time, Larry Rowley introduced me to these organizations. They provided the support and mentoring that I so desperately needed outside of my graduate institution. I also thank one of my most favorite people in the world, H. Richard Milner, not only for contributing to this project but for being a friend as well as a colleague.

Finally, I want to thank all of those individuals who doubted me and who continue to doubt me as a person and a scholar. During my graduate studies, I struggled to make the transition into the rigorous environment of doctoral studies. In addition, I lacked some of the skills necessary for success in graduate school. As a result, I found that some individuals gave up on me and did not take me seriously. Because of my resiliency, I maintained my commitment. Their doubts and lack of support increased my motivation to succeed. I hope that others faced with the same obstacles also find whatever they need from within to achieve at the highest level.

References

Benton, M, A. (2001). Challenges African American students face at predominantly White institutions. *Journal of Student Affairs, 10,* 21–28.

Delgado, L. V. (1998). *Culture shock: Preparing students of color for predominantly white university campuses.* Unpublished manuscript. Colorado State University at Fort Collins.

Delpit, L. (1995). *Other people's children: Cultural conflict in the classroom.* New York: New Press.

Easley, N. (1993). *Black student retention at Colorado State University.* Unpublished manuscript, Colorado State University at Fort Collins.

Sedlacek, W. E. (1999). Black students on white campuses: Twenty years of research. *Journal of College Student Development, 40*(5), 538–550.

Suen, H. K. (1983). Alienation and attrition of black college students on a predominantly white campus. *Journal of College Student Personnel,* 117–121.

PART I

JOURNEY TO THE IVORY TOWER

1

Fred A. Bonner II and Marcheta Evans

CAN YOU HEAR ME?: VOICES AND EXPERIENCES OF AFRICAN AMERICAN STUDENTS IN HIGHER EDUCATION

African Americans have interfaced with academe since the early part of the 19th century. The annals of higher education history show that Edward Jones and John Russworm were the first two African Americans to earn bachelor's degrees from White institutions—Amherst and Bowdoin (Lucas, 1994, p. 158). Although the infusion of African Americans into predominantly White institutions (PWIs) constituted a mere trickle during the formative years of higher education in this nation, it was the development of another separate and supposedly equal institutional type that led to a steady stream in advancing the education status for this population, namely, the historically Black college and university (HBCU). According to Patton and Bonner (2001), "The HBCU has not only served as the exclusive avenue of access to higher education for African Americans with its promotion of a participatory ethos and an open door admissions policy, but it has also provided immeasurable benefits by way of student leadership potential and social development" (p. 18).

Although the establishment of the HBCU has significantly enhanced access to and opportunities for higher education for African Americans, current trends reveal that most African Americans have opted to enroll in PWIs. However, many African American students view the decision to attend a PWI as potentially detrimental to their academic and social identities, mainly because historically the admission of Blacks to predominantly White institutions has been at best tepid and at worst cold (Feagin, Vera, & Imani, 1996). Hence, for African American student populations, finding some sense of agency within these academic enclaves presents a challenge that is at best formidable and at worst insurmountable.

This essay discusses the experiences of the African American students enrolled in PWIs and their on-going struggle to find their voice. We provide a brief overview of the historical and current experiences of the African American students in postsecondary education and explore the impact of postsecondary educational environments, specifically the impact of White academies on the matriculation experiences of African American men compared to those of African American women. In addition, we also treat campus climate and environmental factors, academic integration and mentoring, social integration, identity development, family influence and support, and self-efficacy.

African Americans in Higher Education History

African Americans have traversed a winding and often bumpy road in their pursuit of higher education. Accounts of the historical difficulties experienced by these students who sought an education within predominantly White settings revealed a litany of malfeasance, maliciousness, and mistreatment at the hands of institutional officials and fellow students. According to Lucas (1994), "People of color attending college were nevertheless a rarity in the antebellum period, as indicated by the fact that no more than twenty-seven others [i.e., in addition to Jones and Russworm] were listed in the roster of all Black graduates prior to the Emancipation Proclamation" (p. 158).

Perhaps the greatest obstacle to postsecondary education for African Americans was the prevailing ethos that these individuals were uneducable—intellectually unable to master a collegiate regimen. Ballard (1973) reported a belief common among White Americans that the African was incapable of learning, needing strong and rudimentary safeguards to protect against natural immorality. One categorization of African Americans in about the mid-19th century found them "a childlike race, prone to docility and manageable in every respect . . . the ideal subject for the slave role" (John Hope Franklin, qtd. in Turner, Garcia, Nora, & Rendon, 1996, p. 32). In essence, the calculated development of a mindset promoting African American inferiority had initially reified the institution of slavery and subsequently justified the denial of education to this population.

The most significant factor in changing the national tide about the education of African Americans, particularly higher education, was the establishment of historically Black college and universities (HBCU). Thompson (1973) posited:

> The movement to provide higher education for Black Americans began during the intensely racist-ridden decade after the Civil War. Before that time, the most successful attempts were Lincoln University, established by the Presbyterians in Chester County, Pennsylvania, in 1857, and Wilberforce University, established at Tawawa Springs, near Zenia, Ohio, in 1856, by the Methodist Episcopal Church. (p. 3)

According to Roebuck and Murty (1993), HBCUs are "Black academic institutions established prior to 1964 whose principal mission was, and still is, the education of Black Americans" (p. 3). The establishment of HBCUs substantially in-creased the number of degrees granted to African Americans. Prior to the Civil War, 28 degrees were awarded to African Americans. A recent report in the *Chron-icle of Higher Education* revealed an all-time high of 94,053 bachelor's degrees awarded to this population during the 1997 academic year. Yet despite the increas-ing numbers of African American collegians enrolling in PWIs, the HBCU contin-ues to serve as the top degree producer.

The HBCU continues to serve as a source of pride and hope for African Ameri-cans, many of whom would otherwise have no opportunity to pursue any form of postsecondary education (Carnegie Commission of Higher Education, 1971). Ad-ditionally, these institutions have not only provided exclusive avenues of access to higher education for African Americans but have also provided a supportive insti-tutional climate fostering self-reliance among student populations (Fleming, 1984). Hence, it is the HBCU, with a 20% total national enrollment of African American students but with a one-third national graduation rate for this same population, that will ensure the continued development of future academicians and leaders.

African American Student Voices in PWIs

Despite the widespread gains of African American students in higher education, an array of issues endures to overshadow their success. For the African American col-legian enrolled in the PWI, these issues are acrimonious, exacting, and pointed. Many of these students have vividly described their on-campus experiences in what Smith (1997) has termed the "chilly climate." Isolation, marginalization, and ra-cism are frequently cited as the heads constituting the higher education hydra that these students are essentially asked not only to combat but to also conquer. Ac-cording to Walter Allen (qtd. in Turner et al., 1996), "Past research suggests that the fit between Black students and White colleges is not very good" (p. 179). Al-though *Black Students at White Colleges* (Willie & McCord, 1972) is more than two decades old, the issues it describes are recapitulated by African American students in very contemporary contexts:

> We have discovered that most Blacks came to White colleges expecting to find less prejudice, less discrimination, and more social integration than they actually encoun-ter[ed]. Their confidence and trust in Whites has been shaken by cruel, or, at the very least, thoughtless, insults and insensitivity. (p. 104)

The ostensible outcome for many African American students in these hostile en-vironments is to retreat into enclaves comprised of like-minded and like-complexioned peers. Although these cohorts provide the student with a homoge-neous discourse community, they are often relegated to the periphery of the institution, causing these groups to be viewed as "particularistic," beyond the main-stream of the broader campus-based community, and automatically marginalized.

According to Levine and Cureton (1998), when student groups cleave unto themselves for support without establishing the necessary connections to remain visible within the institutional setting, a mitotic process leading to isolation and estrangement often ensues. Still another and potentially more virulent outcome of this mitotic process is the subsequent loss of "voice" by these student groups.

A pivotal issue that institutions must consider in attempting to meet the academic and social needs of minority students in general and African American students in particular is voice. When students have voice—a viable means of expressing their views and perceptions regarding the challenges and successes they experience during their collegiate matriculation—they become empowered. In *How Minority Students Experience College: Implications for Planning and Policy,* Watson et al. (2002) advocate the use of qualitative methods to uncover the salient topics minority students deal with on campus. These scholars, along with many of their peers, stress the importance of using these methods to get at the true meanings attached to the college-going experience (Kuh & Andreas, 1991). It is only the voices of actual students, engaged in the daily rigors of higher education, that will lead to a genuine understanding of the factors that impinge upon their postsecondary sojourn.

For the African American college matriculant, the PWI often presents certain issues that must be addressed prior to the search for a voice. One of the most enduring and yet most basic issues these students face is developing a sense of trust. Willie and McCord (1972) report, "With more interaction between the races on campus as the number of Black students increases, the level of trust between Blacks and Whites appears to decrease" (p. 103). Consequently, African American student populations will view attempting to create institutional contexts encouraging the use of voice as disingenuous if the issue of trust has been sidestepped.

To build a sense of community, a foundation based on mutual respect and trust must be established. Paralleling Maslow's (1959) hierarchy of needs, the most basic concerns (i.e., safety and trust) must be addressed before students are willing to tackle more advanced issues (i.e., identity and voice). African American students cannot attend to issues of voice until they feel a sense of safety and affirmation within the institutional context. Another critical issue for African American students is to develop a sense of identity. Although, the topic of identity development will be treated in a subsequent section of this paper, it is important to mention this concept in relation to the student's search for a voice. According to Stikes (1984), "The problems, adaptations, changes, possibilities for development, and needs of Black students must be put into perspective in order to move toward ways to assist these students" (p. 70). Helping them understand the various identity developmental processes they will experience during their postsecondary experience is but one of the methods Stikes means. Therefore, an understanding of the developmental processes that African American student populations undergo during their postsecondary engagements should be a necessary component in training both academic and student affairs agents on predominantly White campuses.

A tertiary issue of importance impacting voice among African American student populations is respect. Watson et al. (2002), highlighting the campus-based experiences of the minority populations they interviewed, reported: "A common thread throughout the respondents' statements was the importance of being recognized and respected as a minority student in the higher education setting" (p. 71). Other studies confirm that African American students struggle on various fronts, often without success, to gain respect (Ballard, 1973; Brown, 1994; Fleming, 1984; Roebuck & Murty, 1993; Stikes, 1984; Willie & McCord, 1972). According to Brown, "Some White professors establish a negative learning environment for African American students in the classroom. For example, some professors encourage African American students to comment about Black-related issues but discourage these students from participating in mainstream class discussions" (p. 8).

Many African American students also report on-going tensions with their non-minority peers and their institutions; each of these dynamics affect their attitudes, feelings, and perceptions regarding trust, identity formation, and respect. As a result, the pathway toward voice is often circuitous. When the experiences of African American men are disaggregated from those of their women counterparts, the picture becomes even more complex. Treating these two groups as a unit obliterates their unique encounters with academe. This essay deals with each group separately to shed a brighter light on both the shared and individual circumstances leading to their search for a voice.

African American Men and Women in Academe

Although as men and women, African American students share many of the same struggles in their collegiate matriculation experiences, research has also revealed some unique issues related to their learning, growth, and development. These differences are particularly noteworthy regarding their level of college participation, educational attainment, degrees conferred, and overall trends in higher education (Thomas & Larke, 1989).

The latest statistics cited in *Minorities in Higher Education 2001–2002: Nineteenth Annual Status Report,* published by the American Council of Education Office of Minorities in Higher Education (2002a), indicate a 48.3% increase in the enrollment of minority students in institutions of higher education between 1990 and 1999. Students of color (African Americans, Asian Americans, Hispanic Americans and Native Americans) experienced combined increases in the percentages of degrees earned in 1999: 11.7% at the associate degree level, 5.8% at the bachelor's degree level, 8.1% at the master's degree level, 2.5% at the doctoral level, and 3.4% at the first-professional degree level. While this report indicates favorable trends and positive increases, when African American cohorts are singled out, disparities in educational access, opportunity, and attainment are pervasive.

One of the staggering conclusions of the report is that the gap between the number of African American women and African American men participating in higher education is widening: In 1999, 43.9% of African American women were participating in higher education as opposed to 33.8% of African American men. Whereas African American women's participation has shown an increase of four percentage points from 1990–2000, there has been a significant drop of five percentage points from 38.5 in 1990 to 33.8 in 2000 in African American men's participation. When combined with dismal graduation rates among African American populations, these numbers become even more discouraging. This *Report* also indicates that only 33% of the African American men enrolled in college in 1997 actually graduated, compared to 43% of African American women. Of all African Americans earning bachelors' degrees, just over 35% were males. Currently, 1.7 million African American women hold college degrees compared to 1.2 million African American men (ACE, 2002b).

This decline in African American male enrollment extends beyond undergraduate colleges into post-baccalaureate and professional degrees. In 1997, just over 35% of African Americans earning master's degrees were men, down from 43% twenty years earlier. Furthermore, 222,000 African American men presently hold master's degrees, compared to 454,000 African American women who are degreed at this level. At the professional degree level, African American males in 1997 earned 41% of all first professional degrees, which represents a significant decrease from 1976 when 75% attained that degree. Aditionally, a significant decrease in the number of doctorates awarded to African American males has also predominated. In 1997, there were 41,368 recipients of doctoral degrees. Out of that total number, only 1,656 were awarded to African Americans. African American females received 1,088 (65%) and African American males earned a mere 568 (35%) of all doctorates awarded to African Americans in 1997. Twenty years earlier, African American men had earned 61% of the total number of doctorates (ACE, 2002b).

Yet the story for African American women is quite different. Huhn (1997) found that the number of African American females attaining their first professional degree increased 219% over the last 10 years while, during the past 20 years, the number of African American women achieving a bachelor's degree, has increased by 55%.

Cross and Slater (2000) assert that the reason for the relative decrease in the percentages of male participation and increase in female participation in higher education is partly due to the women's movement, which has encouraged women to participate in higher education and to use this venue as a mechanism for elevating themselves economically, professionally, and personally. Through education, women became more independent and more capable of providing for themselves, thereby lessening their dependence on males as primary breadwinners and caretakers.

In addition, the educational literature highlights a trend suggesting that African American women are more likely to be promoted than African American men (Middleton et al., 1996). Professional education has traditionally been the most popular choice among degreed African Americans, particularly women, who have been extremely visible in teaching and educational leadership (Collison, 2000). This concentration may partially stem from the traditional encouragement to women to pursue caretaker roles (teachers, nurses), while men were primarily encouraged to provide for their families by working in general labor positions requiring little or no postsecondary education.

A study completed by Cross and Slater (1997) attempts to address some of the more salient issues impacting African American males in K–12 education contexts. This study has implications for the matriculation and graduation rates of these students when they seek higher education. Cross and Slater observe that many school officials consider African American young women to be compliant, while they see African American young men as deviant, noncompliant, and unruly. As a resultant, male students are labeled as not oriented toward achievement and are sometimes mistakenly tracked into special education programs, a "diagnosis" which persists throughout their educational careers, thereby lessening their chances of breaking out of a category of low educational achievement. Compounding this trend is an educational system in which the majority of teachers are White, female, and uninformed about the cultural norms and traditions that African American students bring to the education setting. These disparities contribute to a lack of recognition and voice, ultimately leading to the widening gap in the educational attainments between African American males and females.

Another aspect contributing to the significant increase in African American female enrollment in higher education institutions is that major U.S. corporations "court" African American women (Malveaux, 2002). Businesses attempting to increase diversity among their employees seek educated minorities. African American women fit in two minority slots: being of color and being women. Thus, they are often favored for key jobs over their African American male counterparts (Cross & Slater, 1997), due to the dual status their position as women of color accords. Savvy African American women take advantage of this trend by obtaining the education required to occupy these positions. Thus, their numbers in academe continue to increase.

Several additional issues, such as salary and wage inequity, homicide and incarceration rates, and higher rates of death from natural causes loom large in the disparity between African American men and women. Although this section focused on the dire experiences of African American men, we are in no way implying that the experiences of the African American female are not at times perilous (Fleming, 1984). What we have attempted to show is that the two groups have different experiences; and although both have accrued some individual benefits (e.g., higher enrollment and degree attainment), overall representation on campuses nationwide remains dismally low.

Factors Influencing African American Matriculation

Campus Climate and Environmental Factors

An important factor in the success of African American collegians on the predominantly White campus is the actual institutional environment, campus climate, or institutional ecosystem. Clearly it has great power to promote or impede successful matriculation and involvement among African American students (Astin, 1975). Penny Edgert (qtd. in Smith, Wolf, & Levitan, 1994) describes campus climate as "a collage of the interpersonal and group dynamics that comprise the experience of participants in a collegiate setting" (p. 53).

According to Smith (1997), "Campuses of all kinds serve as a microcosm for the issues, efforts, and tensions being played out elsewhere in society" (p. 3). Thus, it is important for campus leaders to be aware of how these various topics are being realized in the institutional context—how they are being addressed and resolved. Also, campuses must remain cognizant of issues involving "climatology" and how these issues impinge upon the development of environments that all students view as inclusive.

Extant literature reports on not only the learning style preferences of various student groups but also on the desired institutional contexts that facilitate their academic achievement. Hughes (1987) asserted that African American students attending predominantly White institutions described their campuses as being intellectually oriented, achievement oriented, independence oriented, and competition oriented. Unilaterally many of these campuses promote rigor by campus-based criterion and standards used to determine academic competence. Yet this approach is counterproductive for the overall happiness and success of many student populations during the college matriculation process. Maurianne Adams (qtd. in Border & Chism, 1992) reports:

> For example, classroom engagement in competitive or assertive behavior, "talking up" in class, and acceptance of grading curves by which one's gain is another's loss are likely to be in conflict with cultures that do not endorse individual success at the expense of one's peers or that value modesty over assertiveness and cross-age tutoring over competitive interpeer debate. (p. 5)

Many African American students attending PWIs experience feelings of incongruence or what Tinto (1975) has called a lack of "student-institution fit." According to Tinto's model, the more students become involved in the college's social and academic systems, the more committed the student will be to the college and the more likely to persist to graduation. In essence, the initial strength of a student's commitment to an individual campus is linked to the successful matching of that student's background and the college campus. Yet matching is problematic when institutions ignore the needs of minority student populations, particularly African Americans, in their attempt to promote equitable campus climates and institutional environments (Sadker & Sadker, in Border & Chism, 1992).

In attempting to find their voice, African American students interfacing with the predominantly White institution must often negotiate many campus climate and environmental factors. Depending on whether these negotiations occur in settings that promote comfort and collegiality rather than discomfort and disingenuousness, students will sense that their voices are not only heard but also respected. One plausible means of determining if African American student voices are being heard and affirmed across campus contexts is to conduct some form of assessment.

According to Edgert, campus climate should be assessed for a number of reasons. Three that are salient to this essay are (a) a better understanding of campus climate and its influence on the achievement of diversity goals (b) a better understanding of how campus climate influences students' performance and their decisions about educations and careers, and (c) the need to assess campus climate in ways that will shift the discussion from isolated events to collective appraisals of institutional life (in Smith, Wolf, & Levitan, 1994, 53–54).

Campus-wide efforts from administration, faculty, staff, and students must be encouraged to ensure that the campus climate promotes pluralism and inclusion. According to Edgert, "the perception of individuals participating in a college or university environment provides the lens for viewing campus climate" (in Smith, Wolf, & Levitan, 1994, 53). PWIs must ensure that this lens and the view through the lens for all student populations is free from obstructions.

Academic Integration and Mentoring

All students who seek scholarly success need to be integrated into the fabric of the institution. Like many other minority students, African Americans students enrolled in PWIs often find this process of integration difficult. Lee (1999) discovered that for African American students "having an African American faculty mentor was less important than having a mentor in their career field. Students reasoned that they could get the cultural connection they needed outside of the university, when necessary, by simply going home" (p. 33). The important point of Lee's research is that the need for mentors transcends cultural and ethnic boundaries; expertise, not ethnicity, is the *raison d'être* for an effective mentoring relationship.

African American students encounter multiple difficulties in academe—poor academic preparation, lack of proper advising, and inadequate financial resources. Each issue exerts an acerbic influence on their integration. Perhaps the most formidable obstacle to academic integration for African American collegians is the absence of a viable role model to serve as a mentor and a guide for them during their postsecondary experience. James Valadez (qtd. in Frierson, 1998) asserts:

> Faculty role models and mentors can provide numerous benefits to students. The faculty may guide, teach, advise, and connect students to academic networks. The mentoring relationship is often complex, and the outcomes are not always positive, but students who have been mentored have access to knowledge and information that may not be as accessible to non-mentored students. (p. 13)

Valadez highlights such key issues as access, connectivity, and guidance—all important aspects of the collegiate academic integration process. From the standpoint of access, mentors give student ways to obtain information and knowledge that would otherwise elude them. A common lament among minority student masses is their lack of access to key information to assist them in their matriculation processes.

Baxter Magolda (1987) found that students who were at the highest levels of complexity in their intellectual development preferred relationships with mentors, primarily faculty, who shared their experiences, provided access to knowledge, and worked with them as colleagues. In addition, connectivity for these students is directly linked to access. Through access channels, mentors effectively provide connections for their students to individuals who know the processes necessary for successful integration into the academy. Both access and connectivity are organically connected through the guidance provided by the mentor. It is the time commitment beyond the traditional "required" engagements that makes these relationships based on academic guidance important (Holland, cited in Frierson, 1998).

African American student voices are intricately linked to their perceived levels of academic integration within the institutional setting. According to Watson et al. (2003), students of color are successful academically when they are comfortable with not only the social environment but also the academic environment on campus. Paul (1998) reinforces Watson et al.'s findings for young African American men; her study found that their expectations of future life success were deeply rooted in experiences within nonminority contexts. College and university settings serve as but one of these contexts and therefore must be aligned in a way to facilitate their academic achievement and help them find their respective voices.

Social Integration Experiences

The social lives and experiences of students within academe are often relegated to offices of student affairs and student personnel. A common belief is that academic matters can be addressed in venues far removed from such less scholarly pursuits as Greek life or student government. In attempt to address this issue, Tinto (1975) developed a comprehensive model of the separate and parallel nature of the academic and social systems. Both deserve attention as important student experiences in higher education.

This bifurcated view of the student as being part academic and part social is exactly what recent student development movements have attempted to dismantle through a concern for the "whole" student. According to one of the guiding documents in the field, the *Student Personnel Point of View* (SPPV), educators must guide the "whole" student to reach his or her full potential and contribute to society's betterment (Evans, Forney, & Guido-DiBrito, 1998). W. H. Cowley also spoke to the importance of addressing student needs holistically, particularly in his description of the job performed by the student personnel workers. According to Cowley, these workers must

> devote their attention to the student as an individual rather than as a mind merely[.] They enhance and supplement the formal instructional programs of the college. They are interested in his emotional and social development, in his health, in his selection of courses as they relate to his personal objectives, in his place of residence, in his extra-curricular activities, in his financial needs, and in any number of other considerations, which bear upon his education broadly considered. (qtd. in Rentz, 1994, p. 43)

Thus, the importance of meeting the needs of the student outside the classroom, beyond the purview of faculty and other campus academic agents, is important in ensuring a balanced matriculation experience. Tracey and Sedlacek (1985), using their "noncognitive variables" rubric also highlight the importance of nonacademic factors that impact student success in colleges and universities:

> Historically, academic success has been viewed as largely related to academic dimensions. But growing evidence indicates that noncognitive dimensions are as important or more important to academic success than are the traditional academic dimensions. (p. 405)

What researchers and campus-based officials are realizing is that students are empowered not only by their successes in the classroom but also by their successes beyond it. For the African American collegian, this process is no different. Unfortunately, what many students of color experience on predominantly White campuses is a lack of success or a lack of integration between their interests and identities with the campus social offerings. These students often struggle to even remotely identify programming initiatives designed to meet their needs. According to Gordon and Bonner (1998), "All segments of the campus in diversity initiatives must be included if a true sense of community is to develop. Initiatives must be viewed as serving not only targeted populations, but also the entire campus community" (p. 50). Social offerings for minority populations, specifically for African American students, must be attuned to their motivations; in response, these students will feel that they are an integral part of the institution. In essence, the institution reveals to these students that they matter and that their voices are being heard. Being heard is summarily translated into programs and initiatives reflective of their worldviews and cultural experiences.

Any attempt at addressing issues impacting the African American student voice through social integration experiences has to take into account these students' prior socializing experiences. Being socialized in an environment that lacks any parallel to the institutional context can create formidable challenges in identifying programming initiatives for these students. Colleges and universities must be cognizant of who these African American students are and what they bring to the institutional context. Institutions must not assume that social integration processes are the same for African American and White students. In essence, the social integration experiences for these collegians must be purposeful, exhibiting a institutional willingness to explore differences honestly. It is through the exploration of differences that the authentic voice of the African American college student will be heard.

Identity Development and Self-Perception

College students undergo a host of identity development processes during matriculation. Whether these processes are connected to gender, race, ethnicity, or moral development, each can be quite taxing, even prohibitive for some students in their attempts to achieve success within academe. Chickering and Reisser (1993) highlight the importance of identity development:

> Identity includes comfort with body and appearance, comfort with gender and sexual orientation, a sense of one's social and cultural heritage, a clear self-concept and comfort with one's roles and lifestyle, a secure sense of self in light of feedback from significant others, self acceptance, and self-esteem, and personal stability and integration. (Chickering & Reisser, 1993)

Understanding college student development is an important process in making college and university environments more responsive to the needs of diverse student populations. What makes addressing identity development as a means of reconstituting how the educational environment is realized is due to the complexities offered by diverse student populations—each presenting a myriad of developmental needs. Understanding these identity issues and their influence on college student success must not be ignored. How students learn, develop, and grow, in addition to how institutional conditions facilitate or hamper success, should be a continuing concern of all academic institutions of higher learning (Evans, cited in Komives, Woodward, & Associates, 1996).

By disaggregating the complexities of student identity development, institutions reveal their commitment to promoting both personal and professional wellness in their students. African American students benefit from the willingness of their universities to view them not as a monolithic group, but as a collection of individuals, each presenting unique combinations and permutations in their development of their identities (Pascarella & Terenzini, 1991). The institution makes a strong statement when it makes an effort to communicate to African American students: "We not only want to know who you are and what your needs are on a grand scale, but we also want to know who you are and what your needs are on an individual basis." This two-pronged approach is a commitment to hearing the students' voice at both a macro and a micro level.

In addition to addressing matters related to college student identity development, institutions must also deal with self-perception issues. Student retention, satisfaction, and stability within institutional settings are often related to how students perceive themselves within these contexts. According to Hughes and Demo (1989), two major dimensions define self-perception: self-esteem and personal efficacy. They found that many earlier studies which portrayed minority students, especially African Americans, as lacking self-esteem were ill conceived. What this population tended to exhibit were lower levels of personal efficacy, the second component in the self-perception link:

> Personal self-esteem is most strongly influenced by microsocial relations with family, friends, and community, while personal efficacy is generated through experiences in social structures embedded in macrosocial systems of social inequality. We conclude that Black self-esteem is insulated from systems of racial inequality, while personal efficacy is not, and suggest that this explains why Black Americans have relatively high self-esteem but low personal efficacy. (p. 132)

The issue for academe now becomes finding ways to create environments that promote positive self-perceptions among African American students. According to Bonner (2001), whether from an academic or student affairs perspective, creating institutional environments that promote inclusion is essential to student development. Positive self-perceptions among African American student cohorts translate into feelings of empowerment which exert a direct influence on student behavior (Silverman & Casazza, 2000), especially motivation and achievement. These behaviors are necessary factors in collegiate success and in finding and using one's voice.

Family Influence and Support

The relationships maintained between collegians and their families are a linchpin holding together an often precarious existence. The student must negotiate life and school circumstances simultaneously with growth and development issues. The overload that can occur often leads to despair and frustration, and sometimes to stopping-out or dropping-out of higher education. The family is invaluable in combatting this sense of overload and bewilderment. Several researchers place the family squarely in the equation involving the students' overall socialization process within the academy (Wilson & Constantine, 1999; Wilson-Sadberry, Royster, & Winfield, 1991).

Serving as a supportive framework, the family provides a safe haven in which students can discuss their academic and social experiences. Despite mixed findings on the family's relative impact on academic achievement, research has documented its positive impact on student matriculation and retention (Walker & Satterwhite, 2002). Louis C. Attinasi (as cited in Turner et al., 1996) found that the family should be included in all efforts associated with Mexican American college students' experience. This important point is highly transferable to other minority groups.

African American students can talk with their families about many experiences in academe that are often atypical of the experiences of their White counterparts (Fisher & Padmawidjaja, 1999; Walker & Satterwhite, 2002). Hence, any steps to involve the family must account for these unique experiences; in essence, listening to the voices of these students and their families is critical. According to Trickett, Watts, and Birman (1994), understanding the student's unique socialization process within his or her family must be "rooted in the diverse ecologies of different groups" (p. 37).

African American students are particularly connected to their home communities. Many times, going to college is seen a collective endeavor with family, church, and community all serving as sources of counsel and support. Any effort to reach the student must accommodate these varied discourse communities who feel some sense of responsibility for the student's ultimate success. The family serves across the life continuum in helping the student with developmental issues, one of which is acquiring and using a voice.

Institutions can serve as coauthors in the development of the student's voice, not trying to supplant the efforts of the family nor trying to short-circuit their responsibility for assisting in this process. Institutions should share the responsibility with the family in helping the student understand why voice is important and how to raise a strong voice of reason in and outside of the academic setting. Doing so will provide immeasurable benefits in student learning, growth, and development. The end result is that African American students can develop a voice that is both intellectualized (speaking to issues of academic importance) and grounded (speaking to issues impacting their local, national, and world communities).

Conclusion

Developing an understanding of the African American student experience in academe—particularly as it relates to finding a voice—requires a commitment to dealing with complex questions that lack simple answers. What we have attempted to do in this essay is to provide a historical structure within which to understand the experiences of African American men and African American women as they are differentially impacted by factors that influence their success in PWIs.

If finding a voice within academe is important for African American students and assisting them in this process is of equal importance to the institution, then each group must find ways to facilitate dialogue that is meaningful and important. We have suggested a number of factors, ranging from campus climate to family influence, as promising points of entry. Our suggestions are not meant to be pedantic nor prescriptive; they merely serve as descriptive commentary, a meta-analysis of sorts. What African American students and institutions can do, in collaboration with all parties invested in the success of this student cohort, is to actively listen to each other in multidirectional dialogical contexts. Perhaps we will then no longer need to ask: "Can you hear me?" but instead respond, "We have heard, and it is done."

References

American Council on Education (2000). *ACE study shows no general education crisis among men.* Vol. 49, no. 19. Retrieved November 5, 2002, from http://www.acenet.edu/hena/issues/2000/10_23_00/men.cfm.

American Council on Education (2002a). *Minorities in higher education 2001–2002: Nineteenth annual status report.* Washington, DC: American Council of Education Office of Minorities in Higher Education.

American Council on Education (2002b). *Students of color make enrollment gains in postsecondary education according to ACE report.* Retrieved October 30, 2002, from http://www.ed.uiuc.edu.news/2002/aceminorityreport.htm.

Ballard, A. B. (1973). *The education of Black folk: The Afro-American struggle for knowledge in White America.* New York: Harper & Row.

Baxter Magolda, M. (1987). A rater-training program for assessing intellectual development on the Perry scheme. *Journal of College Student Development, 28*(4), 356–364.

Bonner, F. A. (2001). *Gifted African American male college students: A phenomenological study.* Storrs, CT: National Research Center on the Gifted and Talented.

Border, L. B., & Chism, N. V. (1992, Spring). Teaching for diversity. *New Directions for Teaching and Learning, No. 49.* San Francisco: Jossey-Bass.

Brown, O. G. (1994). *Debunking the myth: Stories of African American university students.* Bloomington, IN: Phi Delta Kappa Educational Foundation.

Carnegie Commission on Higher Education. (1971). *From isolation to mainstream: Problems of the colleges founded for Negroes.* New York: McGraw-Hill.

Chickering, A. W., & Reisser, L. (1993). *Education and identity.* San Francisco: Jossey-Bass.

Collison, M. (2000, July 6). Studied indifference. *Black Issues in Higher Education, 17,* 32–37.

Cross, T., & Slater, R. B. (2000, Spring). The alarming decline in the academic performance of African-American men. *Journal of Blacks in Higher Education, 27,* 82–87.

Evans, N. J., Forney, D. S., & Guido-DiBrito, F. (1998). *Student development in college: Theory, research, and practice.* San Francisco: Jossey-Bass.

Feagin, J. E., Vera, H., & Imani, N. (1996). *The agony of education: Black students at White colleges and universities.* New York: Routledge.

Fisher, T. A., & Padmawidjaja, I. (1999). Parental influences on career development perceived by African American and Mexican American college students. *Journal of Multicultural Counseling and Development, 27*(3), 136–154.

Fleming, J. (1984). *Blacks in college.* San Francisco: Jossey-Bass.

Frierson, H. T. (Ed.). (1998). *Diversity in higher education: Examining protégé-mentor experiences* (Vol. 2). Stamford, CT: JAI Press.

Gordon, S., & Bonner, F. A. (1998). Best practices in diversity: The student affairs perspective. *College Student Journal, 18*(1), 40–51.

Hughes, M., & Demo, D. (1989). Self-perceptions of Black Americans: Self-esteem and personal efficancy. *American Journal of Sociology, 95,* 132–159.

Hughes, M. S. (1987). Black students' participation in higher education. *Journal of College Student Personnel, 28,* 532–545.

Huhn, S. (1997). Minority applicant numbers unequal: African-American misrepresentation in college still present. *The Review.* Retrieved October 30, 2002, from http://www.reviewe/vdel.edu/archive/1997_Issues/03.07.97/news/story2.html.

Komives, S. R., Woodward, D. B., & Associates (Eds.). (1996). *Student services: A handbook for the profession* (3rd ed.). San Francisco: Jossey-Bass.

Kuh, G., & Andreas, R. E. (1991). It's about time: Using qualitative methods in student life studies. *Journal of College Student Development, 32*(5), 397–405.

Lee, W. (1999). Striving toward effective retention: The effect of race on mentoring African American students. *Peabody Journal of Education, 74*(2), 27–44.

Levine, A., & Cureton, J. S. (1998). Where hope and fear collide: A portrait of today's college student. San Francisco: Jossey-Bass.

Lucas, C. J. (1994). *American higher education: A history.* New York: St. Martin's Griffin.

Malveaux, J. (2002). The campus gender gap—a women's issue. *Black Issues in Higher Education, 19*(2), 38.

Maslow, A. H. (Ed.). (1959). *New knowledge in human values.* New York: Harper and Brothers.

Middleton, E., Bausaldo, F., Fleury, S., Gordon, H., & Mason, E. (1996). Forty years after

Brown: The impact of race and ethnicity on the recruitment and retention of minorities in education. *Proceedings of the National Conference on Recruitment and Retention of Minorities in Education.* 9th conference, Oswego, New York, April 9–11, 1995.

Pascarella, E. T., & Terenzini, P. T. (1991). *How college affects students.* San Francisco: Jossey-Bass.

Patton, L., & Bonner, F. A. (2001). Advising the historically Black Greek letter organization (HBGLO): A reason for angst or euphoria? *National Association of Student Affairs Professionals Journal, 4*(1), 17–30.

Paul, D. G. (1998). Bridging the cultural divide: Reflective dialogue about multicultural children's books. *New Advocate, 11*(3), 241–251.

Rentz, A. (Ed.) (1994). *Student affairs: A profession's heritage* (2nd ed.). Lanham, MD: University Press of America.

Roebuck, J. B., & Murty, S. M. (1993). *Historically Black colleges and universities: Their place in American higher education.* Westport, CT: Praeger.

Silverman, S. L., & Casazza, M. E. (2000). *Learning and development: Making connections to enhance teaching.* San Francisco: Jossey-Bass.

Smith, D. G. (1997). *Diversity works: The emerging picture of how students benefit.* Washington, DC: Association of American Colleges and Universities.

Smith, D. G., Wolf, L. E., & Levitan, T. (1994). Introduction to studying diversity: Lessons from the field. *New Directions for Institutional Research, 81,* 1–8.

Stikes, C. S. (1984). *Black students in higher education.* Carbondale: Southern Illinois University Press.

Thomas, G. E., & Larke, P. J. (1989, May). Gender differences among blacks in education and career orientation. *Education and Urban Society, 21*(3), 283–98.

Thompson, D. C. (1973). *Private Black colleges at the crossroads.* Westport, CT: Greenwood Press.

Tinto, V. (1975). Dropout from higher education: A theoretical synthesis of recent research. *Review of Educational Research, 45,* 89–125.

Tracey, T., & Sedlacek, W. E. (1985). *A comparison of White and Black student academic success using noncognitive variables: A LISREL analysis* (Research Report). College Park: University of Maryland, Counseling Center.

Trickett, E. J., Watts, R. J., & Birman, D. (Eds.). (1994). *Human diversity: Perspectives of people of color in context.* San Francisco: Jossey-Bass.

Turner, C., Garcia, M., Nora, A., & Rendon, L. I. (1996). *Racial and ethnic diversity in higher education.* Needham Heights, MA: Simon and Schuster.

Walker, K. L., & Satterwhite, T. (2002). Academic performance among African American and Caucasian college students: Is the family still important? *College Student Journal, 36*(1), 113–129.

Watson, L. W., Terrell, M. C., Wright, D. J., Bonner, F. A., Cuyhjet, M. J., Gold, J. A., Rudy, D., & Person, D. R. (2002). *How minority students experience college: Implications for planning and policy.* Sterling, VA: Stylus Publishing.

Willie, C. V., & McCord, A. S. (1972). *Black students at White colleges.* New York: Praeger.

Wilson, J. W., & Constantine, M. G. (1999). Racial identity attitudes, self-concept, and perceived family cohesion in Black college students. *Journal of Black Studies, 29*(3), 354–367.

Wilson-Sadberry, K. R., Royster, D., & Winfield, L.F. (1991). Resilience and persistence of African American males in post secondary enrollment. *Education and Urban Society, 24*(1), 87–103.

2

H. Richard Milner

AFRICAN AMERICAN GRADUATE STUDENTS' EXPERIENCES: A CRITICAL ANALYSIS OF RECENT RESEARCH

Recently, I met and spoke with an African American doctoral student* who had not been enrolled in her program longer than a few weeks. She said she was feeling "down." She had considered leaving the program because she did not feel prepared for nor accepted in her program. She felt alienated, as if she did not "belong." Although she held back the tears that made her voice crack, her emotional strain was obvious. Unfortunately, this conversation was not the first time that an African American student had expressed his or her hurt to me as an African American faculty member. No doubt, graduate school experiences for African American students deserve attention at a time when disproportionately low numbers of African Americans are earning doctorate and professional degrees.

Statistics show that although Blacks represent almost 13% of the U.S. population (U.S. Census Bureau, 2001), they receive only about 8% of the master's degrees awarded and about 6% of the Ph.D.s awarded each year (National Center, 2002). Only 2,066 (4.5%) of the 45,925 doctoral degrees awarded during the 1997–1998 academic year went to African Americans with 30,097 (7%) of the 429,296 master's degrees awarded that year to African Americans (U.S. Department of Education, 2001).

In short, the graduate school experiences among African American students are often alienating, unsupportive, and tense; thus, many African Americans do not persist. In this chapter, I outline some of the issues that African American students

---

* I used "African American" and "Black" interchangeably throughout this chapter.

often encounter throughout their graduate school experiences, then discuss how faculty members in higher education might address the matters within their control and think about attending to those issues beyond their immediate control.

African American Students and Graduate School

For the purposes of this chapter, I am considering several negative influences relating to African American students' experiences in graduate school: (a) their feelings of a lack of value and respect (b) their burdens of invalidating stereotypes (c) their issues concerning misconceptions about their expertise, and (d) their feelings of alienation by virtue of perspective.

A Lack of Value and Respect

African American students may find themselves feeling as if their perspectives are not valued, respected, and appreciated in their classes, among their professors, and among their classmates—especially in predominantly White universities. This idea became clear in Delpit's (1995) work as well as my own (Milner, Husband, & Jackson, 2002). During class discussions, for instance, these reactions may become quite apparent, perhaps because the perspectives of African Americans students about diversity often counter those of the White "majority" view. These feelings of disvalue and disrespect often result in African American students becoming discouraged and anxious. Clearly, African American students bring a wealth of "theory" and "knowing" to discussions by virtue of their experience, yet these qualities can be circumvented by others' negative actions suggesting disvalue and disrespect—particularly when the African American graduate student perceptions concern other African Americans. Thus, African American graduate students' ways of knowing may be constructed through their daily analysis as members of the race. They may substantiate their perspectives by examining their own lives and by providing examples that may not be grounded "empirically" or in ways that follow more traditional paradigms around knowing, conceptualizing, understanding, interpreting, and theorizing. African American graduate students often feel that their perspectives related to knowledge are disvalued, disrespected, and consequently ignored.

When this sense of disvalue and disrespect occurs, African American students often withhold their perspectives because of their frustration; such withholding results in what Delpit (1995) calls "silencing," a condition that can be detrimental to their persistence. Such silencing is obviously damaging to their classmates and professors, who could learn significant knowledge from the experience and positions voiced by these African American students. To illuminate, a graduate student in Delpit's (1995) research reported:

> I tell you, I'm tired of arguing with those white people, because they won't listen.
> Well, I don't know if they really don't listen or if they just don't believe you. It seems

like if you can't quote Vgotsky or something, then you don't have any validity to speak about your *own* kids. Anyway, I'm not bothering with it anymore, now I'm just in it for a grade. (p. 21)

African American graduate students, like others, want to feel valued or at least respected as they express their perspectives. Quite often, however, the classroom setting is not organized to foster such an outcome. There are consequences to these feelings, and unfortunately, it could lead to these students leaving graduate programs.

I am certainly not suggesting that areas of disagreement are unproductive. Indeed, there should be substantive and constructive discussion in graduate coursres that could push all students' and professors' thinking to deeper, more appropriate levels. Clearly, such exchanges are one of the benefits of our work in higher education. However, when classrooms are not set up to promote value and respect for divergent, inconsistent thinking among *all* students, African American students detect the inconsistency. They are hurt (and often damaged) as a result. The silencing that may occur from being disvalued and disrespected could cause stress on African American students. Not expressing themselves about issues salient to their experiences, interests, and perspectives can result in overwhelming inner tensions as they fail to voice what they really believe to affirm their own reality. They may become confused. They may feel hopeless. They may then opt to leave these tense and unsupportive environments where they believe that their perceptions are ignored, disvalued, and disrespected.

Coupled with being disvalued and disrespected in classes is the sense of "invisibility" that many African American graduate students encounter outside the classroom (Patterson-Stewart, Ritchie, & Sanders, 1997). One student reported:

I was walking across campus one day, and when I passed a White student, I spoke to him. He ignored me. I felt invisible when he totally ignored my personhood. He made no acknowledgement of my presence. It was like I had no right to be there— like I didn't belong. (Patterson-Stewart, Ritchie & Sanders, 1997, p. 492)

African American students may also encounter such invisibility related to disrespect and disvalue among professors outside the classroom:

I remember a professor who refused to speak to me even when I spoke to him. One day I saw him coming down the hall [,] and I decided that he was going to look at me—see me today. So I spoke to him in a loud voice, which shocked him. He jumped about a foot off the ground. But he looked at me that day. He was a very respected professor at the university. I really respected him—he was a very smart man. I guess I just wanted him to see me. When he refused to speak to me, I felt invisible—like I didn't belong. I used to see him interacting with White students—they belonged, but I did not. (Patterson-Stewart, Ritchie & Sanders, 1997, p. 492)

These instances of being purposely ignored outside the classroom are more than just a missing social interaction. Rather, such deliberate nonrecognitions communicate a sense of disvalue and disrespect. If students are already feeling uneasy about their place in graduate programs, their perceptions of being disvalued and disrespected only contribute to accumulating negativity about their respective programs.

The Burden to Invalidate Stereotypes

African American students' feelings of disvalue and disrespect could be linked to what Claude Steele calls "stereotype threat." Stereotype threat is "a social psychological predicament rooted in the prevailing American image of African Americans as intellectually inferior" (Aronson & Fried, in press). When stereotyped individuals (in this case, African American graduate students) are in situations where the stereotype applies, they bear an extra emotional and cognitive burden. To illustrate, because of the reliance on "predictive" measures (e.g., GRE data) in admissions criteria among graduate schools, many African American graduate students may feel psychologically that they are not "supposed" to be there if their GRE scores are less than "standard." Thus, African American graduate students may not fully accept the reality that there is often a low correlation between these data sources and success in graduate school (Cooksey & Stenning, 1981; Sternberg & Williams, 1997). The burden that accompanies this thinking among African Americans concerns the possibility that they may in fact confirm negative stereotypes (e.g., that African Americans typically do not test well) in the eyes of others or in their own eyes.

Stereotype threat may apply to females who are asked to solve complicated mathematics problems; they are at risk of confirming the widely held stereotype that females are inferior to males in mathematics. It is not necessary that individuals even believe the stereotype personally. Rather, what matters is that the person is aware of the stereotype and cares about performing well enough to disprove or invalidate its unflattering implications (Aronson, Lustina, Good, Keough, Steele, & Brown, 1999).

Obviously stress and anxiety are associated with these feelings, and African American graduate students often find themselves working overtime to demystify or to challenge negatively held stereotypes about other African Americans. The price to pay for such thinking is enormous. They may spend twice the amount of time on assignments to make sure they can prove to their classmates and professors that they are "supposed" to be there. Yet ironically, this burden of overwork and overcompensation, undertaken to challenge and invalidate stereotypes, may result in anxiety that undermines performance (Osborne, 2001). In a series of experiments, Joshua Aronson, Claude Steele, and their colleagues demonstrated that when African American or Latino/a college students are put in situations that induce stereotype threat, their performance suffers (Aronson & Salinas, 1998; Aronson, Steele, et al., 1999; Steele & Aronson, 1995). African American and White undergraduate students in an experiment at Stanford University were told that the test they were about to take would measure their verbal ability. Another group was told that the purpose of the test was to understand the psychology of verbal problem solving and not to assess individual ability. When the test was presented as diagnostic of verbal ability, the African American students solved about half as many problems as the White students. In the non-threatening situation, the two groups solved about the same number of problems. Anxiety and distraction were the main problems reported for the African American students who, I conjecture, were tensely aware of the pervasive stereotypes as they tried to work (Osborne, 2001; Steele, 1997; Steele & Aronson, 1995). Many of these data from this inquiry represent undergraduate students, but they are easily and logically linked to the experiences of African American graduate students.

In sum, African American graduate students may find themselves working overtime and putting forth extra (and often unnecessary) effort to invalidate stereotypes that permeate higher education. This physical work of exerting extraneous energy and effort to complete assignments can be taxing, while the associated emotional burden adds further fatigue and frustration. The physical and emotional consequences together can result in students leaving graduate programs.

Unfair Conceptions of Expertise

In addition to feelings of disvalue and disrespect and their burden of feeling compelled to refute stereotypes, African American graduate students may also become frustrated by their classmates' and professors' expectation that they should be authorities *solely* on African American issues (Ford, Milner, & Sims, in press). African American graduate students are often looked to for responses to the "Black" issue—matters that may or may not be consistent with their areas of interest and expertise. This situation is discouraging for African American graduate students because they cannot be the authority on all Black issues. (Who could?) Thus, speaking on behalf of the group becomes a burden, particularly when their perceptions could be misconstrued and taken out of context. On the one hand, African Americans are "expected" to speak for other Black people in general. On the other hand, when they share their perspectives, African American graduate students are often ridiculed and the legitimacy of their arguments is questioned. Clearly, such reactions are stressful for African American students.

To be clear here, I strongly believe that African American students (and students in general) should be given opportunities to share the authority and perceptions they have derived as a consequence of their experiences. In hooks's (1994) words:

> As a teacher [educator], I recognize that students . . . enter classrooms within institutions where their voices have been neither heard nor welcomed, whether these students discuss facts—those that any of us might know—or personal experience. My pedagogy has been shaped to respond to this reality. If I do not wish to see these students use the "authority of experience" as a means of asserting voice, I can circumvent this possible misuse of power by bringing to the classroom pedagogical strategies that affirm their presence, their right to speak, in multiple ways on diverse topics. (p. 84)

However, African American graduate students are often placed under an inordinate amount of pressure to attend to matters that they may not find appropriate for their own work. The strain from this pressure could leave them confronting a dichotomy that is unproductive and meaningless for their professional growth and maturation. That is, asserting unfair conceptions of expertise where race is concerned and not receiving support for the conceptions after they are shared can leave African American graduate students frustrated, fragmented, and fragile.

Alienation by Virtue of Perspective

In other significant ways, African American graduate students often feel alienated. For instance, during class discussions, African American students may find it difficult to find classmates who share their interests. This is especially true when African American graduate students center dimensions of their work on racial and cultural issues because many of their classmates at public White institutions do not share the African American students' interests. These students often encounter the attitude that some people believe that we (as individuals in multiple roles) should adopt color-blind ideologies despite much compelling conceptual and empirical evidence that counters the idea that race does not matter (e.g., Bell, 1992; Ford, 1996; Gay, 2000; Gordon, 2001; Johnson, 2002; Ladson-Billings & Tate, 1995; Lewis, 2001; McIntosh, 1990; Milner 2002; Paley, 2000; Tatum, 2001; West, 1993). African American students then, because of the nature of their interests and areas of focus, may find themselves feeling isolated because so many of their perspectives contrast with those of their classmates. Graduate work on any level already has the potential of being an isolating experience because of its self-exploratory nature. Discovering research agendas and paths to attend to those agendas frequently requires independent thinking. This is often lonely work. Combining this aspect of graduate work in general with the isolation that can result from African American graduate students' distinctive interests often creates serious issues.

In short, there is an element of loneliness associated with alienation that students may encounter both in and out of the classroom. Inside the classroom, African American graduate students may experience loneliness when they are required to participate in group activities and discussions. Many graduate programs follow social constructivist pedagogy as an epistemology. Finding that their perspectives are inconsistent with those of their classmates can be problematic as these graduate students work to "fit" into the collaborative experience. This isolation can also become evident when African American graduate students speak up during class discussion, only to meet either silence or disagreement. These students feel as if they are fighting relentless and lonely battles, especially when they consciously work for social justice on behalf of those who may not have a voice in discussions (Freire, 2000; Dillard, 1994).

In addition to feelings of isolation inside the classroom, African American graduate students can also experience loneliness and isolation outside the classroom.

When doctoral students, for example, matriculate to the dissertation phases of their programs, they may find it excessively difficult to locate and to join writing groups. Data support the importance of networking and collaboration (both peer and professional) in contributing to the persistence and success of students in general and African American graduate students in particular (Milner, Husband, & Jackson, 2002; Nettles, 1990; Patterson-Stewart, Ritchie, & Sanders, 1997). If there is no network to encourage and guide students through what many perceive as the most important and difficult phase of the graduate school process—completing the dissertation—is it any wonder why so few African American graduate students persevere and complete their programs?

Key Ingredients in Persistence

Despite these obstacles and hostile environments, many African American graduate students do persist and graduate. In this section, I identify key ingredients that are central to such persistence. Indeed, outlining some of the negative experiences among African American graduate students may be helpful. Considering how faculty members who work with African American graduate students and higher education may better assist the students could yield even more insights. Three ingredients that faculty may consider as they work to maximize the success of African American graduate students are (a) making the implicit explicit (b) providing substantive mentoring relationships, and (c) developing culturally appropriate advising.

Making the Implicit Explicit

Making success strategies—the implicit rules and norms of an institution—explicit to graduate students is a task that educators in higher education must consciously and assertively pursue through their work. Delpit (1995) argues: "If you are not already a participant in the culture of power, being told explicitly the rules of that culture makes acquiring power easier" (p. 24). Because African American students often come from different places as cultural and racial beings, they may not understand some of higher education's rules and expectations. I am discussing this idea of power to mean authority over one's own existence and presence where graduate work is concerned. To African American students who operate from very different worldviews, these assumptions are mystifying and nebulous. "Different" worldviews of African American students does not mean good or bad, or more or less effective. Rather, mentoring means divergent, dissimilar from the understandings of how success in graduate programs is structured. Accordingly, explicitly providing African American graduate students with some of the ingredients that ensure success could be central to their persistence.

To illuminate, there seems to be a "rite of passage" mentality among individuals in higher education. Jones (2000) in his discussion of some of the dilemmas inherent in higher education calls it "hazing." African American graduate students may be baffled when they encounter implicit rules that silently govern success. Faculty should do their best to make the rules explicit to students in logical and meaningful ways. And because it is a truism that we are frequently unconscious of our own culture, faculty teaching in higher education should reflect on their assumptions through deliberate, critical, and analytical thinking that may promote a clearer view of the expectations of what is needed to succeed and of how to actualize this success.

I am not suggesting that there is a prescriptive way to address these issues, even through explicit discourse and action. Nor am I suggesting that becoming aware of the implicit assumptions that guide our thinking is simple and unchallenging. Indeed, in Delpit's (1995) words, "Those with power are frequently least aware of—or least willing to acknowledge—its existence" (p. 24). However, faculty who are committed to addressing and mitigating some of the concerns outlined in the previous sections of this chapter may find it helpful to bring their own implicit rules and guidelines about the nature of success for themselves and their students to the forefront of their thinking as they work to make connections with African American students' experiences.

Making the implicit explicit is key as we think about the political nature of graduate programs—educative processes that can clearly be experiences that enable or stifle the progression of any student. The ability to really understand the political nature of academic programs and how to navigate and to negotiate the many issues that plague graduate experiences can be challenging even with explicit guidance. Attempting to navigate through these issues can easily become overwhelming if the rules remain implicit.

Developing Substantive Mentoring Relationships

While mentoring is not a new idea for helping students succeed in graduate school, the potency of its possibility is one that deserves further discussion where faculty and African American graduate students are concerned. Mentoring has been found significant in the persistence of African American graduate students (Milner, Husband, & Jackson, 2002; Smith & Davidson, 1992; Patterson-Stewart, Ritchie, & Sanders, 1997). Effective mentoring relationships, however, do not occur naturally. Rather, it involves a plethora of possibilities in addition to complexities.

Tillman (2001) provides a useful framework concerning the mentoring process of African American faculty in predominantly White institutions (PWIs). For the purposes of this chapter, three of the four considerations she describes in developing and implementing effective mentoring are helpful. While this discussion focuses on African American graduate students, some of Tillman's proposals involving African American faculty would likely require facilitation, planning, and assistance at the administrative level. However, the framework can help faculty as they think about developing key mentoring relationships.

First, Tillman advances the necessity of organized and systematic mentoring for African American faculty. Thus, organized mentor pairs should be developed with more advanced African American students and new African American graduate students. In addition, graduate students should be paired with faculty mentors. Indeed, such mentor-protégé teams could facilitate relationships that might otherwise not develop. In this way, an administrative office might provide workshops and discussions to help both mentors and protégés become more efficient in developing and carrying out meaningful relationships.

A second consideration for Tillman is creating a "list of career and psychosocial functions that are specific to the needs" (p. 322) of the protégé and mentor. This idea is related to the necessity of making explicit the implicit rules and norms of higher education. Third, Tillman (2001) suggests that there be some form of evaluation built into the mentoring process. That is, some form of inquiry is necessary to understand the strengths and weaknesses of the mentoring pair. Mentors and protégés alike must be conscious of what is working and of what needs to be changed. They need tools for deliberately thinking about and exploring the relationship.

Indeed, effective mentoring relationships could be integral to the persistence and resiliency among African American graduate students. Lipschutz (1993) has observed: "Keeping track of students' progress at every stage of the graduate career is almost as important as admitting students" (p. 73). Clearly, mentoring is serious business, and effective mentoring likely involves a combination of frameworks for the benefit of the faculty members and students.

Developing Culturally Appropriate Advising

Baird (1995) maintains that "faculty advisers are the most significant people in students' graduate education, people students usually turn to first with questions about coursework, career planning, publishing, and meeting graduate school requirements" (p. 25). Yet because the experiences of African American students are not the same as those of White students, advising an African American student in a vacuum has a high risk of being detrimental to their persistence. Culturally appropriate advising, then, considers and attends to their cultural needs. Academic advisers may have to accept a learning role when working with African American students because African Americans' life/social experiences may be in conflict with dominant views, perspectives, ideologies, and paradigms.

Obviously, there are some connections between mentoring and advising with regard to African American graduate students. I am purposely discussing them separately. While mentoring can be seen as a "service" provided by faculty, advising is likely one of faculty's professional requirements. Thus, advising might look different from mentoring. Still, advising for African American graduate students can be central to their persistence. And individuals from all ethnic origins can achieve effective advisement with African American graduate students. For instance, in Milner, Husband, and Jackson's (2002) research, successful African American graduate students and faculty had non-African American advisors yet still had appropriate and effective advising relationships. Given the low numbers of African American faculty on university campuses, it is virtually impossible to pair all African American students with other African Americans for advisement. However, this study found that African American students invariably sought out African American faculty for mentoring even when they had European American advisors. African American faculty members are often overworked because African American students seek them out, hoping that they will understand the nature of their experiences more deeply. I discovered no data to suggest that same-race advisement is more or less effective. Thus, the task of effective and culturally appropriate advisement is not impossible for non–African American faculty in higher education.

Fundamentally, academic advisors should consider the reality that African American students bring strengths and weaknesses to the advising relationship that relate significantly to whom they are as racial and cultural beings. That is, to attempt to advise African American students without considerations of their whole person would be to understand and to advise in a fragmented and disconnected manner. So, African American students' experiences and identities need to be considered in advising. These distinctions can be considered as advisors become learners. Again, I am not suggesting that developing effective, culturally appropriate advising is a simple task. Rather, it requires time, effort, energy, commitment, and desire.

Conclusion

African Americans' experience in graduate school can be so negative that it hastens their premature departure from academe. I have outlined some of the factors that can stifle student persistence. It is at least partly the responsibility of the faculty with whom these students come in contact to provide supportive experiences to help them negotiate the difficult times they encounter. I am not suggesting that faculty should take sole responsibility for mitigating some of the attrition in higher education. Some systemic structures that directly influence the experiences of African American students lie far beyond the control of faculty. Faculty, however, can contribute to the enhancement of African American graduate students' experiences. Administrators and other support personnel also play significant roles in their matriculation.

To date, the research findings are clear that the experiences of African American graduate students can often be difficult (Clark & Garza, 1994; Willie, Grady, & Hope, 1991). More attention should be given to their experiences as we work to increase the numbers of them who earn graduate degrees. This attention should include both conceptual and empirical analyses and implications. Indeed, the problems inherent in the experiences of these students are plentiful but solutions will emerge with more understanding of the issues.

Finally, as Malveaux (1996) wrote in *Black Issues in Higher Education:*

> The ideological wars that are being fought in the academy scream [about] the need
> for more [African American] warriors to challenge flawed theories about eugenics,

IQ, race, affirmative action and other issues. . . . These voices are needed outside, as well as inside, the academy. . . . We need to send a signal to the young people we encounter. Wanted: more black graduate and professional students. (p. 44)

Recruiting and retaining African American graduate students is an urgent enterprise. Their contributions can be endless. I am optimistic and hopeful about the possibilities of enhancing the graduate school experiences of African American students. Such enhancement could increase the numbers of African Americans who are actually completing their respective programs. A collective effort with increased concern, commitment, and desire to really make significant progress in eliminating factors that undermine African American graduate students' experiences is needed. The factors and experiences discussed in this chapter help frame the decision-making processes among African American graduate students and could be integral to their tolerance and tenacity to remain in graduate school or to leave. Indeed, to lose one student in the process is far too many.

References

Aronson, J., & Fried, C. B. (2002). Reducing the effects of stereotype threat on African American college students: The role of theories of intelligence. *Journal of Experimental Social Psychology.*

Aronson, J., Lustina, M. J., Good, C., Keough, K., Steele, C. M., & Brown, J. (1999). When White men can't do math: Necessary and sufficient factors in stereotype threat. *Journal of Experimental Social Psychology, 35,* 29–46.

Aronson, J., & Salinas, M. F. (1998). *Stereotype threat, attributional ambiguity, and Latino underperformance.* Unpublished manuscript, University of Texas at Austin.

Aronson, J., Steele, C. M., Salinas, M. F., & Lustina, M. J. (1999). The effect of stereotype threat on the standardized test performance of college students. In E. Aronson (Ed.), *Readings about the social animal* (8th ed.). New York: Freeman Press.

Baird, L. L. (1995). Helping graduate students: A graduate adviser's view. *New Directions for Student Services, 72,* 25–32.

Bell, D. (1992). *Faces at the bottom of the well: The permanence of racism.* New York: Basic Books.

Clark, M., & Garza, H. (1994). Minorities in graduate education: A need to regain lost momentum. In J. J. Manuel, R. Wilson, & L. G. Bjork (Eds.), *Minorities in higher education* (pp. 297–313). Phoeniz, AZ: Oryx Press.

Cooksey, L., & Stenning, W. F. (1981). *The empirical impact of the graduate record examination and grade point average on entry and success in graduate school at Texas A&M.* ERIC Document Reproduction Service. (ED 225 421).

Delpit, L. (1995). *Other people's children: Cultural conflict in the classroom.* New York: New Press.

Dillard, C. B. (1994). Beyond supply and demand: Critical pedagogy, ethnicity, and empowerment in recruiting teachers of color. *Journal of Teacher Education, 45*(4), 9–17.

Ford, D. Y. (1996). *Reversing underachievement among gifted Black students: Promising practices and programs.* New York: Teachers College Press.

Ford, D. Y., Milner, H. R., Sims, D. D. (2002). Counseling high achieving African Americans. In C. Lee (Ed.), *Multicultural issues in counseling: New approaches to diversity* (3rd ed.). Alexandria, VA: American Counseling Association.

Freire, P. (2000). *Pedagogy of the oppressed.* Trans. Myra Bergman Ramos. New York: Continuum. Originally published in 1970.

Gay, G. (2000). *Culturally, responsive teaching: Theory, research, & practice.* New York: Teachers College Press.

Gordon, B. M. (2001). The criticality of racism in education at the dawn of the new millennium. In S. H. King & L. A. Castennell (Eds.), *Racism and racial inequality: Implications for teacher education.* Washington, DC: AACTE Publication.

hooks, b. (1994). *Teaching to transgress: Education as the practice of freedom.* New York: Routledge.

Johnson, L. (2002). "My eyes have been opened": White teachers and racial awareness. *Journal of Teacher Education, 53*(2), 153–167.

Jones, L. (2000). Introduction. *Brothers of the academy: Up and coming black scholars earning our way in higher education.* Sterling, VA: Stylus Publishing.

Ladson-Billings, G., & Tate, B. (1995). Toward a critical race theory of education. *Teachers College Record, 97*(1), 47–67.

Lewis, A. E. (2001). There is no "race" in the schoolyard: Color-blind ideology in an (almost) all White school. *American Educational Research Journal, 38*(4), 781–811.

Lipschutz, S. S. (1993). Enhancing success in doctoral education: From policy to practice. *New Directions for Student Services, 80,* 69–80.

Malveaux, J. (1996). Wanted: More black graduate students. *Black Issues in Higher Education, 13,* 44.

McIntosh, P. (1990). White privilege: Unpacking the invisible knapsack. *Independent School, 49,* 31–36.

Milner, H. R. (2002). Affective and social issues among high-achieving African American students: Recommendations for teachers and teacher education. *Action in Teacher Education, 24*(1), 81–89.

Milner, H. R., Husband, T., & Jackson, M. P. (2002). Voices of persistence and self-efficacy: African American graduate students and professors who affirm them. *Journal of Critical Inquiry into Curriculum and Instruction, 4*(1), 33–39.

National Center for Education Statistics. (2000). *Digest of Education Statistics.* [On-line]. Available from: http://www.nces.ed.gov/pubs2001/digest.html.

Nettles, M. T. (1990). Success in doctoral programs: Experiences of minority and white students. *Education, 98,* 495–522.

Osborne, J. W. (2001). Testing stereotype threat: Does anxiety explain race and sex differences in achievement? *Contemporary Educational Psychology, 26,* 291–310.

Paley, V. G. (2000). *White teacher.* Cambridge. MA: Harvard University Press.

Patterson-Stewart, K., Ritchie, M. H., & Sanders, E. T. W. (1997). Interpersonal dynamics of African American persistence in doctoral programs at predominately White universities. *Journal of College Student Development, 38,* 489–498.

Smith, E. P., & Davidson, W. S. (1992). Mentoring and the development of African American graduate students. *Journal of College Student Development, 33,* 531–539.

Steele, C. M. (1997). A threat in the air: How stereotypes shape intellectual identity and performance. *American Psychologist, 52,* 613–629.

Steele, C. M., & Aronson, J. (1995). Stereotype threat and the intellectual test performance of African Americans. *Journal of Personality and Social Psychology, 69,* 797–811.

Sternberg, R. J., & Williams, W. M. (1997). Does the Graduate Record Examination predict meaningful success in the graduate training of psychologists? *American Psychologist, 52,* 630–641.

Tatum, B. D. (2001). Professional development: An important partner in antiracist teacher education. In S. H. King & L. A. Castenell (Eds.), *Racism and racial inequality: Implications for teacher education* (pp. 51–58). Washington, DC: AACTE Publications.

Tillman, L. C. (2001). Mentoring African American faculty in predominantly white institutions. *Research in Higher Education, 42*(3), 295–325.

U.S. Department of Education, National Center for Education Statistics. (2001). Tables 271, 268. Downloaded in early 2000 from http://nces.ed.gov/pubs2001/digest/dt268.asp.

U.S. Census Bureau (2001). *Profiles of general demographic Characteristics: 2000 census of population and housing.* Washington, DC: U.S. Department of Commerce. Downloaded in early 2000 from http://nces.ed.gov/pubs2001/digest/dt268.asp.

West, C. (1993). *Race matters.* Boston: Beacon Press.

Willie, C. V., Grady, M. K., & Hope, R. O. (1991). *African Americans and the doctoral experience: Implications for policy.* New York: Teachers College Press.

3

Joy L. Gaston

PREPARING FOR THE PROFESSORATE: WHAT AFRICAN AMERICAN GRADUATE STUDENTS SHOULD KNOW

As I reflect on my graduate school experience, I often wonder if my program truly prepared me for faculty life at a research university. In most cases, the answer to my inquiry is yes; however, I had to deliberately include experiences that would prepare me for survival as a faculty member of color in the academy. For instance, my classroom experience did not prepare me for teaching graduate level courses. Very rarely do students take courses from the perspective of the professor. To be frank, as a student, I did not think that my professors prepared as much for classes as I now know they did. Additionally, writing papers for my classes did not teach me how to write for publication. Not only was the feedback insufficient, but writing for publication is a different process altogether. How then does one focus on obtaining the type of education that will help him or her acquire and sustain a faculty position at a research university where research reigns supreme?

This chapter critically examines the transition from graduate school to obtaining and sustaining a faculty position in the academy. What types of experiences will help prepare African American doctoral students for faculty roles in the academy? How might students go about obtaining such experiences? This chapter addresses these questions by drawing upon the research literature as well as my own experience as a graduate student of color. The importance of obtaining an education, not just a Ph.D., is reinforced by providing suggestions for African American doctoral students on how to navigate their programs to prepare for a career in the professorate at a research university.

Experiences of African American Graduate Students

Although African Americans, especially African American women, have had an increasing presence in graduate school, the numbers still lag far behind the majority population. According to the National Center for Educational Statistics (2001), only 6.6% of doctoral degrees were conferred on African Americans in 2000. This number is strikingly low when compared to the number of doctoral degrees conferred on Whites (82%). More importantly, the experiences of African Americans in doctoral programs are not always positive.

Despite the slow increase in the numbers of African American doctoral students, their experience in graduate school at predominantly White institutions (PWIs) is seldom positive. H. Richard Milner's essay in this volume extensively discusses some of the negative experiences that African American graduate students encounter, such as a lack of value and respect, the burden of dispelling stereotypes, and feelings of alienation. Other research suggests that African American graduate students often feel isolated and alienated from faculty and peers (Nettles, 1990) and are less likely to have mentor relationships with faculty members (Smith & Davidson, 1992). Unless African American doctoral students are willing to work twice as hard to overcome such barriers, they often find that they are not prepared to assume and sustain faculty roles in the academy after earning a Ph.D.

African American graduate students are often overlooked in terms of research and teaching assistantship appointments. A survey of African American graduate students indicated that 3.7% held teaching assistantships, while only 3.5% held research assistantships (Allen, 1982). In a study of the experiences of minority and White graduate students, Nettles (1990) called for more support mechanisms for African American graduate students. Specifically, Nettles suggested that African American graduate students were in desperate need of more fellowships, teaching assistantships, and research assistantships, which would reduce the financial burden of attending graduate school and provide more opportunities for interaction with faculty members. These experiences are crucial for the preparation and success of doctoral students who aspire to hold faculty roles, especially at research universities. If African American students are not acquiring teaching and research skills in their doctoral programs, their chances of obtaining and succeeding in a tenure-track faculty position are lowered as a result.

Earning a Ph.D. is not an easy feat. About half of all students entering Ph.D. programs actually complete the doctoral degree (Isaac, 1993). Isaac identified two main reasons for high attrition rates: (a) the structure, or lack thereof, associated with most graduate programs, and (b) heavily individualized programs of study. Other than a core set of courses designated by a particular program of study, most programs allow students to put most of their program together individually. Without proper guidance from a mentor or advisor, students often overlook courses that could potentially prepare them for faculty roles. Likewise, doctoral students have the liberty of selecting their own topic of interest within a given field of study; but without proper guidance and direction from a faculty mentor, this process can be very overwhelming and cumbersome.

Characteristics of Faculty Life

The number of African Americans in faculty positions is daunting, to say the least. In 2001, only 4.9% of all college and university faculty were African American ("News and Views," 2001). When broken down by type of institution, the numbers were even lower. Only 3.5% of faculty at PWIs were African American. The number of African American faculty at the most prestigious institutions (e.g., Harvard, Yale) decreased to a mere 2%.

Some have attributed these minute figures to the low numbers of African American students pursuing Ph.D.'s, a phenomenon frequently called the "pipeline defense" ("News and Views," 2001). This defense is, however, only an excuse, since research data document that the number of African American earning Ph.D.'s is steadily increasing. In 1999, more than 1,500 African American earned Ph.D.'s, more than 13% of them in the hard sciences ("News and Views," 2001).

Another area of concern is the low number of African American faculty who earn tenure and promotion at rates equivalent to their non-African American peers (Brown, 1994). Menges and Exum (1983) offer three explanations for the low numbers of minorities in the professorate. First, the pool of potential candidates is small, due to the high cost and time-consuming nature of graduate education. These factors often cause minorities to pursue positions in other areas that are more immediately lucrative. Second, affirmative action has been unsuccessful in improving the number of minorities in the professorate, largely because its guidelines are inadequate in implementing or creating ways to provide opportunities for women and minorities. Last, but most important, are the obstacles that minorities encounter during the tenure and promotion process:

> Sustaining a career in academia requires more than securing a junior position. It also requires surviving promotion and tenure reviews. Not only do such reviews determine whether one may stay at a particular institution, but, with today's severely restricted mobility, they may also determine whether one remains in the academic profession. . . . Many faculty say that the criteria are unclear, inappropriate, or unrealistic. (p. 130)

Although tenure and promotion are processes that *all* tenure-track faculty must undergo, the processes are extremely cumbersome and often problematic for minority faculty members. The road to tenure and promotion is also unusually challenging for African American faculty, who are often reunited with a familiar, but heightened, sense of alienation, discrimination, and lack of respect for their work. Turner and Myers (2000) identified seven key issues facing minority faculty members in the academy: (a) tenure and promotion, (b) working twice as hard, (c) credential recognition over color/ethnicity, (d) tokenism, (e) lack of support, (f) the expectation that they will handle all minority issues, and (g) being the only one.

One can easily discern that the problems and issues faced by African American graduate students do not simply go away after earning a doctorate degree and obtaining a faculty position. In most cases, the problems escalate to new levels at a higher cost—tenure and promotion. The purpose of this chapter is not to discourage African American graduate students from pursuing faculty positions; rather, it is to enlighten or uncover the "hidden curriculum," which is very rarely discussed as a formal part of graduate programs.

Unfortunately, the workload as a faculty member does not decrease as a result of earning a Ph.D. Instead, the workload increases under the tick of the tenure clock. The good news is that there are ways African American graduate students can prepare themselves for success as a faculty member while pursuing their terminal degree.

Preparing for Faculty Life

To increase the likelihood of success in the academy, graduate students should acquire certain experiences before completing their doctoral degrees. This "unwritten curriculum" is just as important as the formal curriculum in terms of surviving the academy. The *unwritten curriculum* includes experiences that are not necessarily attainable in the classroom. Rather, these lessons are conveyed through mentors, networking, major professors, and professional development experiences, to name a few.

Understanding Faculty Life

Before completing the doctorate and applying for faculty positions, graduate students should familiarize themselves with the tenure and promotion process (in general) and the type of institution in which they intend to work comfortably. Faculty members are expected to contribute to their discipline through research, teaching, and service, which are defined differently by individual fields of study and institutional type. Moreover, during the tenure and promotion process, professors are evaluated based on research, teaching, and service. Whicker, Kronenfeld, and Strickland (1993) characterized tenure and promotion in three phrases: (a) merit reward, (b) career motivator, and (c) job security. Accordingly, earning tenure and promotion "is a merit reward for a job well done" in research, teaching, and service (p. 9). Tenure is also a career motivator because senior faculty have more freedom than junior faculty in their research agendas. Lastly, tenured faculty have more job security than junior faculty in cases of downsizing. The general rule of thumb in these situations is "last hired, first fired." All too often African American faculty were the last hired.

Various institutional types prioritize teaching, research, and service differently. In other words, depending on the type of institution (e.g., public, private, research, liberal arts), the order in which teaching, research, and service are emphasized changes. Research universities, for example, place the heaviest emphasis on research followed by teaching and service. In contrast, community colleges and liberal arts colleges place heavier emphasis on service and teaching. For instance, community colleges usually have heavier teaching loads but expect less in terms of research and publications. Graduate students need to become familiar with what constitutes "scholarly contributions" within their discipline and at the type of institution where they aspire to hold a faculty position. Knowing about the demands of various institutions in terms of teaching, research, and service can help students make informed decisions about faculty life accordingly.

Faculty and Peer Mentors

It is important for African American graduate students to find faculty and peer mentors early in their programs. Clark and Garza (1994) highlight distinct differences between faculty mentors and advisors. Given the high attrition rates and the length of time to degree associated with graduate school, especially for minorities in graduate school, there is a need for faculty mentors with whom these students can develop a personal relationship. Cusanovich and Gilliland make this distinction:

> [Faculty mentorship] involves professors acting as close, trusted and experienced colleagues and guides. . . . It is recognized that part of what is learned in graduate school is not cognitive; it is socialization to the values, norms, practices, and attitudes of a discipline and university; it transforms the student into a colleague. (qtd. in Clark & Garza, 1994, p. 308)

It is also important for graduate students to identify other potentially supportive faculty in forming a dissertation committee, yet often graduate students are familiar only with faculty from whom they have taken courses. Graduate students should make a point of seeking out other faculty members who might share their particular area(s) of interest and begin to build relationships outside of their classroom experiences. Finding a faculty mentor can also help with this process because he or she can recommend other faculty members who work well together and share similar interests.

Mentorship is of paramount importance, not only to the successful completion of the doctoral degree, but also to ensure adequate preparation for the professorate. Milner, Husband, and Jackson (2002) introduced the idea of "cultural vicarious experiences," which they defined as an enhanced level of efficacy through "observations of and interactions with other African Americans who have successfully executed similar tasks" (p. 38). The graduate students in their study gained confidence in their ability to successfully complete their programs by watching the successes of others (i.e., faculty and peers) who were similar to them in cultural background.

This kind of mentor-protégé relationship is important for African American graduate students to establish and maintain throughout their programs of study. Milner et al. (2002) expressed how the mentor relationship extended from faculty members who mentored doctoral students who mentored a master's student and vice versa. The mentor relationships were not linear; instead, they were reciprocal, similar to a three-way relationship.

Professional Development

Professional development opportunities are also part of the unwritten curriculum; therefore, African American graduate students should start to engage in such activities before the completion of their doctoral programs. For the purpose of this discussion, professional development includes, but is not limited to, attending and presenting papers at professional meetings, participating in college and university governance structures, volunteering to serve on committees, and writing for publication.

Some graduate programs have support systems in place for minority graduate students. For example, Ohio State's College of Education has a program called Project PROFS (Providing Research Opportunities for Future Scholars), which was created for the professional development of minority graduate students. Project PROFS provides opportunities for minority graduate students to interact with minority faculty members in the college, develop a support network of peers, and work collaboratively on scholarly papers and presentations. Moreover, the program provides assistantship opportunities and a place in which minority students can voice their frustrations, concerns, triumphs, and victories, relative to their graduate school experiences in a supportive environment.

Although not all graduate programs may have such programs available for minority students, there may be other opportunities for support and professional development. Most institutions have a specially designed annual graduate student research forum at which graduate students present their research. The forums are unique because faculty are often solicited to be judges and give feedback on individual papers. In most cases, authors of outstanding paper presentations receive some type of monetary award. Students can then use the money to offset some of the costs associated with presenting at professional meetings.

Institutions and graduate programs vary in terms of the types of programs and support services offered to and for graduate students. The key for African American graduate students is to seek out these opportunities by reading bulletin boards and staying abreast of what is happening around the college and the university.

Teaching and Research Experience

When doctoral students are finishing up their dissertations and preparing to apply for faculty positions, the curriculum vitae becomes an important document. Graduate students should start to build their curriculum vitae as early as possible during their doctoral programs. There is no one format for developing a curriculum vitae; however, all vitae should be similar in content. One suggestion is to look at the curriculum vitaee of the faculty in the department as models. Usually, students can find this information on a professor's Web-site, or in the college or department offices.

Most often search committees at research universities are looking for evidence of teaching and publication on curriculum vitae. Although writing articles and teaching courses are not automatically a part of most graduate programs, it is expected that new Ph.D.'s have some experience in both areas.

With that said, graduate students should find ways to incorporate teaching and research into their programs of study. When I was in graduate school, I co-taught a course with my advisor. I designed the course from beginning to end, which included creating the syllabus for the course and selecting the readings. My advisor shadowed the process, and we team taught the class for ten weeks. Not only did this experience provide me with teaching skills to highlight on my vita, but it also increased my confidence in teaching graduate-level courses.

There are also other ways in which graduate students can gain teaching experience. Often, community colleges hire part-time instructors to teach some of their courses. Some universities allow graduate students with at least a master's degree to teach certain undergraduate courses (i.e. study skills, career planning, college orientation, etc.).

Evidence of publication is also important. Search committees want to know that potential candidates understand the publication process. All other things being equal, a candidate with at least one publication is more likely to be selected over a candidate without publications. Some ways that graduate students can begin to think about writing for publication might include approaching professors and/or other students with similar interests, or start writing on their own. Attending professional meetings is an excellent way to meet colleagues (e.g., students, professors, and administrators) who share a particular area of interest. Writing book reviews for professional journals is an excellent entry into publishing for graduate students. Professional associations also publicize writing opportunities through periodic newsletters and on their official Web sites. As a note of caution about writing for publication, graduate students should keep in mind which types of publication(s) (e.g., books, book chapters, refereed articles, book reviews) are valued more, in terms of tenure and promotion, in their particular discipline.

Conclusion

As we move into the 21st century, the number of African American doctoral students earning terminal degrees and obtaining faculty positions, as well as the number of African American faculty earning tenure and promotion must increase. At a time when affirmative action is at risk and resources are scarce, we African Americans must continue to pursue higher education in numbers proportionate to our representation in the population, despite social and cultural barriers. This chapter outlined some of the issues facing African Americans in graduate school and the professorate and offers suggestions on how to prepare for success as a faculty member of color in the academy. However, the preparation and success of African American graduate students should be a united effort.

Graduate programs should actively recruit and support African American graduate students. Historically Black colleges and universities serve as an excellent avenue for recruiting African American graduate students. But recruitment is only part of the equation. Support programs should also be in place and supported by the college to ensure the success of African American graduate students. Graduate programs should make a concerted effort to place African American students in teaching and research assistantships in order to enhance the quality of their graduate school experience. Further, faculty should be actively involved in the mentoring process.

By the same token, African American graduate students must find ways to enhance their graduate school experience. Often times, graduate programs will not have support programs in place to retain African American graduate students. In such unfortunate cases, African American graduate students must work harder to ensure that they are successful and prepared after the graduate school experience is complete. Smith and Davidson (1992) reported that, in the near future, about one-third of the college professors will need to be replaced. This prediction implies the urgent need to increase the number of African Americans in graduate programs and assure that they are prepared to obtain and sustain faculty positions in the academy.

References

Allen, W. R. (1982). *Black students in U.S. postgraduate education.* Unpublished manuscript, University of Michigan, Ann Arbor.

Brown, S. V. (1994). The impasse on faculty diversity in higher education: A national agenda. In M. J. Justiz, R. Wilson, & L. G. Bjork (Eds.), *Minorities in higher education* (pp. 314–333). Phoenix, AZ: Oryx Press.

Clark, M., & Garza, H. (1994). Minorities in graduate education: A need to regain lost momentum. In M. J. Justiz, R. Wilson, & L. G. Bjork (Eds.), *Minorities in higher education* (pp. 297–313). Phoenix, AZ: Oryx Press.

Isaac, P. D. (1993). Measuring graduate student retention. *New Directions for Institutional Research* (Vol. 80, pp. 13–25). San Francisco: Jossey-Bass.

Menges, R. J., & Exum, W. H. (1983). Barriers to the progress of women and minority faculty [On-line version]. *Journal of Higher Education, 54,* 123–144.

Milner, H. R., Husband, T., & Jackson, M. P. (2002). Voices of persistence and self-efficacy: African American graduate students and professors who affirm them. *Journal of Critical Inquiry into Curriculum and Instruction, 4,* 33–39.

National Center for Education Statistics (2001). *Digest of education statistics.* Retrieved October 22, 2002, from http://nces.ed.gov/pubs2002/digest2001/tables/dt274.asp

Nettles, M. T. (1990). Success in doctoral programs: Experiences of minority and White students. *American Journal of Education, 98,* 494–522.

News and views: "No Blacks in the pipeline"; The standard explanation for low percentage of Black faculty continues to be much of a red herring. (2001). *Journal of Blacks in Higher Education, 33,* 77.

Turner, C. S. V., & Myers, S. L. (2000). *Faculty of color in academe: Bittersweet success.* Needham Heights, MA: Allyn & Bacon.

Smith, E. P., & Davidson, W. S. (1992). Mentoring and the development of African-American graduate students [On-line version]. *Journal of College Student Development, 33,* 531–539.

Whicker, M. L., Kronenfeld, J. J., & Strickland, R. A. (1993). *Getting tenure.* Newbury Park, CA: Sage Publications.

4   *Cassandra Sligh DeWalt*

IN THE MIDST OF A MAZE: A NEED FOR MENTORING

Mentoring has been defined as the process of a more experienced individual pro-viding support, guidance, and direction to an individual with less experience (Smith & Davidson, 1992). Some authorities argue that mentoring may increase and retain graduate students in programs (Blackwell, 1989; Dickey, 1996; Sligh DeWalt, 1999, in press 2003; Smith & Davidson, 1992), but there is a dearth of re-search about the needs of graduate students during the beginning, middle, and end phases of a specific program (Faison, 1996). In recent years, research has also focused on minority students pursuing graduate education, master's and doctoral programs (Blackwell, 1989; Dickey, 1996; Parker, 2002; Sligh DeWalt, 1999, in press 2003; Smith & Davidson, 1992).

Issues in Mentoring

In my doctoral dissertation, I noted that women and minorities might have differ-ent needs than other students (Sligh DeWalt, 1999). For instance, I postulated that, if a mentor does not understand a student's culture and values, a problem might develop in the mentoring relationship. Such problems can pose serious ob-stacles, especially if a minority student has issues related to culture and values as he or she pursues a graduate degree.

McNairy (1996) reported that recruiting certain students might be a challenge at predominantly White institutions (PWIs), stemming from these institutions' inability to retain minority students, and suggested three ways to increase retention: (a) try to recognize students from more than one area such as race (b) try to not force students to acculturate, and (c) try to make the institution as diverse as possible to attract students. White and Shelley (1996) argued that for students to have the "ability to identify, create, and maintain supportive learning communities, . . . they must be encouraged and allowed to critique and challenge collegiate culture. . . . Furthermore, the staff that work with them should facilitate and join that critique" (p. 32).

Brinson and Kottler (1993) observed the lack of minority faculty to mentor minority students at PWIs and argued that minority faculty mentors can serve as great sponsors and role models, helping the minority student negotiate his or her way through the academic bureaucracy. Studies done by Smith and Davidson (1992) and Sligh DeWalt (1999) found that some minority graduate students at PWIs are not receiving or benefiting from many professional development activities such as presenting a paper at a conference and submitting a paper to a journal for publication.

Case Scenarios

In arguing that mentoring is a promising option for retaining graduate students, I draw on three situations I encountered as a Ph.D. candidate at a large, predominantly White, Midwestern university. The first characterizes the beginning phase of my graduate work, the second the middle, and the third my final stages.

Don't Holler at Me

At the beginning of this class, I noticed that all of the White students (a majority of the class members) seemed very supportive of one another. In contrast, I and the other African American woman seemed isolated from the entire group, but not by choice. We had to fight to be heard during the discussion sessions and frequently had the feeling that we were invisible.

Over the course of the class, the other African American students seemed to become disillusioned because of feeling ignored. One of the students even stated, "I am not coming back next semester." After one particular class period, she exclaimed, "I can't take it anymore"—by which she meant the unremitting struggle to prove that she was intelligent and worthy of a Ph.D. I tried to convince her to stay in the course, but she dropped out before it ended. I had interacted with this student more than any other in the class, and now I felt alone, without support.

In addition to the feeling of being invisible and inaudible, I was troubled by another situation. One day the White professor seemed quite irritated at my level of knowledge about a particular area of research. When she posed a question, I answered it briefly. Obviously annoyed, she stated, "This is not a competition!" I stared at her in disbelief. I felt that my right as a student to be treated with the same

amount of respect as any other student in the class had been violated. I was participating in the class discussion like all of the other students but this White professor
seemed to be intimidated by my knowledge level.

I handled the situation carefully as I needed this class in order to go through
phase II of the program. I said merely, "I am only responding to your question."
The next thing I heard, the professor had told another professor in my department
about the incident. I inferred that she must have realized that the nature and tone
of her response were inappropriate and reported it to protect herself. My departmental professor asked to meet with me and, in essence, gave me several helpful
suggestions to defuse a potentially prickly situation.

After this incident, I knew I had to have a mentor that could help me through
the Ph.D. process because I had about three more years to go. As I began actively
searching for a mentor, I found someone who filled that personal and professional
role. In fact, I give a large percentage of the credit for my Ph.D. to this African
American woman. As I told her about this incident, she counseled me to take this
situation as a learning experience. She stated, "Whatever happens do not think that
you are not qualified or not worthy. Sometimes, these things can happen because
the person may be intimidated. Keep going. We can process things like this as they
happen." I followed her advice exactly, did not withdraw from the class, and decided which battles I would fight.

This incident, however, posed two questions that I continued to process: (a)
Why did I continue my Ph.D. program? and (b) How was I able to continue
when the environment was so discouraging that another student felt she could
not continue?

Why Didn't I Get This Information?

During the middle phase of my program, I was enrolled in a class that required
group participation to complete most of the projects. I knew some students from
other cultures in my class and initially thought that everything was okay. However, as the group progressed, I noted that only one person, an Asian Indian,
would work with me on assignments. When assignments were due, I had to use
this student to get the group assignments required for the class. What I found even
more interesting was that the White students were apparently not intimidated by
my Asian friend but seemed intent on minimizing or avoiding interactions with
me, an African American woman, who was very confident about her knowledge,
skills, and expertise.

I have to admit that at first I was really frustrated at not being accepted as a part
of the group. I found myself reexamining myself as a competent and confident African American woman. I became disillusioned and found that I had to work extremely hard to keep myself motivated and interested as I found myself being isolated and alienated from some of my peers.

To continue to pursue my Ph.D. studies, I made it an objective to find students
who could help me remain motivated and socialized within this environment. I

consciously searched for student mentors in my own program and in other areas as well. I joined two African American organizations, a move that helped me with socializing in the community. By immersing myself in each organization, I met other African American men and women who were all having similar issues at this PWI. This realization brought a sense of relief and resolution. In fact, it became a standard part of my schedule to attend the organizations' monthly meetings and the Friday night dinners. Finally, I had found a group where I felt a sense of community!

"Where Were My Research Opportunities?"

During the concluding phase of my program in a meeting with my personal and professional mentor, I asked: "Where are my research opportunities?"

Sympathetically but clearly, my mentor explained that sometimes, no matter how hard you try to become a part of the majority group, you just may never receive the same opportunities as a majority student. She shared her own earlier experience as a Ph.D. candidate, never being offered a research opportunity and being isolated and alienated by her White peers. If she had not had a well-known female mentor, she probably would never have had opportunities for teaching and research. She added that her early research opportunities came from peer networking and meeting other influential lay people, faculty, and administrators at major conferences in the counseling field.

After this conversation, I began to develop my own research agenda so that I would not be dependent on collaborative research. I developed a research agenda. I then determined short and long-term goals, objectives, and measurable outcomes to reach my research goals. I initiated a strategic plan for myself based on four questions and began immediately working out the answers:

1. *What research area do I want to pursue?* I chose mentoring as my long-term research topic because I had concentrated on it so specifically to survive my Ph.D. program, and it was a topic that I felt I could be passionate about for at least a decade.
2. *How will I strategically pursue my research agenda over a long period of time?* In response, I designed a research action plan so that I could concentrate on one or two areas for a considerable period of time. Each year I could submit theoretical articles and/or experimental articles for publication.
3. *Who will be my personal and/or professional mentors?* I appraised and evaluated those who had been supportive of me while I pursued my Ph.D. studies. I learned to not rely on all people you know as references; but thanks to my female mentor, I learned that I could file my references and letters of support in one university office so that I did not need to repeatedly contact faculty for new letters of recommendation.
4. How will I motivate myself when I become disillusioned or when people seem intimidated by me? I decided that I had to use resources that are sources of af-

firmation for me, e.g., prayer, mentoring, and taking care of myself physically and emotionally. During the Ph.D. process, I sometimes neglected these two areas of health, even though they were extremely essential in my ability to continue my program.

Implications of Mentoring

Throughout my Ph.D. experience (e.g., the beginning, middle, and ending phases), I had to be instrumental in finding my support outside and inside the university environment. Blackwell's postulate (1983, 1989) about the importance of mentoring for minority students was absolutely true in my case. I found that having a mentor during my program was very important to my psychosocial development. Without this support, I would have left the university at a much earlier time, possibly dropping out of my degree program. Like McNairy (1996), I agree that some universities may fail to have adequate measures or interventions set up to assist and retain graduate students.

It was important to be mentored by someone who resembled me in race, cultural group, and gender. As an African American woman, the mentoring I received from another African American woman was invaluable. Like me, she had received her Ph.D. at a PWI and therefore shared examples with me with which I could identify closely. Several researchers have also found benefits in being mentored by someone from the same culture, race, and/or gender (Knackstadt, 2001; Sligh DeWalt, 1999; in press 2003).

Blackwell (1989), Smith and Davidson (1992), and Sligh DeWalt (1999, in press, 2003) have postulated that the number of mentors may be necessary in obtaining significant research opportunities and achieving an adequate publication record to be considered for tenure. As I continue through the "maze" of academic promotion and tenure, I still feel the importance of having a mentor's assistance.

In my Ph.D. process, I was disillusioned at times when, despite my efforts to collaborate with other faculty members, such invitations went to my White male counterparts. I had to seek assistance from my African American female mentor to understand that I should not accept defeat but rather continue and promote my own research. I also definitely agree about the important role that attending conferences and being a member of professional organizations play in receiving mentoring and professional development opportunities (Blackwell 1989; Smith & Davidson, 1992, Sligh DeWalt, 1999, 2003). As I became active in professional organizations, I observed how publishing opportunities can be extended to students and faculty who are members of such an organization. Not being an active member of a professional organization or failing to attend regional, national, and international conferences can make the difference in being well published or not published in a professional area.

Conclusion

Mentoring can be a great way to assist graduate students through graduate programs as it gives a less experienced person the benefit of a more experienced person's sponsorship and advocacy. I have found that certain experiences, such as the three cited from my Ph.D. program, have shaped me into the person I am professionally. I now understand what I have to do to succeed in my field. My graduate experiences have shown me that, no matter what stage I am in during my professional career, it can be beneficial to seek a personal and professional mentor to advocate on my behalf.

I also understand that a lot depends on me to succeed professionally. I must remain motivated, determined, and persevering, despite intricate and negative situations that may occur during my professional career. Overall, as I continue in my career as a professor, I can see how experiences that seemed difficult when I was a Ph.D. student actually shaped me into the person I am now. From my Ph.D. experiences, I can continue to pursue my professional goals.

References

Blackwell, J. (1983). *Networking and mentoring: A study of cross-generational experiences of Blacks in graduate and professional school.* Atlanta, GA: Southern Foundation.

Blackwell, J. (1989). Mentoring: An action strategy for increasing minority faculty. *Academe, 75,* 8–14.

Brinson, J., & Kottler, J. (1993). Cross-cultural mentoring in counselor education: A strategy for retaining minority faculty. *Counselor Education and Supervision, 32,* 241–253.

Dickey, C. (1996). *Mentoring women of color at the University of Minnesota: Challenges for organizational transformation.* (Report No. 120). Minneapolis: University of Minnesota Press.

Faison, J. (1996). *The next generation: The mentoring of African American graduate students on predominantly White university campuses.* Paper presented at the annual meeting of the American Educational Research Association, New York City.

Knackstadt, J. (2001). Organizational mentoring: What about protégé needs? *Dissertation Abstract International, 62.* University Microfilms International.

McNairy, F. (1996). The challenge for higher education: Retaining students of color. In I. Johnson and A. Ottend (Eds.), *Leveling the playing field: Promoting academic success for students of color* (pp. 3–13). San Francisco: Jossey Bass.

Sligh DeWalt, C. (1999). *Black and White graduate and professional students' perceptions of mentoring.* Unpublished dissertation. University of Iowa.

Sligh DeWalt, C. (2003). Mentoring graduate and professional students in rehabilitation counseling. *Annals.*

Smith, E., & Davidson, W. (1992). Mentoring and the development of African-American graduate students. *Journal of College Student Development, 33,* 531–539.

White, E., & Shelley, C. (1996). Telling stories: Students and administrators talk about retention, In I. Johnson and A. Ottens (Eds.), *Leveling the playing field: Promoting academic success for students of color* (pp. 15–30). San Francisco: Jossey-Bass.

WHY ARE THESE WHITE WOMEN TRYING TO RUN MY LIFE? ONE BLACK WOMAN'S EXPERIENCE TOWARD EARNING A DOCTORATE

I remember spending many hours in the kitchen with my father as he prepared meals for the family. I especially enjoyed watching him prepare sautéed cabbage. He would carefully clean out the kitchen sink, complaining all the while that we (his children) didn't do a good job cleaning the kitchen after washing the dishes and that he shouldn't have to clean the kitchen sink every time he wanted to cook.

We had a stainless steel double sink with a one-handle faucet. He would spend approximately five minutes scrubbing the sink with a sponge and dishwashing liquid. "Don't use a scouring pad; you'll scratch the sink," he reminded me. He would spend the majority of the cleaning time rinsing the sink to ensure that no soap residue would taint the vegetables to be cleaned.

After this meticulously cleaning, he would half-fill one side of the sink with plain water. He would proceed to cut up the cabbage, green pepper, and onions and rinse the cabbage in the basin of water. He would rinse the peppers and onions. separately, in the colander and place each of the cleaned vegetables in separate bowls.

After this point, he might take a break, but I always knew he was ready to cook when he reached inside one of the lower cabinets and pulled out the big metal pot. This was the pot my parents used for all of the large dishes usually prepared for Sunday dinners and other special occasions. The only other time I ever saw my dad pull out this pot was for preparing cabbage. He would rinse out the pot, turn on the front burner, and place a one-pound block of 100% butter inside the pot to be melted. When the butter was nearly all melted, he would drop in the sliced onions and sprinkle it with seasoning salt and black pepper. Anyone in the house could smell the aroma of the butter and onion mixture. It was mental preparation for what would be part of a delightful meal.

When the onions were nearly translucent, he would add the peppers. Approximately one minute later, in would go the cabbage, nearly filling the large pot. He mixed in additional seasonings, gently stirring continuously until the cabbage was nearly wilted yet crunchy. Then he poured the savory dish into a serving bowl with a light sprinkling of paprika on top.

All the while, my mother might be balancing the household budget, helping her children with homework, or cutting the grass if it were a spring, summer, or fall afternoon. Usually, one of us children would gather the grass clippings with a rack while another one would place them in a trash bag. This might be the same bag in which we gathered fallen leaves in the autumn, once we swept them up, piled them high, and played in them.

All of the 1970s feminist rhetoric was not lost on me. When the tenth anniversary edition of Betty Friedan's *The Feminine Mystique* (1974) appeared, I was ten years old. According to bell hooks (1984), "Freidan was the principal shaper of contemporary feminist thought" (p. 3). At this point in my life, I had been declared smart by my teachers and talented by friends and fellow church-goers. But my parents, especially my father, didn't understand why I questioned everything and why I was prone to view actions and reactions through the lenses of fairness. For me, it was simple. I believed everyone should be treated equally.

I have always been in favor of equal rights. And that included women. In retrospect, my girlhood persona was feminist. hooks (2000) defines feminism as "a movement to end sexism, sexist exploitation, and oppression" (p. viii). Feminism said I could have a career as illustrious as Ida B. Wells's. Feminism said I could speak my mind as freely as Elizabeth Cady Stanton. Feminism said I could protest as strongly and as proudly as the courageous founders of my sorority did on March 13, 1913. At 10, I didn't know much about what was termed "women's lib." But I did believe, like many others, that girls were equal to boys. According to hooks (1984), this was how most people defined feminism. However, to desire education, independence, and equality with men was to be unfeminine (Friedan, 1974).

As a child, I was likely to be regarded as the biggest tomboy on the block. I could run, jump, swim, and play just as hard as any guy. And, if pushed too far, I could also fight my way to my own concept of justice and win. I fought often. I believed I had the right to be free to be. And I would not allow anyone to jeopardize my freedom. I would fight when other kids made fun of my name because I believed I had the right to be called what I wanted. I would fight when (usually) boys would pull my hair because I believed I was free to wear my hair as long as I chose. I would fight when kids would deliberately try to hurt me because I believed I was free to exist in time and space as long as my existence did not cause hurt, harm, or danger to anyone else.

And because I believed I was free (and still do), it didn't bother me one bit that many people didn't believe I had the right to fight for what I believed in. "Don't settle your disagreements with fighting; it's not ladylike to fight," some adults would say. Hmmm. Free people don't think about what other people believe should or should not be done. My gender did not establish boundaries for me in that way. I believed I could be anything I chose because I was free.

Many of my strongest role models were teachers. In many ways, I dreamed of emulating these women in style and class. They were articulate, polite, cheerful, sensible, and strong. And not one of them was afraid to speak her mind regarding any issue. One of my best-remembered teachers was my fourth grade teacher, Mrs. Ewell. She is a tall, brown-skinned, African American woman who often dressed in what we refer to today as business casual. She had shoulder-length hair and a warm smile that lit up her face. I remember her pleasant disposition and the way she took the time to greet each student every day as we entered the classroom in the morning. As she became better acquainted with each of us, she would add an inquiry relevant to something we may have said in class the previous day.

Two things stand out clearly in my mind when I remember her. I remember her recommendation that I become a safety guard. Safety guards, usually referred to as "safeties" by the children, were students who "assisted" the school crossing guards to ensure that children traveling to and from school crossed the neighborhood streets safely. I was excited about my appointment as a "safety" and was anxious to tell my parents the good news, only to have my mother tell me that my primary responsibility was to walk my sister home from school. Kim, who is three years my junior, insisted that she was old enough and able to walk home by herself. However, my mother did not agree.

When I told Mrs. Ewell about my mother's decision, she applauded my maturity and responsibility. She deemed it admirable that I was mature and responsible enough to ensure my sibling's safety first. It was during this conversation that she mentioned the second thing I remember about her. She has a daughter my age and her older brother was responsible for her safety. I thought it was so cool that my teacher had a daughter my age. I rarely saw her after fourth grade but her daughter, Holly, and I became acquaintances in high school. This past summer, I sat and talked with Mrs. Ewell for the first time in my adult life. And I was in fourth grade again, gleaming the whole time.

But I didn't want to teach because that was considered woman's work. I aspired to be a writer and a musician. I wanted to travel the world. I wanted to learn to speak two or three foreign languages. I wanted to be an ambassador of the world. I wanted to do everything, except teach. I had no desire to do what was labeled as woman's work.

However, I found that many of the activities I engaged in and part-time jobs I did from middle school through college were related to education. When I was in high school, I spent many hours after school assisting in my mother's classroom. In seventh grade, I spent my work-study week in the classroom of my first-grade teacher. And, in college, I held such jobs as English tutor and resident advisor. During the years I spent at my second undergraduate school (I transferred schools after my first two and half years in college), I was able to develop and enact a curriculum that espoused us, as college students, as whole and diverse individuals. Aside from my duties as advisor, counselor, confidant, and facilities manager, my role as resident advisor allowed me to conduct workshops and seminars on such topics as sex and sexuality, conflict resolution, study habits and time management, multiculturalism, and cultural diversity. These workshops required organization, leadership and delegation, lesson planning, and presentation skills among others; and it was the part of the job I enjoyed most because (a) the students, through an informal survey, selected the topics for workshops and discussion, and (b) these workshops provided opportunities to meld the academic (theory) with the social and political (practice). I was a budding critical race feminist.

I did not find it surprising or unusual that I was drawn toward—and subsequently advocated—critical race feminism. Critical race feminism, with its historical and developmental roots in the law, is a multidisciplinary genre based on the need to voice a distinction in the experiences of men of color (which critical race theory tends to focus on) and White women (which feminist theory addresses). It draws from the "writings of women and men who are not legal scholars" (Wing, 1997, p. 5), as evidenced through the social and political writings of such scholars as Derrick Bell (1997), Patricia Hill Collins (1990, 1998), Richard Delgado (1995), bell hooks (1990), and Adrienne Wing (1997).

My experiences throughout my education have brought me to this place. And while it bears some resemblance to the feminism of the 1970s of my childhood, critical race feminism is the personal and theoretical perspective of my adulthood because it examines the intersections of race and gender in relationship to power (Wing, 1997). It addresses my issues as an African American and as a woman. It allows me to co-exist in the multidimensionality of whom I am and helps me to deal with the multidimensionality of all women of color. It does not exclude my Blackness in favor of my womanhood or vice versa. Although both feminist theory and critical race feminist address issues related to male domination and power, feminist theory relieves itself from issues of race.

> As a group, Black women are in an unusual position in this society, for not only are we collectively at the bottom of the occupational ladder, but also our overall social status is lower than that of any other group. Occupying such a position, we bear the brunt of sexist, racist, and classist oppression. At the same time, we are the group that has not been socialized to assume the role of exploiter/oppressor in that we allow no institutionalized "other" that we can exploit or oppress. White women and Black men have it both ways. They can act as oppressor or be oppressed. Black men may be victimized by racism, but sexism allows them to act as exploiters and oppressors of women. White women may be victimized by sexism, but racism enables them to act as exploiters and oppressors of Black people. Both groups have led liberation movements that favor their interests and support the continued oppression of other groups (hooks, 1984, p. 15).

Feminist theory and critical race feminism both deal with combatting sexism and sexist exploitation. For me, this is where the commonalities end. Friedan

(1974) deals with such oppression solely for the benefit of White, upper-middle class or middle class homemakers desiring to escape the confines of house and home to find intellectually fulfilling endeavors. "Privileged feminists have largely been unable to speak to, with, and for diverse groups of women because they either do not understand fully the inter-relatedness of sex, race, and class oppression or refuse to take this inter-relatedness seriously" (hooks, 1984, p. 14). Critical race feminism addresses these intersections of existence for women of color and does not negate one aspect of our being in favor of another. My Blackness does not work in opposition to my womanhood. They are in concert with one another as two of various parts of the whole.

My journey as an African American female doctoral student was full of missed-understandings for those who attempted to guide me along the way. These individuals often tried to hide their confusion and found my Black womanhood mystifying. At times, they found my whole being exotic and intellectually erotic. "Tell me more, please. Elaborate," I would hear as if they were attempting to dissect my inner workings, my very soul, for their gratification.

Initially, I tried to explain my understanding, my positionalities, and my Black womanhood wisdom lenses of the work we explored and created. One example was an assignment given in my very first class. The context of the course was culture. We, the students, were to conduct a brief study of culture in the classroom. Well, since I knew I wanted my dissertation study to examine teacher preparation and African American women, I decided to conduct an observational study of interactions in teacher preparation classes with African American women at my own university.

"What do you think you're going to find? I just don't think you'll find out much," the professor cautioned.

Although her implications angered me, I mustered every ounce of politeness in me that very moment to tell her I believed she was wrong.

"Okay," she commented. "We'll see."

Near the end of the quarter, the assignment was completed, turned in, and returned. The day she returned my paper, she read portions of it to the class. After class, she apologized for judging so hastily and commented on how well I had analyzed and interpreted the data I had collected. "I had no idea we treated African American women in our teacher education programs so poorly," she added. "Your insights are valuable."

However, when my words, my understandings, and my musings, boggled their minds, I was dissed, dismissed. One professor made attempts to understand my positionalities through reading a few of the works of a few critical race feminists. For weeks, she would come to class attempting to integrate her understandings of what she read into the class discussion. But when I disagreed with her viewpoints, rather see my views as different among multiple views, I was just plain wrong.

The very worst was when confusions led to assumptions of feminism. That's right. The confusion and mystification came from women, White women. These

White women, with their liberal, uplifting, self-glorifying, compassionate patronizing ways, tried to put my roundness into their squareness. My spherical being was in pain. They were trying to make my round world flat. They were more interested in our commonalities than in appreciating and honoring our differences. They were interested in homogenizing Black womanhood, as if we're all the same. As such, they could accept my middle-class upbringing. They loved the fact that I had traveled half the world. My long, dark, permanently straightened hair made them feel comfortable. My ability to speak German and French fascinated them. One professor bonded to our commonality of having attended an all-girls high school. All were looking for ways to attach themselves to me as if we were kindred spirits. And they wanted my work to reflect those commonalities. This was where the war began.

As a result, I encountered battles in the long-standing war for recognition of *my* Black womanhood. Yet the fights were unfair because I was ill equipped. I didn't speak the language. I didn't know the rules. I couldn't see the barriers. Months went by before I realized I was asking for admittance to a socially exclusive club called the academy. I thought I was getting an education. I was. But not the kind I thought I was getting. And thus the battles played out.

~ ~ ~

Here I am
Set upon a journey and
unsure, uncertain I can
achieve, accomplish, acquire as I began,
commenced, embarked upon this road and
walked, slowly, steadily, as stranger in a strange land.
I am looking, searching each face, each man
each woman,
Who might, who can
as a member of the merry band
of academics, lead me,
and guide me to their home so I can say
Here I am.

Enter one.
Known only by name.
She came
to me as a message on the wire.
She came
to me as a voice on the wire.
She came
to me as liquid on a paper.

She came
to me through the words of others.
I came,
Entered her space,
occupied her time,
Breathing, breathing, breathing,
short, long, longer,
deeper
meanings of words I wasn't sure she understood.
I wasn't sure she would
but she could.
For our lives were somewhat reminiscent, somewhat the same.
And I only knew her by her name.

Our lives,
somewhat alike
were filled with strife
by men who lied.
And we survived.
Outcomes now abide.
Part of her life she hides
sometimes, in safety's light.
All of my life is seen both day and night.
My Blackness as a woman cannot take flight.
"Tell the stories where I do not have might."
"I'll tell the stories that strengthen me inside."
And, just as I began to gain insight,
like a flash of light,
she was out of sight.

Here I am
Set upon a journey and
unsure, uncertain I can
achieve, accomplish, acquire as I began,
commenced, embarked upon this road and
walked, slowly, steadily, as stranger in a strange land.
I am looking, searching each face, each man
each woman,
Who might, who can
as a member of the merry band
of academics, lead me,
and guide me to their home so I can say
Here I am.

Enter two.
Energetic, exuberant.
Enlightened?
Enormous enthusiasm.
Effervescent.
Ever-efficient.
Engaging?
Endearing?
Easily approachable?
Ever-present, egotistical, educational evil-lene.
Eagerly awaiting entering doctor of education students.
"You can't know everything about everybody and everything."
"It's the educative process." "Every woman. . . ."
"My ebony essence is essential to the educative process."
"Elaborate, elaborate, elaborate—please."
"Explain ME? Eat me."
"Mind your elders."
Elementary mentality.
Elephantine insecurity.
Emerging conflict.
"I am not EVERY woman."
Emotionally abusing.
Emotionally abused?
Ejected from my educative efforts.
Eminent, unfortunate ending.
Here I am
Set upon a journey and
unsure, uncertain I can
achieve, accomplish, acquire as I began,
commenced, embarked upon this road and
walked, slowly, steadily, as stranger in a strange land.
I am looking, searching each face, each man
each woman,
Who might, who can
as a member of the merry band
of academics, lead me,
and guide me to their home so I can say
Here I am.

Enter three.
She entered late, along this journey she came.
She entered late, just as I was about to go insane.
She entered late, after others had bastardized, bitch-slapped my name.
She entered late, revealed the unspoken rules of the game.

She entered late, for she knew *we* had much to gain.
She entered late.
"These institutions are so fuckin' lame."
She entered late.
"When One was here, things were not the same.
I can't believe I came
Here"
and stayed
Here
and played
got played
Here.
I felt betrayed
Here.

"Where the hell have you been,
as I wallowed in this den
of deceit and sin."
Come in.
Listen
And learn
For I yearn
to know what you know so I can know, you know.
For the women I know
are from places knee-deep in snow,
most, dirt po'
in rural places where few go,
classed as low.

I want to know,
Know more about you and yours,
wealthy and poor
and exist in worlds I'll never know."

The deal was made.
The agreement set.
We would share.
Laid in bed
like politicians and their fellows
with mounds of paper
and miles in the air as pillows
to comfort my steps along this journey.
Bitter Sweetly.

Here I am
Granted
permission to join this merry band
of academics, friends and foes across the land.
As I stand
feet firmly planted
I know I can
As a woman
of color.

❧ ❧ ❧

As a graduate student in a private institution in the U.S. Midwest, I was pleasantly surprised about the number of female scholars in my desired field of study. I dreamed of days like my childhood. Equality and fairness. But as I moved through this program, I discovered that these White women (who articulated that they believed they always meant for the good), wanted me to be like them, and emulation was not my goal. After all, I am a free woman. I have chosen my identity, and I alone will choose to alter it to suit my needs. I recognized the adulthood that is my critical race feminism. Thus, I was resistant to their direction because I discovered that it accepted only the woman of me. I resisted their direction because I discovered I was being asked to choose my womanhood over my Blackness. They rejected, intentionally and unintentionally, the rich majesty of my African descendants. Their seemingly well-intended direction was not willing to fully accept the intersections of race and gender and all of the multi-dimensionality that lay therein. I wanted to be free to be all of who I am. Free to walk through any doors and stand victorious. Free to seek out my heart's desire. Free to enter any place in life without requiring permission.

But to enter the academy, I found I had to endure conflict, live in isolation, and give of myself in order to gain access. To get in, I had to give in—to a point. I had to learn the rules, speak the language, and play the game. I had to find allies—White, Black, male, and female—to help me to gain access to the tools I needed to gain entry. I had to be willing to explain me, over and over again. But I didn't give up my work. That was the proverbial line in the sand. In return, I am now one more African American woman living in the crossroads in the academy.

References

Bell, D. (1997). Introduction. In A. K. Wing (Ed.), *Critical race feminism: A reader* (pp. 1–6). New York: New York University Press.

Collins, P. H. (1990). *Black feminist thought: Knowledge, consciousness, and the politics of empowerment*. New York: Routledge.

Collins, P. H. (1998). *Fighting words: Black women and the search for justice*. Minneapolis: University of Minnesota Press.

Delgado, R. (Ed.) (1995). *Critical race theory: The cutting edge*. Philadelphia: Temple University Press.

Friedan, B. (1974). *The feminine mystique*. New York: Dell Books. Originally published 1963.

hooks, b. (1984). *Feminist theory: From margin to center*. Boston: South End Press.

hooks, b. (1990). *Yearning: Race, gender, and cultural politics*. Boston: South End Press.

hooks, b. (2000). *Feminism is for everybody: Passionate politics*. Cambridge, MA: South End Press.

Wing, A. K. (Ed.). (1997). *Critical race feminism: A reader*. New York: New York University Press.

6

Sherick Hughes

BEYOND THE SILENCED DIALOGUE: WHAT WE TELL OURSELVES WHEN THE WHITE ACADEMY AIN'T HEARIN' US

Prologue

In graduate school, I perceive my place to be betwixt and between as a "native" son, a homeboy who has individual educational accomplishments for which the Black community hoped, and struggled. I also perceive myself as a source espousing and acting out new understandings to my own family that sometimes confirms current family practices and sometimes challenges them—a situation that can breed suspicion, defensiveness, questions about my naiveté, and their hopes that I have not gone too far in the White academy to approach *real*-life situations productively. I am plagued with why the latter generation of African American Ph.D. candidates faces the same or similar struggles while attending what seem to be, on the surface, more liberal predominantly White institutions (PWIs). Possible answers may lie in the study of the educational plight of this particular community.

This essay discusses the educational struggles, resiliency, and hope of African Americans students on the journey to the professorate. It is my attempt to maintain a conscience. It is an attempt to offer a perspective necessary to question the creation and re-creation of environments that perpetuate the systemic silencing of African American graduate students. It is a commencement of a journey to not lose sight of my impetus to promote and seek understanding that helps the social reality that produced me, a reminder to be cautious of my imminent elite status, and an attempt to expose any shallow tributaries to the sea of knowledge about the graduate education of African Americans at PWIs.

Throughout this paper, I use Black and African American interchangeably for three reasons. Generally, *Black* is one current ethnic identification of brown-skinned, U.S. citizens with African heritage who share a generational history of slavery and oppression in the New World. Second, *African American* is also a current ethnic identification of brown-skinned U.S. citizens, which embraces DuBois's notion of "double consciousness," an ambivalent and dynamic ethnic sense of self as African and yet American. Finally, all of the graduate students whose experiences are interpreted in this article identify themselves as Black and/or African American.

☙ ☙ ☙

During a banquet honoring graduate students for achieving monetary awards from outside funding sources, a White semi-retired professor asked where I was in my work. Our table was filled with other honorees who attended the banquet with either their faculty sponsor or significant other. I told the professor about a regression model that I had completed using race as one independent variable and third-grade math test scores as a dependent variable. The White professor told me rather loudly that one could not perform a regression with race as an independent variable. Now, I knew better and explained to him that I had the model checked with a public policy statistician—a White female faculty member whom I think he had been partially responsible for hiring. He again stated that my procedure was flawed and turned to his Asian male graduate student for backup. At that point, I was working on one of my two master's degrees en route to the professorate. Although I had been sure of myself, my confidence began to wane, until the male Asian graduate student said in broken English, "You can use race as independent variable. It is dummy variable." Although the technical term "dummy variable" had slipped my mind, I knew that I had performed this procedure, which requires one to assign numbers to race categories. And the statistical software is programmed to allow researchers to say for example that 0 = "White" and 1 = "Black," when race is an independent variable.

The White professor then said, "Oh. Oh, yes. Uh, you will have to be careful with your analysis, though, and say that it is a dummy variable." The White professor then added insult to injury by saying, "Well, you have to ask him [the Asian student] about statistics. He's the one who knows." He never apologized for embarrassing me at a banquet in my honor in front of my wife, his Asian student, and others at the table.

How could he have the nerve to tell me at a banquet in my honor that my research was flawed, that an Asian student would know more about my research than me, and then fail to apologize for being altogether wrong?

He was older, tenured and White, his student was Asian, and I was Black. That's how.

John, a soft-spoken African American doctoral candidate who also coordinates a precollege program, reveals his experiences at a popular predominantly White institution in the South:

I get a sense that some White faculty don't know what to say to me. I perceive that they're very calculated in the way they approach me. For example, one faculty member likes to prepare to talk with me, but the person doesn't have to with White students.

I came in thinking they [Whites] would be different. I had heard about [this town and this school] and I expected things to be somewhat different. They are liberal, but it's hard to know where they stand. The [White] people I grew up with, I know where they stood. With this group, *they* don't know where they stand, or where they draw the line. They don't seem to know their limitations [when dealing with non-Whites]. They operate under a color-blind policy, which is racist. Not recognizing your limitations can be problematic.

I presented at a conference in the state. After I presented a White woman said, "You're not who I expected you to be, but you were really good." I perceived her comment to mean that she had not expected someone who was a young Black male.

But my negative experiences, I think, come from a lack of [White] interaction with African American males. Sometimes White professors speak to me and acknowledge me when they pass. Sometimes they don't. They think they're so liberal, but I don't think they realize, in a sense, how lonely this endeavor is [as a Black male] working toward this degree.

Keisha's graduate school experiences on the road to a Ph.D., although at a different predominantly White institution in the South, are unsurprisingly similar.

[My] negative responses [experiences] include: study groups that were held with certain groups or cliques without any minority students being invited or made aware that group sessions were held; exclusions from certain activities by not making us [African American students] aware of such activities; and discrimination between the treatment of minority students, especially Black in comparison to other minority students. One faculty member advised me to get a second master's degree in physical education instead of school administration. He thought I might enjoy P.E. better as a career. Sources of negative responses [to me] include the mindset that some still possess that Blacks are an inferior race and do not deserve or need to progress.

Some may be intimidated or feel inferior to Blacks and feel as if we are here to take jobs or promotions which were meant for them. An underlying desire for Black students not to be successful also [comes from] . . . the belief that minorities are admitted to [this predominantly White institution] because they need *so many* Blacks within the program. We are considered as those who were accepted based upon affirmative action processes and not for our academic prowess. There is also the refusal of some to consider us a member of the "cohort" [that] we are so frequently lectured about.

Delpit's (1995) "The Silenced Dialogue: Power and Pedagogy in Educating Other People's Children," a chapter in her *Other People's Children: Cultural Conflict in the Classroom,* offers the anecdote of a Black woman principal who is also a doctoral student at a well-known university on the West Coast. She reports her experience in a lecture from a White professor on issues concerning educating Black children:

If you try to suggest that that's not the way it is, they get defensive, then you get defensive, then they'll start reciting research.

I try to give them my experiences, to explain. They just look and nod. The more I try to explain, they just look and nod, just keep looking and nodding. They don't really hear me.

Then, when it's time for class to be over, the professor tells me to come to his office to talk more. So I go. He asks for more examples of what I'm talking about, and he looks and nods while I give them. Then he says that that's just my experiences. It doesn't really apply to most Black people.

It becomes futile because they think they know everything about everybody. What you have to say about your life, your children, doesn't mean anything. They don't really want to hear what you have to say. They wear blinders and earplugs. They only want to go on research they've read that other White people have written.

It just doesn't make any sense to keep talking to them. (pp. 119–120)

Unfortunately, similar atrocities in doctoral schools of education occur daily and throughout the county. Delpit (1995) laments: "The saddest element is that the individuals that the Black educators speak of in these statements are seldom aware that the dialogue has been *silenced*. Most likely the White educators believe that their colleagues of color did, in the end, agree with their logic. After all, they stopped disagreeing, didn't they?" (p. 121). The portion of Delpit's highly acclaimed book that discusses the silenced dialogue goes on to discuss power and pedagogy in educating other people's children. But what can happen to our psyche? What existential questions do we ask ourselves and ultimately answer in pursuit of the doctorate in predominantly White institutions? One must dig even deeper to explore the question of internal messages of hope and resiliency during the current struggle to become a Black doctoral-degree holder from a predominantly White institution. It was in pondering these questions that I selected my title: "Beyond the Silenced Dialogue."

It appears that for the African American doctoral candidate, one's person is sometimes in a state of DuBoisian double consciousness where career and social concerns clash. This essay began as a graduate class project in a course designed to explore multicultural education experiences. More specifically, the essay documents some of the existential dilemmas faced by African American doctoral candidates in the new millennium at predominantly White institutions in the United States. It sheds light on current internal challenges facing these fledgling doctoral candidates as they negotiate what and how they speak, act, and think to accommodate their peers, instructors, administrators, family, and perhaps, most importantly, themselves. I structure the essay around considerations of narratives from the interviews of two Black men and one Black woman who are on the road to becoming doctors of philosophy. I use pseudonyms to protect the privacy of all the candidates because they are still matriculating at well-known PWIs in the South. Their reflections and resolution highlighted here pay homage to their predecessors and offer insight, inspiration, and consolation by exposing the hidden consequences of this path to others walking or intending to walk it. This is essentially the story of four of us (I am also a doctoral candidate) who represent all of us who have been silenced, the dilemmas we face, and what we tell ourselves when the White academy "ain't hearin' us."

Their Dilemma, Our Dilemma

For, on an Aristotelian view, the questions posed by the moral philosopher and the questions posed by the plain person are to an important degree inseparable. (Alasdair MacIntyre, qtd. in Richardson, Martinez, & Stewart, 1998, p. 47)

Existential moral dilemmas oftentimes arise when personal concerns conflict with social concerns. The conflicting concerns of plain persons may manifest in their asking: "What is my good?" and "What actions will achieve it?" (qtd. in Richardson, Martinez, and Stewart, 1998, p. 47). And if we, as African American plain persons in a country still racked with racism, ask persistently what is the good at stake for us here and now in our particular situation, we must ask a further philosophical question: "What in general is the good for African Americans with our kind of history in this kind of situation?" An ethical dilemma that consistently challenges us as we attempt to answer questions like these involves our decision to become doctoral candidates at predominantly White institutions.

Upon graduating from a predominantly White undergraduate institution, Andre accepted a graduate teaching fellowship to a historically White private institution to pursue his goal of becoming a university professor. The fellowship granted Andre the opportunity to "practice" being a professor and gave him a glimpse of what his career choice entailed. This practice period raised his consciousness about the seemingly distinctive conflict between personal concerns and social concerns as experienced by other African American graduate students and professors of higher education. Around this time, Andre began to think that "the personal concern is to beat the odds, to *represent*, to achieve the individual status and power to empower those who have your kind of history, but perhaps were not as fortunate to be in your kind of situation."

This social concern involves two stages in Kohlberg's ladder of moral development: (a) law and order, and (b) social contract. African American graduate students along the road to the professorship often struggle through these stages as they attempt to make good on their social duty, obligation, and/or contract to other African Americans as well as fight for justice and rights for all marginalized minority groups (Barger, 2000, p. 1).

John: The overall experience keeps me here to finish my dissertation. I'm the first male in my family to get a college degree, first ever to get a Ph.D. It's not all for me. It's for my whole family. My family is waiting for me to finish, but they don't really understand what it takes to get this done and the hard work that goes into it. And it raises the bar of responsibility back to them, my cousins, my brother, but they don't see it that way. They have created a false picture of me. I'm the *smart* one. But my grades suggest I did barely enough to finish undergrad. And it's reflected on my sons. Gregory can do this "because he is my son." But he does this because I read and work with him. [There's] an expectation that my son should do more because I'm going to be a doctor. But most Blacks know [that] this is what you need to do. They just may not do it.

This conflict of personal/social concerns can also be discussed as an individual vs. community "right vs. right" dilemma. Andre offers additional insight: "My interests as an African American seeking the highest degree in my field to empower myself are pitted against my interests as part of the larger African American social group or community."

Alternatives and Consequences

Let us examine the first question underpinning our individual, existential ethical dilemmas: What good is at stake for me here and now in my particular situation? In other words, "What is good and best here and now for me at my stage in the education of my capacities to do?" (MacIntyre, qtd. in Richardson, Martinez, & Stewart, 1998, p. 52). On the one hand, we consider our social obligation and/or contract to participate in grassroots/hands-on efforts to help African Americans in need here and now with the education that we have amassed at this point. On the other hand, we foresee a utilitarian future of "the greatest good for the greatest number," and we believe that we will be able to do that with the credentials that society has accepted as the peak of academic educational preparation—a Ph.D. (Bowers, 1984, p. 16). In this light, the doctoral degree is recognized as one of the most important of the master's tools that will be used to tear down the master's house. To this end, Andre pursues the teaching aspect of the university professorship as the means of empowering him to "introduce an anti-oppressive way of thinking and acting to hundreds of individuals, including but not limited to African Americans" (Freire, 1998, pp. 27–28).

Keisha, who had attended all HBCUs during her undergraduate work, also seems to espouse a utilitarian ethic as she first expresses her decision to enroll in a predominantly White institution and then relays her plan to use "the master's tools" to benefit all African Americans. At that point,

> a professor within my history program at [my HBCU] suggested that I attend a predominantly White university for this degree in that the exposure to the way Caucasians think, maneuver, operate, and the type of education which [the PWI] offers would help me to become stronger in personality and a better thinker. He did not imply that the degrees from the HBCU were not commensurate to [the PWI's], but [rather that] this would be a way for me to step out of the comfort zone which I had become accustomed to. The academic arena in which I want to work will be predominantly White. This was something I had to become more familiar with. This has helped instill [in me] an even stronger desire to succeed, even knowing that there are many who smile at me and are friendly but who do not want me to succeed. The prayers from my family help to give me strength in knowing that this too shall pass, and no matter what, God is with me in all of my endeavors.
>
> The only methodology I know to change the negative responses is to always do my very best in the manner which I conduct myself in public, . . . being professional and articulate at all times, and working closely with the university and its

administrators to educate them [about] the needs, desires, and thinking of African American students.

The second more encompassing philosophical question of our dilemma inquires: "What in general is *the* good for African Americans with my kind of history in this kind of situation?" It seems that we have decided what is *the* good for all African Americans in our situation by continuing the pursuit toward the Ph.D.; but as Andre admits, "I often consider alternatives, choices that others similar to me have made and the consequences subsequent to those alternatives." As we struggle through these dilemmas, it is important for us to be comfortable with the existential ethical approach we have taken and to discern what type of person we have to become in order to achieve our desired outcomes with that approach.

The Decision

In reflecting on my own experiences as a silenced doctoral candidate, I began to explore explanations for why we choose to stay the course. The utilitarian or consequentialist ethical approach appears to at least partially explain our decision to proceed with the doctoral candidacy. The ethical principle of this approach can be referred to as EndRight. It is a teleological method of reasoning, in which the ends are good; therefore, the means are right if they lead to desired consequences.

With the utilitarian approach, some of us seem to justify our decisions to continue the course toward the Ph.D. rather than leaving school to become involved in some grassroots/hands-on peace and empowerment education program. Upon meeting Arun Gandhi, the grandson of Mahatma K. Gandhi, Andre's interests in participating in large-scale efforts to promote alternatives to our current paradigm of world domination peaked. Arun is the founder of the M. K. Gandhi Institute for Non-Violence, an international peace organization that also serves to empower people of color. Andre recalls, "The decision to stay in school and not join such an international or even domestic effort was difficult, but local efforts seem to me equally as important. And as a professor, I can have an impact in a local arena, but also, the knowledge that I will gain from and be able to share with students could proliferate." Students can and do spread the seeds of knowledge as they move on through life, and therefore, the professor can really have no sense of the impact that he or she has on the world during his or her tenure, or whether that impact is negative or positive.

> **John:** Yes, certainly, it's [the doctorate] worth it. It's worth it, not in the sense of course work but the independent learning that I did. For example, Dewey prevails here, but there is no talk about Du Bois *[The Souls of Black Folks]* or Asante (the Afrocentric paradigm]. I read Du Bois in undergrad. But I really didn't get it until I was in graduate school. The benefits come for me doing independent study for myself in light of the coursework.
>
> **Keisha:** Education is definitely useful for Black graduate students. It is the only way in which we can enter . . . the playing field with other professionals. As Blacks, we

are the first [to be questioned about] . . . our authenticity. Having the education opens the door and may allow the opportunity to receive a chance. It is up to us whether or not we score a home run or strike out. Education also provides the opportunity to experience things that others are accustomed to because of who they know and who they are related to. It is my belief that education is the only option for Blacks to succeed and maintain within the White-collar world of academics and high profile jobs.

Because the mission of achieving a doctorate is positive, it justifies the required means of remaining in school. Andre offers insight on this point:

Because both doctoral schoolwork and grassroots work can require an extreme amount of intensity and perseverance and can be physically and mentally taxing, I am unwilling to tackle them simultaneously at this time. The thought of being a service-oriented professor as an end seems more plausible to me, and it would perhaps place me in a better position to balance work with the local commitment to healing the ills of social hierarchy.

As Fleming Bell (1998) explains, "We say that a person is ethical if he or she behaves in ways that we think right or good" (p. 3). The key phrase of Bell's statement seems to be "ways we think right or good." We must remember that only some African Americans and their allies may positively acknowledge doctoral candidates' plight and reward them along the way for a job well done. Others will undoubtedly argue that their decision is not the right choice or not as right as it *should* be. Those dissenters have rebuked those like Andre for "acting White" or referred to such an educational decision as "selling out" or not being true to oneself—but who are we all?

We are who we think other people think we are. Our thoughts, feelings, beliefs, emotions, and actions are bound up by and with others. This is true even of our criticisms and our oppositional communicative behavior. So perhaps our decision to stay the course is no more of a sell-out than the decision of individuals who do little tangible work to benefit the community beyond their family but are quick to announce and enforce criteria for intraethnic rights and wrongs, do's and don'ts. The current situation in our society presents African American students as disproportionately behind other Americans in measures of educational achievement. To eradicate the causes and transgenerational effects of the high proportion of negative educational outcomes in our community, we will need African American leadership of all creeds and complexions, of all classes and castes. Therefore, it appears to be as imperative for some African Americans to stay and fulfill the requirements of the doctorate as it is for others to pursue concomitantly grassroots efforts.

Negotiating Our Candidacy at PWIs

Thus, it is important to continue theorizing on the researchers' multiplicity of identities and the implications of this for qualitative research in education. As members of marginalized groups assume more privileged positions in the educational socioeconomic structures of hierarchy, people who were once merely the exotic objects of inquiry are the inquirers—the ones formulating and asking the questions. (Villenas, 2000, p. 90)

> **Andre:** I identify myself as a man, a Black or African American man, a husband, a son, a brother, an uncle, and a male representative of a Black or African American Southern, rural upbringing.
>
> **John:** I identify myself as an African American, male heterosexual father. It's interesting. I was thinking about that earlier today in relation to my dissertation.
>
> **Keisha:** I identify myself as an African American Christian female with strong roots and beliefs within the African American culture.

Growing up African American or Black locates us in a distinct place geographically, racially, ethnically, politically, and socially. We all live with the same common thread, under the same racial subjugation as the Black family members we study, experiencing much of the same discrimination from mainstream society that comes from being a numerical minority. As Villenas (2000) so poignantly expressed it: "I share the same ethnic consciousness and linguistic experiences" as those deemed participants (p. 75). Most of us are first-generation doctoral candidates and only a few generations removed from slavery. Geographically, our developmental environments were filled with messages of hope and struggle. Ethnically and racially, we are many shades of brown-skinned Americans of African descent. Politically, we are African American or Black with all the rights, privileges, and denial thereof. Socially, we are *educated* African American adults like me for whom Whites enabled the social mobility to move *from* a lower middle-class, country Black boy, living in a trailer home where neighbors often valued and revered doctoral education as abstract but not as a reality-based goal, *to* the middle class, where my ABD status in education is valued as crucial for climbing success ladders and making money in a predominantly White America (Payne, 2001, p. 59). We were groomed to succeed in the White middle-class school by default when entering public school as the often over-achieving, expectation-exceeding kindergartners in racially desegregated classrooms.

In our early educational worlds, it was crucial for us to gain survival and success skills to exist in both the living spaces of the impoverished and a post-desegregation public elementary school. We learned to excel in a school system that was not created for children who looked like us, while maintaining ties with our less cultural-code-switch equipped homies. More often than us, our home-boys/homegirls sometimes broke key White middle-class school rules by such behavior as laughter when disciplined (a way to save face), loud argument with the teacher (signs of highly participatory cultures that distrust authority), angry responses (based on fear, which may stem from loss of face), inappropriate or vulgar comments (reliance on casual language or lack of knowledge of formal language), physical fighting (seen as more or less of a man or woman if one avoids fighting), distrust and lack of conflict resolution skills, belonging by having one's hands always on someone else (a heavy reliance on nonverbal data and touch), and difficulty in following directions and rules at White schools (home discipline is more direct) (Payne, 2001, p. 103; Delpit, 1995). Our multiple identities come into play as we endure the silenced dialogue, both to motivate us and to help us consider our problems and how to help our peers.

As African American doctoral candidates at predominantly White institutions, we oftentimes must negotiate our identities to speak, act, and think to accommodate peers, instructors, and administrators. Of course, such negotiation fuels the existential dilemma and produces internal strain with negative emotional and physical consequences. This negative existential dilemma, I contend, produces a life-stressing condition that is distinct and specific to African American doctoral candidates. This condition is often ignored or misdiagnosed as paranoia by most White and some Black professors at predominantly White institutions. The condition stems from our existence as "potentially both the colonizer . . . and the colonized, as a member of the very community that is made other" evidenced by our learned skill to use "they" to describe people who are essentially an indispensable part of us (Villenas, 2000, p. 75).

Like Delpit (1995), Black doctoral candidates at predominantly White institutions appear to want to make power more explicit by critiquing both White conservatives and liberals who live under color-blind blankets where "acknowledging personal power and admitting participation in the culture of power is distinctly uncomfortable" (p. 123). Like Shujaa (1994), we sense that Blacks received too much schooling in doctoral programs and too little of the knowledge indicative of education. In education, not schooling, lies the tools for exposing the relativity of truth and how "White educators had [have] the authority to establish what was [is] to be considered 'truth' regardless of the opinions of the people of color" who are "well aware of the fact" (Delpit, 1995, p. 123). Unlike Shujaa, some of us do not plan to seek an independent African-centered school as necessary and sufficient to eradicate oppression of the educational apparatus, although we fully understand and respect Shujaa's impetus for a point of departure. We believe that, if *schooling* is more indicative of *education,* as Shujaa argues it should be, there is hope for eliminating the atrocities of the current learning infrastructure of doctoral candidacy. Like Shujaa, we name power and expand the possibilities for an anti-oppressive education apparatus by contributing to change in our public and private predominantly White institutions. These institutions must consistently:

1. Instill skills based on a realistic and thorough understanding of the political system, and support such skills by promoting questioning and critical thinking skills.
2. Provide historical overviews of the nation, the continent, and the world which accurately represent the contributions of all ethnic groups to the storehouse of human knowledge (Shujaa, 1994, p. 15).

I find our present positionality as African American doctoral candidates at White universities as one of negotiating identities and brokering personalities on the

border of an African American upbringing and a White academy that measures optimal, exemplary, and worthy citizenry. We are wearily toeing the line that separ-
ates our familial color of ethnic integrity from mainstream academic dignity and
structural mobility. Our early constructed reality led us to consider the Black community, not as a site of failure or naivete, but rather as an ethos of hard work, community, spiritual faith, and a thirst for pragmatic knowledge that provided a gateway for educational hope and resiliency. Like the "emissarial" Black identity
explained by Grant and Breese (1997), we appear well versed in the norms of
achievement in the dominant culture and have "used them to [our] advantage . . .
even though there [were] several painful racist incidents" in our lives before we entered college (p. 198).

> **Keisha:** I offer to any Black graduate student that others before you have succeeded
> and survived and that others [you] can too. Oftentimes, Blacks are afraid to try for
> fear of failure. We have failed from the beginning when we do not try. Blacks must
> understand the unwritten rules of the game, and we must learn to use the system
> to our advantage as others have for many years. Deadlines serve a purpose. Those
> who do not meet the deadline are eliminated from the beginning. Who is it that
> has difficulties meeting these deadlines and following the instructions completely?
> It is us! That is how we are eliminated so easily. Then we want to cry racial dis-
> crimination when we are our worst enemy. We have to wake up and be intelligent
> at all times. This is truly a White male's world, but Blacks and other minorities can
> live in it successfully also.

Despite the more public and internal identity politics, we "are comfortable with
Anglo-Americans," and we have reached a university educational level that even
most Whites have not achieved (Grant & Breese, 1997, p. 198). Are traditional
White American successes, where progress is seen as a means toward an end of *control over* rather than *harmony with* organic and inorganic existence, what we want to
pursue? In light of the complexities of our histories, as Black, White-university educated, doctoral hopefuls, we enter our work daily as colonizer/colonized, insider/
outsider, mainstream homeboy and homegirl.

Conclusion

The individual narratives of the students highlighted in this chapter offer a critique
and perhaps a revised yardstick for the self-proclaimed White liberal academic professor and advisor. These students matriculate in graduate schools that often silence them. Our dialogue must include naming instances of African American humiliation and suffering. As Delpit (1995) unveils, this silenced dialogue involves a
phenomenon in which

> liberals (and here I am using the term "liberal" to mean the White liberal, progressive
> mystique of those whose beliefs include striving for a society based upon maximum
> individual freedom and autonomy) seem to act under the assumption that to make

any rules or expectations explicit is to act against liberal principles, to limit the freedom and autonomy of those subjected to the explicitness. (p. 123)

Therefore, African American doctoral candidates at predominantly White institutions should anticipate silencing, even by our liberal White peers and professors. We should anticipate internal dilemmas when considering our options and actions. We must also anticipate learning to rely upon ourselves and to draw from the positive energy and intellectual prowess of our predecessors to fulfill the requirements of the doctoral program. We must struggle, but we must do as our ancestors did so ardently—cling to hope with each daily accomplishment. There is no life to the struggle without hope as discussed by the late famed Brazilian educator Paulo Freire.

Struggle is not *the* tool that produces improved social conditions. Participation in struggle is not the improvement in and of itself. There must be hopefulness. In arguing that hope is a fundamental human need, Friere (1996) cautioned against separating hope from the action of struggling: "The idea that hope alone will transform the world . . . is an excellent route to hopelessness, pessimism, and fatalism" (p. 8). Hope is what sustains the struggle for a better condition for Blacks in the academy—a better academy and a better world. As Freire explains, "The attempt to do without hope, in the struggle to improve the world, as if that struggle could be reduced to calculated acts alone, or a purely scientific approach, is a frivolous illusion" (p. 8). Without a minimum of hope, we cannot so much as begin the arduous struggle. "But without the struggle," he contends, "hope . . . dissipates, loses its bearing, and turns into hopelessness" (p. 9). As Oakes and Lipton (1999) conclude, "Hope sustains the actions, and people must act or the hope turns against them—empty" (p. 32).

> John: I think the future depends on how the Black students come to the program. If they come as an independent individual, it can be discouraging. The future is encouraging though, [when] there are Black individuals and organizations reacting and emerging and reaching back, so you can get over that loneliness. And that's why it's so important to reach back.
>
> Keisha: I think the future looks very bright for the Black graduate student. With diversity being the current theme, many schools are soliciting the Black student to come and pursue graduate degrees at their university. This is not to say that they will continue to accept us with open arms, . . . but the challenge will be succeeding and graduating. The minority student must produce 200% of the time and always present their best skills at all times. Many will challenge us, not to discredit us, but to see how we will handle the challenge. It is up to the student to be knowledgeable and resourceful on the content area of their expertise. The sky can truly be the limit; however, we must persevere and forge forward despite the many obstacles we are presented [with]. Achieving the degree is not the end. We as African Americans and future educational leaders are presented [with] the challenge of opening the door for those who follow behind. We must be trail blazers and trend setters for many. This responsibility must be accepted willingly and dealt with accordingly.

It seems that African American doctoral candidates like Andre, John, and Keisha have adopted what Cornel West has called prophetic pragmatism, "a combination of democratic faith and a critical temper that keeps track of social misery, solicits and channels moral outrage to alleviate it, and projects a future in which potentialities of ordinary people flourish and flower" (qtd. in Oakes & Lipton, 1999, p. 369). These doctoral candidates seem to know that social justice is not merely an end state that is "out there" to be achieved someday through persistent struggle. Rather, it is an overdue birthright. They appear to find hope—as well as joy and satisfaction—from the everyday process of working to change the condition of others like them (see also Oakes & Lipton, 1999, p. 379). And when the continuous struggle and educational hope toward upward academic and economic mobility for themselves and others reaches fruition, it must ultimately render positive benefits that can be felt by the entire Black community, the United States, and the world. Martin Luther King Jr. alludes to the exponential positive influences of such struggles for social justice as that endured by Black doctoral candidates in predominantly White institutions:

> It first does something to the hearts and souls of those committed to it. It gives them new self-respect; it calls up resources of strength and courage that they did not know they had. . . . To become the instruments of a great idea is a privilege that history gives only occasionally. (qtd. in Oakes & Lipton, 1999, p. 373)

White institutional faculty, staff, administration, and students, often "ain't hearin' us," but our soul, persistence, potential, and actual positive influences on higher education are loud and clear.

References

Barger, R. N. (2000). *A summary of Lawrence Kohlberg's stages of moral development.* Notre Dame, IN: University of Notre Dame. Retrieved on January 23, 2001, from http://www.nd.edu/%7Erbarger/kohlberg.html.

Bell, A. F., II. (1998). *Ethics in public life.* Chapel Hill: Institute of Government, University of North Carolina—Chapel Hill.

Bowers, C. A. (1984). *The promise of theory: Education and the politics of cultural change.* New York: Teachers College Press.

Delpit, L. (1995). *Other people's children: Cultural conflict in the classroom.* New York: New Press.

Freire, P. (1996). *Pedagogy of hope.* New York: Continuum.

Grant, G. K., & Breese, J. R. (1997, July). Marginality theory and the African American student. *Sociology of Education, 70,* 192–205.

Oakes, J., & Lipton, M. (1999). *Teaching to change the world.* New York: McGraw-Hill.

Payne, R. (2001). *A framework for understanding poverty.* Rev. ed. Highlands, TX: aha! Process.

Richardson, W. D., Martinez, J. M., & Stewart, K. R. (1998). *Ethics and character: The pursuit of democratic virtues.* Durham, NC: Carolina Academic Press.

Shujaa, M. J. (Ed.) (1994). *Too much schooling, too little education: A paradox of Black life in White societies.* Trenton, NJ: Africa World Press.

Villenas, S. (1996). The colonizer/colonized Chicana ethnographer: Identity, marginalization and co-optation in the field. In B. M. Brizuela, J. P. Stewart, R. G. Carrillo, & J. G. Berger (Eds.) *Acts of inquiry in qualitative research.* Cambridge, MA: President and Fellows of Harvard College.

Washington, B. T. (1900, 1901). *Up from slavery: An autobiography.* Garden City, NY: Doubleday.

PART II

WHAT IS IT LIKE TO BE AN
AFRICAN AMERICAN
FACULTY MEMBER?

7

Paul F. Bitting

SO GROWS THE TREE: SOME ASSUMPTIONS UNDERLYING THE COLLEGE PROFESSORATE AND THEIR REPERCUSSIONS ON HIGHER EDUCATION

> *Playing with metaphors can evoke new perspectives on a problem. One strategy for exploiting metaphors is to identify some features from the research domain that are discernible in another domain—perhaps another discipline or area of activity. Attention is shifted to the new area (the metaphor), which is then closely examined. From this examination, the researcher may discover some variables, relationships, or patterns that can usefully be translated back to the research problem.*
>
> A. W. WICKER, 1985, p. _ _ _

The human tendency to think recurring thoughts limits our theories and research. I would like to make an analogy between the experience of beginning law students and that of those entering the college or university professorate, so that our perspectives of the former might contribute to better understanding of the latter. Although there is abundant research in psychology, educational psychology, sociology, philosophy, and adult education on numerous facets of learning, law, and mental health, there have been only minimal attempts to integrate findings across boundaries of these disciplines or fields to shed any light on the "professorial experience."

Consideration of the effectiveness of transitioning young professors into American higher education involves many issues: motivation and learning theory; evaluation of the methods and systems used to provide for the transition, especially in their effects when used during the most intense first-year period; examinations of the kinds of people who self-select for the professorate, their survival and the ways in which they are influenced by the experience; and the questions of justification of the more painful aspects of advancing through the higher education system, which its traditional defenders claim are part of learning to "think and act like a professor." Finally, assuming that all else supports the status quo, or, at least, no one actually dies because of the experience, to evaluate its effectiveness, there is the question of the purpose of that experience, the ultimate value question: If the transitional experience of the new professor is necessary to produce professors who will be functional in our current higher education system, is this the higher education system we want?

In attempting to address just some of these issues, this chapter will (a) describe the current system of graduate philosophical education through its most significant elements, (b) describe the climate created by the graduate philosophy department system, (c) compare this system to the process involved in the transition from graduate school to the professorate, and (d) argue that, in addition to lacking an end that justifies the use of means that degrade human beings, a new way of looking at an old problem suggests more effective strategies for preparing young higher education professors for their careers in the academy.

Some caveats are appropriate. I am biased. First, from one who transitioned into higher education after many years of teaching and administration in a secondary school, my verdict may be emotional rather than rational—reactions programmed into my personality. The resulting implied wrongness of fit may indicate a deficit in me rather than in the system. Second, as an older graduate student and entering professor with life experience, I was statistically expected to weather the attack on my identity and self-esteem better than my younger colleagues. But I had been a secondary school teacher, too. And it was that which made me seriously question the system for transitioning young professors into the academy.

The Philosophy Department Experience

Paper Chase is a film about law students at Harvard, which reputedly depicts pretty fairly the law school experience. The philosophy department with which I am familiar had its own professorial caricatures, including its "Perini"—an imposing figure who would colorfully convey a sense of his understanding of a particular passage from Wittgenstein by sketching a cat on a mat on the chalkboard and who, for twenty years, had terrorized students merely by calling on them to recite in the alphabetical order in which they appeared on his seating chart. I still remember this experience twenty years after it occurred:

> September 23, 1981: Today he picks our side of the room. "Mr. Bitting," he calls, and I stand, determined not to be intimidated. "Please tell us, sir, about Wittgenstein's Picture Theory of Language. Address his ontology within the context of picture theory. . . . Thank you very much, Mr. Bitting.

"Mr. Anderson (next target, sitting next to my right), please tell us about Wittgenstein's Picture Theory of Language."

I sit down, heart pounding. Did I leave something out? Did I get the theory or its underlying reasoning wrong? What does it mean that he is asking another student the exact same question he has just asked me? From somewhere outside of my buzzing head, I hear my friend Mr. Anderson's voice reciting at about two registers above normal.

Where I suspect *Paper Chase* fails in verisimilitude is in its comedic treatment of its subject. Though humor abounds, the Philosophy Department experience was not amusing, the first year least of all. Additionally, it must be noted that while the professor terrorized students who would rather die than admit in front of their peers that they were "unprepared," he also drew their unanimous respect because he never failed to respect them. His teaching does not represent the kind of preparation being criticized in this essay.

Some earmarks of the Philosophy Department, as I remembered it, are: (a) the combined Socratic and case-study methods for presenting information, (b) reliance on the final exam or term paper for the only grade for a course, (c) the practice of class ranking, which required that for me to do well *you* must do poorly, and (d) the encouragement of competitiveness. The sum effect of these characteristics is that "learning the game" outstrips any nobler goal as the ultimate purpose. These moments of performance become the hidden agenda of being in school. In the view of a more advanced student who already held degrees in other disciplines but who nearly flunked out his first year:

> The professors throw us into a sea of philosophy. We can't stop swimming, but we don't know where we're going. Everyone tries to take a cue from someone else, but "Finish" is nowhere in sight. The teachers watch us with detachment from the shore: "Who can keep up? Who's the fastest? And who can't swim at all?" (Lee Allen, personal interview, September 2002).

How do students respond to such conditions? A collection of first-year law student responses gathered by James R. Elkins (1985) provides examples. Elkins asked students to keep a journal of their experience and feelings in law school in various courses which he taught. He got the idea from Robert Coles's *Children of Crisis: A Study of Courage and Fear,* who in studying children attempted to "locate his body and mind where certain *citizens* are up against difficult times, so that their lives, like those of the sick, may have something to teach the rest of us" (qtd. in Elkins, p. 28). For Elkins, "the suffering of the few is a valuable source for understanding a pedagogy and curriculum that purports to serve the many" (p. 28).

Words that commonly appear in the accounts of Elkins's students are: tension, stress, apprehension, anxiety, doubt, fear, intimidation, terror, and impending doom. "Apprehension is so much a part of the experience," Elkins says, "that one student remarked: 'I begin to feel scared because I was not feeling scared'" (1985, p. 32).

Entering the Professorate

Are there marked similarities between the experiences of the graduate student in philosophy or law and the experience of being initiated into the professorate? I propose an approach to preparing young professors in higher education that is based on reinforcement and kindness, a change derived from the observation that there are marked similarities between new professors and students trying for the first time to master a discipline in a deep and scholarly way. Both have new skills to master. When new professors enter the highly ritualized initiation process in higher education, they are confronted with a complex, multidimensional world. The young professor is asked to leave the security of a "relatively" known world, a world in which certain tasks have been mastered, supportive relationships formed and maintained, and ways devised to keep self-esteem and identity. As a new colleague of mine expressed it: "I had prepared myself as well as possible for what I knew was to be a difficult transition from a competent, responsible, knowledgeable graduate student to that of a floundering, doubting, questioning professor in the eyes of the more experienced faculty in our department."

The need to develop totally new skills in both the early stage of graduate study and the early stage of the professorate results in both groups experiencing an extremely high level of anxiety. Such anxiety leads to an unusually strong emotional reliance on a teacher (if a graduate student) or a mentor (if a young professor), a heightened receptiveness to ideas and readiness to learn, and last, a strong need to internalize incoming new information.

Furthermore, the anxiety experienced by newly minted professors, stimulated by the total unfamiliarity of their environment, is exacerbated by the fact that when, again like beginning graduate students in philosophy, new professors need to establish an emotional bond with someone whom they regard as a mentor, senior professors are often notoriously unapproachable.

Initiation into professionalism has frequently been described as a painful experience, and the ritual of becoming a university professor is no exception. A major change occurs in the process of becoming a professor. The "troubles" of the new professor are a mirror reflecting the hidden, human depths of the higher education initiation rites. Entering the professorate is a powerful, transformative experience in which the soul as well as the mind is at stake. This is the *"deformation professionelle,"* "the possible distortion of character that derives from participation in the world of work" (Taylor, 1975, p. 251). In fact, both the professorate and academia may suffer due to the prevailing transformation system.

It would take a very simple intervention to effect a major change in easing the transition of young professors. The source of this change is discoverable by watching graduate students entering a new discipline, because there are striking similarities between the ecological relationship of each group of learners to their respective environment. Both are on the frontier of literacy: "professorial thinking" is a kind of literacy. Both experience anxiety and stress due to the strangeness of the new world they are entering and the expectations of others. Both have great need for a "guide"—a teacher or mentor whom they can trust. Both are in a state of heightened receptivity to new ideas and of heightened ability to synthesize bits of incoming information. However, because so much of the input is new, both feel an intensified need to internalize incoming information and attach it to their pre-existing conceptual framework. What all of this means in terms of success in the profession and in learning can be expressed in two points: The concepts and skills to be mastered for success must appear to be of value to the learner, and the learner must feel that he or she is capable of learning them (Bettelheim, 1982). Analogizing between new professors and new graduate students in philosophy could help higher education administrators and senior professors move toward success.

In recent years, observers attempting to identify the stressors of the entering professor have produced a lengthy list: the heavy work load (teaching, research, advising, committee assignments, university and community service); the high level of competition, isolation and loneliness, the emphasis on professionalism rather than on humanistic or philosophical issues; and the paucity of ongoing positive reinforcement (Taylor, 1975).

As the result of these stressors, a general pattern of anxiety, fear of failure, and depression may emerge. In response, the new professors assume a stance adaptive for survival that Elkins (1985) described as "routinization" and "compartmentalization" (p. 41); the professor becomes indifferent to his or her surroundings and alienated from his or her own emotions.

Must this happen? Are the stressing elements of the system crucial for effective professorial work? Is it "right" that the young professor, crumpling under the stress, finds that he or she is not "the stuff whereof professors are made"? Is it possible that the system of transitioning initiates into the professorate may be damaging to an individual whose self-esteem depends on continuous demonstrations of success? In support of this idea, popular wisdom maintains that any good system trains losers as well as winners, so that setbacks will be no more than temporary. Observing that the same stressful factors exist for all entering professors, I suggest that "sub-optimal coping" in some but not all results from the way in which the individual structures and perceives his or her experience. New professors who expect the transition into higher education to be difficult may have less than the anticipated difficulty while those less braced for stress may suffer more.

Just as the jousts of chivalry prepared the medieval knight for the carnage of battle, so the tensions, competitiveness, and work load may prepare the professor for the cool battle of wills required by the system of transitioning into academe. And just as the dissecting room forces the fledgling medical doctor to suppress and conquer his or her emotional reactions to bodily violation, so may the procedures of preparing the newly hired Ph.D. force fledgling professors to suppress and conquer their moral reactions to their students' cause.

"Suppress and conquer their moral reaction to their students' cause"? Does this statement of an educational goal represent a desirable community value? In the service of objective truth and justice, professorial transitioning strives to develop certain intellectual traits—skepticism, objectivity, and analytical acumen.

Such development involves the deification of intelligence. The deification begins with the interview process, in which candidates are chiefly appraised on and rewarded for their intelligence. And in calculating the candidate's eligibility for such glittering prizes as the tenure-track assistant professorship, the deification continues. Meanwhile, many equally sterling virtues—moral awareness, social commitment, emotional stability—are ignored.

The definitive study on the new professor *qua* person has not been undertaken, yet such a study may well hold the key to the long-term changes that would enhance higher education.

References

Bettelheim, B., & Zelan, K. (1982). *On learning to read: The child's fascination with meaning.* New York: Random House.

Elkins, J. R. (1985). Rites de Passage: Law Students "Telling Their Lives." *Journal of Legal Education, 35,* 27–55.

Taylor, J. B. (1975). Law school stress and the *deformation professionelle. Journal of Legal Education, 27,* 251–267.

Wicker, A. W. (1985, October). Getting out of our conceptual ruts: Strategies for expanding conceptual frameworks. *American Psychologist,* 1094–1103.

8

Robin Hughes

THE DWINDLING POOL OF
QUALIFIED PROFESSORS OF COLOR:
SUBURBAN LEGENDS

The number of doctoral degrees awarded to students of color has remained significantly low over the past 25 years. Understandably, the number of students who graduate from doctoral degree granting programs affects the total number of faculty members of color. For instance, in 1986 only 804 or 3.5% of the 22,984 doctoral recipients were African American. In 1991, although the pool of doctoral recipients increased by over 10%, doctoral recipients of African descent remained at a steady low of 933 or 3.8% of the total degree recipients (Hacker, 1992). Ten years later, the *Chronicle of Higher Education* (2002) reported a 1% increase in doctoral degrees awarded to students of African descent. Given this trend, it should come as no surprise that the number of doctoral degree recipients entering the professorate has also remained virtually unchanged.

These numbers translate into shortages throughout the academy where African Americans constitute only 4.5% of the professorate (*Chronicle*, 2002, p. 232); Ladson-Billings, 1998). Even more astonishing is that, when disaggregated from the total, Blacks comprise approximately only 1% of the faculty in predominantly White colleges and universities (PWIs) while HBCU's account for the remaining 3.3% (Ladson-Billings, 1998). When it comes to professional administrative positions, only 186 of the nation's total 3,070 CEO's of institutions of higher education are African American (American Council, 2000). Accordingly, it comes as no surprise that Whites hold 90.7% of the faculty positions and 89.7% of all administrative positions in American colleges and universities.

While these figures should suggest to everyone that immediate attention be given to increasing the minority representation in education, not only to help the sharply waning economic growth of the United States—the more politically correct non-offensive sound bite—but also to ensure democratic plurality (the hegemonic reality) for groups that have traditionally been marginalized and subsequently forced out of the labor market and continue to lag in educational and economic growth. However, such has not been the case, specifically for institutions of higher education.

University policy has been characterized by media and other stakeholders as unfairly admitting and recruiting"unqualified and undeserving" faculty members and students of color who routinely "steal" the spots that other more "qualified" faculty are "entitled" to (Duster, 1993, p. 232). Although the stereotypical image of the gray-haired White male professor remains statistically intact and universities remains predominantly White (Hamilton, 2002), White students are increasingly taking universities to court with the cry of reverse discrimination based on the premise of the "dwindling pool" of "qualified" applicants.

The "pool," which many have come to read as code for the number of people of color is undeniably a direct result of the pool of doctoral degree recipients. However, if every one of those newly minted African American doctorates went into the academy, they would have a negligible effect on the proportion of African Americans in the professorate (Ladson-Billings, 1998). This leaves many institutions in quite a quandary. How does one increase the number of applicants in the so-called pool?

The most frequently noted solution includes simple mathematical accountability rhetoric in which one's future employment is reduced to a few simple mathematical and logic fundamentals. Simply put: not enough in, not enough out. And certainly, if not enough "adequate" in, then this condition further diminishes the number of"adequate" out. These flawed and rather simplistic conclusions clearly draw upon very crude statistical theories of inadequate sample size. Unfortunately, a consequence of such misinformation, is that this one-dimensional and flawed logic encourages the public to assume that people of color (African Americans in this context), who obtain advanced degrees, are inadequately prepared to assume the faculty role. Further, this analysis suggests that the actual quantity of "good" candidates from people of color is insufficient to make a determination for employment. Simply put, there were not enough applicants from that particular ethnic pool to make a "good" selection.

However, the pool logic is riddled with some fundamental flaws. First, the pool is a mirage at best. It assumes meritocratic experiences and equally a meritocratic employment system. It assumes that no one benefits from legacy. It assumes that certain protected groups benefit from a skewed description and perception of affirmative action that privileges one group over another. It assumes that the protected group does not have credentials equivalent to the majority group. It assumes that one group is more "merited" and "qualified" than another. But most importantly, it amalgamates into one simple, "objective," monolithic explanation of a phenomenon that is far more complex than Darwinian accounts of ability, sample size, and fittest logic.

I argue that the size of the pool is a complex and political debate that demands intricate analysis and exposure of the many hegemonic variables that may play a role in why or why not people of color are selected. This essay, based solely on my personal experiences, will address and interrogate the myth of the dwindling pool of minority applicants for positions in higher education. Accordingly, it will address some of the many obstacles that students and faculty of color must negotiate before placing a toe in the sometimes-chilly pool.

The Myth of the Level Playing Field

An incorrect assumption underlying the image of the pool is that of, to use another image, the level playing field. This more politically correct term was used to covertly lead the initial attack on affirmative action, the mention of which has historically caused much turmoil. Most recently, educational affirmative action policies have come under sustained attack (Milem, 1999; Schmidt, 1998), particularly as applied to admissions policies and standardized scores (Gose, 1998). The theme heard frequently among students is that affirmative action policies undercut the university's traditional color-blind, equal opportunity approach to recruitment (Duster, 1993). Universities have provided new fuel for the anti-affirmative action fire by their interpretations of court rulings on affirmative action.

Texas has taken the lead on such rulings. In *Hopwood v. Texas,* the Fifth Circuit Court of Appeals ruled that raced-based admissions policies at the University of Texas were unconstitutional. However, Texas extended the ruling by instituting anti-affirmative action policies throughout its higher educational system. This action not only set the tone for admissions policies but also extended anti-affirmative action policies to include non race based financial aid, and scholarships. In addition, all programs supporting minority students operate through guidelines created in response to the *Hopwood* ruling.

Other states have followed this trend, changing the weather of the racial climate throughout the United States. The University of Washington will no longer use race as a criterion in admissions decisions. At the University of Michigan, a student contends that he was denied admission to law school because of race-based preferential treatment. At the University of Maryland and the University of Oklahoma, students have filed suits alleging that their university kept standards low to admit minority students. The underlying premise is that such behavior subverts the university's meritocratic principles. As a result, the schools unfairly admit "unqualified" and "undeserving" students who steal the spots to which "qualified" students are "entitled," thereby unleveling the field.

However, the image of the level playing field in admissions does not hold up to statistical realities. Universities that have, for the most part, only recently admitted students of color in significant numbers, routinely allow and encourage preferential treatment under the rubric of legacy (Duster, 1993). This term means that more White students have entered the gates of the 10 most elite American institutions of higher education through "alumni preference" than the combined number of all of the Blacks and Hispanics who entered through affirmative action (Duster, 1993). Furthermore, according to Nettles, Perna, and Millet (1998) only 342 of the nation's 1,808 four-year colleges and universities are likely to use affirmative action (p. 103). The rest admit most students who apply; questions of selectivity are not particularly relevant. Of those 342, only about 120 are serious affirmative action institutions, meaning that they are the institutions that have admitted the greatest number of Black and Hispanic students in the past decade or so. Of the top 120 institutions under consideration, many expanded the size of their freshman class by at least as many as the number of Black and Hispanic students they had admitted in the last decade.

Still, some students of color are affected by misinterpretation of the level playing field. They return obsessively to the agonizing question: "Do I really belong here?" I recall wearing my credentials on my sleeve daily as part of the necessary armor to fend off the doubts of classmates and professors. This armor typically consisted of one's GRE scores neatly tucked into one's long-term memory but ready to be retrieved at any moment. Often, the discussion of some standardized score, specifically GREs, emerged as a way in which one could be "academically outed" in hopes of justifying one's presence.

This is not say that my experiences are universally generalizable. In fact, I hope that many African American students who attended PWIs can claim that they wrestled with few or no issues of racism on campus. However, my own experience in graduate school was not so sunny. One professor claimed that a class assignment for a lesson on affirmative action (one in which I was to portray the resident and stereotypical Black person, was designed to incorporate readings that should satisfy me and my Blackness. Another suggested that I more than likely would not need to purchase graduation regalia, because that right was reserved for those who were thinking of pursuing the professorate.

However, the experience that remains most vivid in my memory occurred during a class in which my classmates, all of them White, swapped stories of at least one person they had known who had been directly affected by some form of reverse discrimination—either by not getting a job or not being admitted to a particular school. Some of the stories came from distant relatives or friends from years gone by. Their point was an indictment of the current system of affirmative action (or what they called affirmative action) and a call to readjust the playing field. Many told me how lucky I was to be a double minority protected by affirmative action. They were not being hostile (although they were certainly patronizing and insensitive), because they stressed that they were glad that at least someone they knew was worthy of benefiting from affirmative action, even though it was an unfair system. They knew I really struggled and worked hard, plus they knew me, so I deserved it. In fact, they assured me, that it would be so much easier for me to get a job. (They were wrong about that, too).

For what seemed to be an eternity, I listened to these heartfelt stories of some distant relative or friend of a friend who had experienced alleged reverse discrimination. I was reminded of the cynical response to Clarence Thomas's emotional story of pulling himself up by his bootstraps: "All Black people have a story." Yes, they do. And many have several stories a day.

As the conversation on race continued, a White male friend in the class finally had enough. He explained that, while he appreciated these stories, he hardly construed them as reverse discrimination and instead saw the conversation as racist. He pointed out that I was the only person of color in our program and in the class, that I had the highest GRE (another issue) scores in the cohort, and that many of them, except for the Hispanic students, were mid- to upper-level administrators on campus. I was certainly qualified to fill one of these same coveted positions but lacked the necessary connections to "call in a favor" to get one.

He and I later debriefed, as we often did. We concluded that I was a classmate, not a colleague—not quite a friend—so it would be difficult for me to prove that I had the sociological credentials of "face validity"—in this case, a phenotypic likeness. Second, a major contributor to this academic ontology was the institution's idiosyncratic nature: a campus population of well over 40,000, predominantly White students from rural Texas counties; it enrolls less than 3% African American undergraduates and roughly 1.5% African-descended graduate students. Not only was I the only African American in the program at the time, there were only 128 Black doctoral students on the entire campus of 50,000 and only 35 Black faculty members on a campus with over 1,500 faculty and staff—at least, the university claimed 35 African American members. However, accounting for all 35 of them seemed to be more difficult and require more sophisticated mathematics than that which is used to approximate the whereabouts of the legendary electron cloud (see the electron density argument in Lincoln & Guba, 1985). Finally, the university is located in a still-segregated town with predominantly Black and Hispanic neighborhoods on one side of University Street and Whites on the other. One does not have to travel far between the two sides of University Street to experience firsthand the lack of diversity. Less than a five-minute trip in either direction takes the visitor to the town's ethnic extremes in grocery shopping, fashion, hair salons, and eateries. For instance, while everyone knows that Shannon's serves the best soul food on the north side of town and routinely attrracts a diverse crowd from the entire city, located on the other side of town is an equally popular student bar, the Dixie Chicken, where the crowd tends to look rather homogeneous.

My experiences in the department (though not the institution in general) have been good. My mentors have been stellar. I have presented at several national conferences and with an international scholar. Yet I am still awaiting that phone call from all of those universities looking for a double minority.

The Doppelganger Effect: Not a Myth

Another important fact that has been overshadowed in the debate about affirmative action is that affirmative action groups, including Blacks, Latinos, sometimes

Asians, veterans, the disabled, and Native people, make up about 70% of the population (Staples, 1995). However this figure is not reflected in the employment picture, in which White males, the alleged victims of affirmative action, compose about 30% of the population yet still hold about 75% of the highest earning occupations in this country and 95% of the very top (Staples, 1995). And, although many would like to believe "the debate to be a Black-White issue, the fact is that White women are more likely to benefit from affirmative action policies than any other group" (Staples, 1995, p. 4) due in part to sheer numbers.

I am often reminded of an international woman scholar in a leading Texas university who could not be inducted into a distinguished professorship before she was placed "on trial" by a jury of her peers—all males, all White. This policy, set by the academic governing board, reeked of the same politics of that of the private Georgia golf course that had no Black members until 1990 and no female members at the time of this writing. At least its officers were forthright in explaining that, as a private club, its membership does not include women at this time. In contrast, this particular higher education institution is public, supported by the tax dollars of men and women from all walks of life; but it too had unwritten rules that are very clear. This scholar was its first woman member, and it has yet to induct a person of color. In essence, that field, although it appears to be more level, is slanted as well.

The level playing field myth is further perpetuated by the rhetorical sound bite, "Women and minorities are encouraged to apply." In reality, I found that this statement includes several hidden statements, including: We say we encourage you to apply, but because we must include this statement. You are encouraged to apply, but we are not committed to recruiting faculty or administrators of color because it is not that important. You are encouraged to apply, but we already have a [faculty of color, female, other protected group], and one is enough to fulfill our duty in the diversity department. We encourage you to apply, but the organization is likely to hire minorities who, despite their color, will blend into the fold (Cose, 1993). As an example, consider the incident that occurred at Harvard University where Cornel West, an internationally known Black scholar and professor, was scrutinized because he did not blend in well. According to West, the president of Harvard attacked his integrity and questioned the academic merit of his work (Wilson & Smallwood, 2002). Perhaps the president overlooked the fact that West was one of the 14 academicians on Harvard's campus out of 2,000 to hold the title of "university professor."

I am certain that many of us can add other items to this list. The bottom line is that while *some* organizations may promote a commitment to hiring minorities, they are unwilling to purposefully recruit (Hughes, 2001), support or facilitate minority members' transition to a majority White organization. (Mabokela & Madsen, 2002). This is not new. Many organizations boast a history of recruiting and retaining people of color; however, many also suffer from the psychological tendency to hire a Doppelganger ("double"), well-known in educational literature as the existence and promulgation of homogeneity in organizations.

Why are institutions, both public and private, homogeneous? The reason most typically given is that individuals are generally attracted to and selected by organizations already filled by members with values similar to their own. People tend to hire people who look and act like themselves. Consequently, Whites, the majority of the population, have a distinct advantage. If a the majority of institutions, both public and private, are led by a particular ethnic or cultural group, then it is more likely that officers of those institutions will hire people with similar backgrounds. The inevitable results is that organizations are more homogenous than heterogeneous (Chemers & Murphy, 1995).

An argument that counters the advantages of diversity is that employers should have the freedom to hire whomever they wish. The basis for the argument is in part upon who reads and interprets the Constitution and in part due to the misconception that a meritocracy exists—when in fact the framers of the Constitution did not have Blacks in mind during that writing. The flaw in the meritocracy argument is that it is a hegemonic illusion. This presumed existence of a meritocracy subconsciously (and perhaps consciously) excludes cultural and ethnic groups that have historically been excluded. Although a racial- and/or gender-pure organization may not be a purposeful conspiracy, it is most certainly an end result, because people tend to hire themselves: the doppelganger effect. As a result, entire groups are inadvertently yet routinely excluded from employment, housing, and other inalienable rights that would be afforded to everyone in a genuine meritocracy.

Institutions of higher education are not immune from the doppelganger effect. Many Americans find their jobs through a network of friends and kinfolk. The doppelganger effect is further confounded by a phenomenon like spousal hires in institutions of higher education. Although such institutions boast a level of democracy and plurality not reflected in the larger society and make a committed effort to seek qualified minority employees, offices of student affairs, campus administration, and faculty continue to remain virtually homogenous.

During my time in graduate school and after, I heard about the many phone calls made to friends in the field who knew other friends, that help still more friends find employment. This system seems perfectly fine; however, it becomes very difficult when you are not a part of that very powerful network. I am personally aware of an African American administrator with over ten years of experience and scholarship in student affairs who was not hired. Instead, a person with absolutely no experience or education in student affairs was selected for the position, simply because of phone calls from a network of students, administrators, and former students. The university yielded to the pressure. Actually, I learned from participants that the administers responsible for making the final decision were thrilled to hire "one of their own." Ironically, their "own" left after only a year, a year described by many as "awful" for the university, for the students, and for his staff. He was not qualified by either education or experience, but he looked like the university.

Perhaps, again, this event was unique to the idiosyncratic institution that I described previously. Nevertheless, the doppelganger effect is not confined to one region. During most of my interviews, in all cases but one, I was greeted by an all-White faculty. In one instance, I heard that the department had embraced diversity because they had indeed hired one person of color, explaining, "The pool was so shallow, we really lucked out."

One of my most interesting interviews occurred at a small liberal arts college on the East Coast. One of the interviewers explained to me in more detail than I cared to know that their last hire had been an African American woman who "caused problems" for the entire staff. She just did not fit in. They would all close their office doors when she arrived at work. As an African American woman, I understood why this story had to be shared with me: This college would not be hiring me if he had anything to do with it. Even after this explanation, I reminded myself that my interview with the director had proceeded without a flaw, that he seemed to be honestly committed to creating a diverse staff, and that he had seemed impressed by his two-day visit with me. The director was and is an internationally known scholar, well respected by many people of color. Besides, the college was hiring for two positions, and I was one of three finalists. I liked those odds. However, I learned that the first position would certainly be filled by the son of the director's long-time friend, while the final candidate had the distinct advantage of being another White male. The odds were suddenly stacked against me. I continued to hope until Sunday when the director called to reiterate how much he had enjoyed interviewing me and that, if he had to make the decision solely on hunches and without input from the other staff, then I was perfect. But the bottom line was that the doppelganger received the job. Again, I debriefed, this time with two students and several professors in the program. They all told me that he had something that I did not have on my vitae: "He looks like them." They are not committed to diversity because they are scared of change and apparently do not see the merits of diversity.

During this period when I was contemplating a life-long career with a national copying chain, I remembered a study I conducted as a graduate student. A White student asked whether there were any Black professors on campus, because he had taken classes only from White professors. I explained that the school reportedly had 35 Black faculty members but that they had never been specifically identified. He pointed out that the university is somehow able to recruit Black football players but seems unable to recruit Black professors. In his book, the university was communicating that it cared about diversity on its athletic teams but was not equally committed to diverse faculty representation.

This student's observations were astute. According to the Office of Institutional Studies and Planning (1998), Blacks filled 15 executive administrative positions, or 4.82% of the total 311 available positions. However, Blacks accounted for 40% of service and maintenance positions, Hispanics 31%, and Whites only 27%. These figures are even more interesting in light of the fact that Whites comprise 70% of the total staff employed by the university. In other words, out of a total of 782 Blacks employed by the institution, 65% work in service and maintenance positions, but fill only 1.91% of the executive administrative staff. In contrast, of 3,409

Whites employed in nonfaculty positions, only 8.8% are employed as service maintenance staff.

Interestingly enough, the demographic make-up of the urban region serving this university suggests that the university disproportionately employs Blacks in nonprofessional positions. According to the U.S. Census Bureau figures for 2000, Blacks and Hispanics comprise 30% of the total 134,213 population, with Blacks numbering 16,418 and Hispanics 23,840.

Color-Blind Classroom: Another Myth

Faculty are routinely perceived as marching in the vanguard of liberalism, implying that America's higher education teachers are collectively better able to participate in discourse that includes social, cultural, economic, and political ways of understanding; racial and ethnic critiques of intellectual and knowledge production activities; and views of knowledge through a variety of lenses, not from a singular perspective (Lincoln, 1999). Unfortunately, it appears that no group on campus is less involved in the diversity agenda than the professorate (Levine, 1993); and of those involved, typically the majority are minority faculty members. At institutions that have been identified as most diverse, few teach about or engage in scholarship concerning diversity or seem concerned about diversity. Almost none are engaged in co-curricular activities dealing with diversity (Levine, 1993). Still, some professors believe that the problem of racism is virtually a thing of the past; therefore, any special attention to ethnic minorities would be a form of reverse discrimination.

Paradoxically, the majority of professors reported that they had been brought up under conditions in which discrimination against Blacks was accepted and even endorsed by parents and other significant people in their environment. They lived in environments where there were no Blacks and had very few Black acquaintances or friends. This lack of exposure should make them keenly aware of their own potential blind spots; and certainly the horizon has changed since 1950s. However, many faculty continue to look away from the problems of race (Katz, 1991). This attitude alone contributes to missed opportunities on the part of both minority and White students and White faculty members to become better aware of the discourse of race.

In that graduate classroom where I was the only African American listening to a chorus of stories about reverse discrimination, conspicuously missing from the discourse was the voice of the professor. He purposely did not engage in the conversation, although he told me at the end of the semester that he had launched the discussion on affirmative action specifically to accommodate me as a Black person. It was the only class discussion the entire semester on race. No doubt I failed to be as grateful as he expected.

While many would like to believe that race doesn't matter, the color-blind classroom and campus are fictions. I find claims of color-blindness absurd, given how many professors grew up under conditions in which discrimination against Blacks was accepted and even endorsed by parents and other significant people in their environment (Katz, 1991). The university environment perpetuates this mindset. According to a Levine (1993) study of 14 universities, no institution, with the exception of a Black college and an institution historically committed to diversity, had a faculty even remotely matching the minority population of its region or the nation. Nearly all colleges now lack the critical mass of underrepresented peoples to make diversity visible to colleagues, to reduce the level of complacency, to encourage discourse, to provide models for students, and to serve as a catalyst for action. Not only are Black students affected, but Black faculty claim that they bear the brunt of the responsibility for Black students and their success or failure while in college (Blackwell, 1996). According to some faculty members, whenever a minority person is hired in a faculty position, he or she automatically becomes role model, advisor, counselor, advocate, and a sympathetic listener for minority students. Moreover, students of color are frequently in greater need of mentoring than their White counterparts even while many faculty do not believe that they are responsible for giving any special attention to minority students (Blackwell, 1996). However, such a position ignores a critical part of a teacher's job description: to do whatever needs to be done to meet the needs of the student. Teachers who have abandoned the "one size fits most" theory of pedagogy (Estaban Alvere, personal communication, August 2001), still seem to believe that "one size fits all or most" in mentoring. This attitude is a disservice to the academy and the profession, as well as failing to serve students.

Mentoring creates a stronger involvement with the university for students, stimulating their interest in what it means to be a faculty member (Boyer, 1990). An "intrusive" strategy of mentoring students has been found particularly effective when advising and mentoring students of color (Blackwell, 1996; Kobrak, 1992). Intrusive advising means being duly concerned about the academic affairs of one's students. It requires that the faculty members, administrators, and advisors take an aggressive approach, requiring the student to come in for advising at frequent intervals. (Bennett & Okinaka, 1989; Sedlacek, 1987). Historically, intrusive advising has been used as a form of mentoring and retention at HBCUs, and the persistent rates of Black college students at HBCUs attest to its effectiveness. In fact, intrusive advising may help to explain why, even though there are only 118 HBCUs, they account for over 20% of all Black students enrolled in institutions of higher education and award a greater percentage of all degrees earned by Black students (Blackwell, 1996; Feagin, Vera, & Imani, 1996; Fleming, 1984; Nettles & Perna, 1997). I am the beneficiary of intrusive advising. Those weekly "come to Jesus meetings" between my mentors and me were often harsh, but they have been critical to my experience as a new assistant professor.

African American students are particularly vulnerable in faculty-student relationships, and these relationships have frequently been unhelpful to Black students while professors seem more receptive to White students. According to Trueba (1998), "Many times White students are more frequently cultivated, guided, and supported, because they know how to obtain support and exhibit the appropriate behaviors at every inch of the journey" (p. 87). It would seem clear that all institutions that hope or need to move toward a more diverse faculty and student body should adopt intrusive advising. In fact the university should lead the charge that would incorporate a sense of reciprocity between the institution, the professor, and the student—students of color in general and African American students in particular.

Indeed, some universities have recognized this need and have begun to make significant policy and institutional changes to this end. One of my mentors told me years ago of his conscious resistance to the "natural" impulse to hire a familiar candidate. He described interviewing an African American candidate who was so unlike the rest of the candidates and the faculty that he was unsure whether she would fit in. He supported her nomination for exactly that reason. He was fifty, a full professor at a Research I institution; she was African American, barely thirty. She was different, and her research agenda was different, but my mentor knew the importance of diversity and that his college needed to diversify its faculty. He told me that they had hired plenty of people who looked and acted like him and that was enough. However, many institutions have not begun this change process, regrettably perpetuating the enduring image of the gray-haired professor who walks the paths of forever fall campuses, wearing brown tweed jackets with leather patches. Yet "institutions which fail to diversify their faculties and students will quite simply be left behind, footnotes and afterthoughts in the cultural and organizational history, sad monuments to a forgotten orthodoxy" (Lincoln 1999, p. 21).

References

American Council on Education Corporate Database. (2000). College and University Chief Executive Officers, by Institutional Type: Race/Ethnicity and Gender: Table 2A. Washington, DC: ACE.

Bennett, C., & Okinaka, A. (1989, April). *Factors related to persistence among Asian, Black, Hispanic and White undergraduates at a predominantly White university: Comparison between first and fourth year cohorts.* Paper presented at the annual meeting of the American Educational Research Association, San Francisco.

Blackwell, J. (1996). Faculty issues: The impact on minorities. In B. Townsend (Ed.), *Racial and ethnic diversity in higher education* (pp. 315–336). ASHE Reader Series. Needham Heights, MA: Simon and Schuster.

Boyer, W. (1990). *Scholarship reconsidered.* Princeton, NJ: Carnegie Foundation for the Advancement of Teaching.

Chemers, M. M., & Murphy, S. E. (1995). Leadership and diversity in groups and organizations. In M. M. Chemers, S. Oskamp, & M. A. Costanzo (Eds.), *Diversity in organizations: New perspectives for a changing workplace* (pp. 157–190). Thousand Oaks, CA: Sage.

Chronicle of Higher Education (2002, September). *Almanac: Characteristics of faculty members with teaching duties by type of institution, fall 1998* [On-line]. Available http://chronicle.com/weekly/almanac/2002/nation/0103102.htm.

Cose, E. (1993). *The rage of a privileged class.* New York: HarperCollins.

Duster, T. (1993). The diversity of California at Berkeley: An emerging reformulation of "competence" in an increasingly multicultural world. In B. Thompson and S. Tyagi (Eds.), *Beyond a dream deferred: Multicultural education and the politics of excellence* (pp. 231–235). Minneapolis: University of Minnesota Press.

Feagin, J., Vera, H., & Imani, N. (1996). *The agony of education: Black students at White colleges and universities.* New York: Routledge.

Fleming, J. (1984). *Blacks in college: A comparative study of students: Success in Black and White institutions.* San Francisco: Jossey-Bass.

Gose, B. (1998, September 18). A sweeping new defense of affirmative action. *Chronicle of Higher Education,* p. A46.

Hacker, A. (1992). *Two nations: Black and White, separate, hostile, and unequal.* New York: Charles Scribner's Sons.

Hamilton, K. (2002). Race in the classroom. *Black Issues in Higher Education, 19*(2), 32–36.

Hughes, R. (2001). *Student development and change: Student and parent expectations and experience.* Unpublished doctoral dissertation, Texas A&M University.

Katz, J. (1991). White faculty struggling with the effects of racism. In P. Altbach & K. Lomotey (Eds.), *The racial crisis in American higher education* (pp. 187–196). New York: University of New York Press.

Kobrak, P. (1992). Black student retention in predominantly White regional universities: The politics of faculty involvement. *Journal of Negro Education, 61*(4), 509–530.

Ladson-Billings, G. (1998). Just what is critical race theory and what's it doing in a nice field like education? *Qualitative Studies in Education, 11*(1), 7–24.

Levine, A. (1993). Diversity on campus. In A. Levine (Ed.), *Higher learning of America: 1980–2000* (pp. 333–343). Baltimore, MD: Johns Hopkins University Press.

Lincoln, Y. (1999). *Toward a postmodern university: Land-grants in the new millennium.* Paper presented at the University Distinguished Lecture Series, Texas A&M University, College Station, Texas.

Lincoln, Y., & Guba, E. (1985). *Naturalistic inquiry.* Newbury Park, CA: Sage.

Madsen, J., & Mabokela, R. (2000). Organizational culture and its impact on African American teachers. *American Educational Research Journal, 37*(4), 849–876.

Milem J. (1999). The educational benefits of diversity: Evidence from multiple sectors. In M. Chang, D. Witt, J. Jones, & K. Hakuta (Eds.), *Compelling interest: Examining the evidence on racial dynamics in higher education* (pp. 1–41). Stanford, CA: American Educational Research Association and the Stanford University Center for Comparative Studies in Race and Ethnicity.

Madsen, J., & Mabokela, R. (2000). Organizational culture and its impact on African American teachers. *American Educational Journal 37*(4), 849–876.

Nettles, M., Perna, L., & Millet, C. (1998). In G. Orfield & E. Miller (Eds.), *Chilling admissions: The affirmative action crisis and the search for alternatives* (pp. 97–110). Cambridge, MA: Harvard Civil Rights Project and Harvard Education Publishing Group.

Office of Institutional Studies and Planning (1998). *Texas A&M University profile reports: Staff by category, gender, and ethnicity.* [On-line]. Available at www.tamu.edu.opir?stat_cat.gif in September 2002.

Schmidt, P. (1998, October 30). Affirmative action: The next battleground. *Chronicle of Higher Education,* p. A32.

Sedlacek, W. (1987). Black students on White campuses: 20 years of research. *Journal College Student Personnel, 28*(6), 484–495.

Staples, R. (1995). Black deprivation—White privilege: The assault on affirmative action. *The Black Scholar, 25*(3), 2–6.

Trueba, H. (1998). Race and ethnicity in academia. In L. Valverde & L. Castenell Jr. (Eds.), *The multicultural campus: Strategies for transforming higher education* (pp. 71–34). Walnut Creek, CA: AltaMira Press.

Wilson, R., & Smallwood, S. (2002, January 18). Battles of wills at Harvard. *Chronicle of Higher Education,* p. A8.

9

Lisa D. Hobson-Horton

AVOIDING THE CLOCK STOPPERS: HOW TO PREPARE FOR, ENDURE, AND SURVIVE THE FIRST YEAR OF THE PROFESSORATE

The first year of teaching can be an interesting experience of learning new roles, preparing new content, and facing new challenges. In this essay, I discuss experiences from my first two years as an African American woman teaching at a primarily White institution (PWI), identify some of the behaviors and micro-aggressions that novice minority faculty may encounter, and suggest ways in which novice minority faculty and graduate students entering the professorate can positively navigate the university environment without internalizing negative experiences. This conversation transcends lamenting the negative experiences to include how individuals can respond proactively to implement some concrete suggestions that can eliminate or reduce some potential difficulties.

Demographic Descriptive Profile of Minority Faculty

Several researchers have documented the limited number of minorities obtaining Ph.D.'s as well as the limited number of minorities employed on the university level. Statistics for 1997–1998 show that only 16.8% of minorities had obtained doctoral degrees, with percentages awarded to each minority group as follows: 5.4% awarded to African Americans, 3.2% to Hispanics, 7.7% to Asian or Pacific Islanders, and .5% to American Indians/Alaskan Natives. Additionally for first professional degrees,[1] 22.6% of the degrees were received by minorities, with 5.4% awarded to African Americans, 4.6% to Hispanics, 10.1% to Asian or Pacific Islanders, and .7% to American Indians or Alaskan Natives (U.S. Department of Education, 2001b).

Regarding statistics on the distribution of instructional faculty and staff by race at all "public and private not-for-profit Title IV participating, degree-granting institutions" in the 50 states and the District of Columbia show that .7% are American Indian/Alaskan Native, 5.8% are Asian/Pacific Island, 5.1% are Black (non-Hispanic), 3.3% are Hispanic, and 85.1% are White (non-Hispanic) (U.S. Department of Education, 2001a).

A number of reasons can be attributed to explain the lack of minorities in both areas.

Cress and Hart (2002) acknowledge that minority professors on majority campuses may face include discrimination in hiring; poor professional, affective, and financial support for minorities; lack of respect and rewards; isolation from colleagues; and inadequate grievance processes. Even after minorities obtain positions in the university, a number of factors interfere with their success. For example, Allen, Epps, Guillory, Suh, and Bonous-Hammarth (2000) document two obstacles: the overburdening of minority faculty with teaching and service responsibilities and unrealistic research/publication expectations from administrators. Minorities have difficulty with publications, not because of insufficient writing ability, but because they are often employed at universities that emphasize teaching instead of research and often have high teaching loads (Allen et al., 2000). Minority faculty also have heavier advising loads than White faculty members that typically require minority faculty to spend more time with students. The time demands of such advising include providing social support for students, writing letters of recommendation, and helping them with such post-undergraduate activities as job seeking and selecting graduate/professional schools (Allen et al., 2000).

On a national level, professors, associate professors, assistant professors, instructors, and lecturers spend 57% of their time on teaching, 15.3% on research, 13.4% on administrative responsibilities, and 14.2% on other responsibilities (U.S. Department of Education, 1999). Even for tenure-track faculty, full professors, associate professors, and assistant professors spent 53%, 55.3%, and 56.9% of their time respectively, according to figures reported for the fall of 1998. In the same time period, full professors, associate professors, and assistant professors spent 18.2%, 17%, and 17.3% of their time on research (U.S. Department of Education, 1999). The amount of time devoted to these different activities definitely impacts the rate of writing, and therefore the number of publications and the acquisition of tenure status.

White faculty are three times more likely be tenured than African American, Hispanic faculty, or Asian Americans (Lee, 2002). The National Study of Post-Secondary Faculty (NSOPF) data show that 80% of Asians and 66% of Whites have doctorates or professional degrees. More Asian Americans are in the natural sciences, mathematics, and engineering than Whites (Lee, 2002).

Data for 2000–2001 from the 2002 Institutional Report identify only 12% of the faculty in the College of Education at my institution as minorities. For the current academic year, there are only nine minority teaching faculty and three minority faculty serving in administrative, nonteaching positions in my college.[2]

Black Professor at a PWI School: A Personal Report

After completing my doctorate, I accepted an appointment during my second year at a south central university as assistant professor in a department of curriculum and instruction. I have learned a lot about being a Black woman assistant professor at the university, and my experiences resonate with other studies on the experiences of minority faculty at PWIs. I can recall being very excited about teaching, excited about working with colleagues, and enthusiastic about being an assistant professor. But the excitement dissipated quickly after I received my first set of student evaluations, when a student went to the provost because one of my colleagues accused her of cheating, and when I encountered negative experiences with coworkers.

I realized that colleagues who were teaching without a doctorate received more respect than a minority faculty member with a Ph.D, both from students and from other faculty members. The instructors tended to exert significant effort to please and follow the directions of the White professors, even performing personal errands for them. Although my doctorate came from a more prestigious university college of education than those of any colleague, as rated by *U.S. News & World Report*,[3] I had the feeling that my degree meant nothing except perhaps to make the university look good on NCATE reports or to impress prospective faculty members.

Early on, I found that, when I gave students information, they would not believe me and would ask a White colleague to verify it. Once I received feedback from a cooperating teacher that her elementary education methods block students had the impression that they did not have to follow my directions and that I had no influence on their field work grades, an idea communicated to them by a non-doctorate-holding White male instructor. The White instructor never corrected of refuted this impression. I also observed that some White students called the non-doctorate-holding instructors "Dr." yet called me "Ms."

During another semester, I had a group of students who consistently came late to class. I was aware of the policy regarding tardiness and had already commented to the block director about the students' lateness. The following week after I handed back a graded test, two students reported to the practicum and methods director (she was not my supervisor but another assistant professor) that I was allowing students to come in late without taking any action. I became aware of the complaint only after I solicited the information from the director.

In another example, I returned a graded exam characterized by very poor grammar and punctuation. Only after taking the test and receiving the grade did the student tell me that I was discriminating against him/her because of his/her disability; he/she had dyslexia. Each semester, the former provost sent a memo to faculty about how students with disabilities (or students who thought they did but had not been professionally diagnosed) should communicate with the Student Support Services Office to arrange for accommodation of their condition. Fortunately, I had printed the document and shared it with the student, pointing out that, by policy, accommodations cannot be made until after Student Support Services conducts an assessment and provides suggestions on how to best support the student's disability. Even after this meeting, the student made no effort to have his/her disability, if any, recognized by the university.[4]

Student evaluations are used to determine ratings on annual reviews and are also considered in promotion and tenure decisions. Teachers experience pressure from both sides on evaluations. Administrators urge them to reduce the number of A's given during grading, but professors who do grade more rigorously are penalized on the evaluations. During the first semester I taught in the department, one of my colleagues accused a student of cheating. Her parent sent a memo to the provost announcing that "a woman of another race" had been harassing their daughter all semester. When I realized that the parent meant me, I felt disappointed and betrayed, for I had gone out of my way to give that student support all semester.

I also remember numerous instances where majority colleagues have made derogatory comments, used stereotypes, or exhibited micro-aggression against other minority groups including African American, Native American, and Middle Easterners. Micro-aggressions, according to research on the experiences of minority students at PWI's, are indirect, racially motivated comments that are delivered verbally, nonverbally, and/or visually (Solarzano, Ceja, & Yosso, 2000). At my university, micro-aggressions have occurred apparently because their perpetrators are unaware of the inappropriateness. For example, posted on the office door of a White colleague is the article "How to Improve Black America" by Clarence Page, an African American. Although the article may be positive, it would probably be inappropriate even for me, as an African American woman professor, to post an article of that nature in a PWI and possibly in a historically Black college of university as well.

I have noticed other subtle differences in how I have been treated as a minority faculty member. I rapidly noticed that the opportunities for networking, socializing, and mentoring were very different from those I received in comparison to a White woman professor with a Ph.D. who entered the department at the same time I did. While she received informal advising from other colleagues, I learned the university and college advising procedures by reading and asking lots of questions. Senior faculty invited her to write grants with them, while I had to seek out co-writers and grant opportunities. She was also invited to socialize with colleagues outside of work hours, while I was not. My experiences are similar to those of most minorities in the academy. One semester at the request of a non-doctorate instructor, the textbook was changed for all of the students taking that course, including students in my sections. I was the professor of record for the class, but I was not consulted or even informed of the change.

Some students will spend each class period all semester sitting with either angry or apathetic expressions, no matter how interesting and relevant I attempted to make the class. Others will hold conversations with neighbors during the whole time while I taught, or participate only grudgingly and with manifest hostility from the first day of the class through its end. There would be no plausible reason for this behavior, at least no reason I had control over. After I once reprimanded a White student for swearing in a conversation with her peers in my presence, she gyrated her lower extremities and told me, "My taxes pay your damn salary." The university took no action against her, but she withdrew from the program.

Although administrators at the university have orally commented about the insistence on publishing at least one article per year, support has not been included that would facilitate focus on research. The College of Education institutional report relates to the statement that "The Unit provides extensive instructional and research support for candidates and for teaching and research faculty in the Unit. Candidates and faculty have complete access to the [library]" (College of Education, 2001, p. 78). The document further describes, in detail, the library resources and campus computer labs. In my opinion, having computer labs and a library does not provide sufficient support for research. A lack of support for research is evidenced, in my opinion, by the lack of student workers and the lack of supervision of student workers to complete clerical duties, like providing/obtaining office supplies, copying materials, and typing routine documents—as opposed to the professor having to perform the responsibilities. Regarding advising, the paperwork is excessive, the rules change frequently, the burden of ensuring the paperwork is completed is placed on the advisor (not the advisee) and much of the work is clerical in nature (for example, calculating GPAs and highlighting courses completed on student transcripts before they are able to be admitted to the college, ensuring that their letters of recommendation come from educators, ensuring that they have passing Praxis scores, securing copies of their Praxis scores, etc.). Additionally, being one of three black teaching faculty in the department and one of two black elementary education faculty, I get requests to serve as the advisor to minority students and majority students not assigned to me. My experiences confirm Cress and Hart's (2002) findings that students faculty of color spend more time advising students even discussing career and personal issues.

The area of curriculum I teach in requires a substantial number of meetings. My program area meets two or three times a month every month while other program areas may not even meet each month. There are also monthly departmental meetings. My experiences confirm Allen et al.'s assertions (2000) regarding how faculty time is primarily used for teaching and service responsibilities.

Negative experiences like these can generate anger, hurt, bitterness, resentment, disappointment, and disgust. I have certainly experienced such emotions; however, I believe that I have learned some valuable strategies through these experiences that will help other minority assistant professors avoid the mistakes I made and become more productive. I do believe that some colleagues and students are malicious and purposeful in their attempts to belittle a minority professor; still there are ways of preventing negative experiences. Also, minority professors should not allow such experiences to affect them personally or erode their confidence.

Clock Stoppers: Factors That Prevent Tenure

I refer to any interference with productivity as a "clock stopper," an activity, meeting, professional responsibility, or other task that prevents a faculty member from using his or her time on activities that help secure promotion and tenure. As a result, the faculty member is hindered in moving to higher levels of faculty rank. In contrast are "clock advancers" that help a faculty member complete activities, committee assignments, or other responsibilities that help secure promotion and tenure.

One of the major clock stoppers includes resolving supposed emergencies. In many instances, students, faculty, staff, and superiors will require the faculty member's immediate attention. In many instances, having one's attention can actually be delayed to a later time. A so-called emergency is actually an "I don't feel like waiting—my time is more important than yours" distraction. Not only will office time be affected, but also home time. Students will call the professor at home to request additional time for turning in assignments or to inform the professor of a planned absence. Constant "emergencies" prevent the faculty member from being productive.

A second clock stopper is how my college has organized student advisement. In my opinion, the paperwork is excessive, the rules change frequently, the burden of ensuring that paperwork is completed is placed on the advisor (not the advisee), and much of the work is clerical in nature (for example, calculating GPAs and highlighting courses completed on student transcripts before they are able to be admitted to the college, ensuring that their letters of recommendation come from educators, ensuring that they have passing Praxis scores, securing copies of their Praxis scores, etc.).

I don't want to imply to anyone that I don't take advising seriously, that I don't like advising, or that I don't value good advising. I work diligently to help all of my assigned advisees, students requesting me as an adviser, and any other students who come to me for assistance. However, the paperwork required for advising, as it is currently organized, is tedious; advisees and the dean's secretary (only the one who handles admission to the college) could certainly assume more responsibility in the process. Additionally, being one of three Black teaching faculty in the department and one of two Black elementary education faculty, I get requests to serve as the advisor to minority students and majority students not assigned to me. My experiences related to Cress and Hart's (2002) findings that faculty of color spend more time advising students, even discussing career and personal issues.

A third clock stopper is excessive meetings. Faculty in my curriculum area meet two or three times a month while other program faculty may not even have monthly meetings. There are also monthly departmental meetings. My experiences reinforce the findings of Allen et al. (2000) about how faculty time is used for teaching and service responsibilities.

On the other hand, there are several "clock advancers," activities/committees/responsibilities that facilitate a faculty member's completing acts that help secure promotion and tenure. Clock advancers are discussed in detail below.

Clock Advancers: Strategies, Policies, and Adaptations for Novice, Minority Faculty

Given the college's passive support for research, writing, and publishing, I have discovered that faculty should be proactive, creative, and determined to minimize the number of clock stoppers they handle and to increase the number of clock advancers. Here are the coping strategies I learned as a novice minority professor, sometimes more slowly than I should have, to generate more productive time.

Clock Advancer #1: Preserve your time. Do not allow yourself to be detained in the office by activities that prevent you from publishing or seeking and/or seeking grants. Tactfully inform students, coworkers, book representatives, etc., that they may visit you during your office hours. Post your office hours outside your door, on your syllabus, and on your voice-mail greeting. Respond with considerable restraint to pleas of "emergencies." I learned to confine meeting times with students to my posted office hours after several experiences in which a student asked for a special appointment time that required altering my schedule yet failed to arrive and did not call ahead or apologize afterward.

I also learned to refer students to their own advisors and save advising for students assigned to me or to those who request me as an advisor. At my university, advising consumes a substantial amount of time because of the endless paperwork. I now save advising information on my computer so that I can email documents answering frequently asked questions and listing detailed procedures.

When students ask about information that does not relate to my job responsibilities, I quickly refer them by phone or e-mail to the correct office. For example, I received an e-mail from a student asking how he could get student identification so he could obtain football tickets. I always want to help students, but the e-mails, calls, and drop-ins will destroy one's research and grant writing time. Cooper and Stevens (2002) comment that professors should "clarify expectations and manage your time." The policy is sometimes hard to follow, but the novice professor must make time preservation the rule, not the exception.

Concerning departmental and university responsibilities, carefully chose committees you will serve on, participating on those of personal benefit to you, those that will give you status and prestige at the university, or those that will allow you to interact with powerful stakeholders. Network with those in the institution in a position to help you professionally.

Cooper and Stevens (2000), the editors of *Tenure in the Sacred Grove: Issues and Strategies for Women and Minority Faculty,* recommend: "Be a visible and active member of the academic community" (p. 228). I agree that the novice minority professor should be rigorous about meeting office hours, should observe the behavior of other faculty members to get a sense of the norms for presence, determine whether he/she is expected to attend every meeting, analyze whether the meetings are productive, and most importantly, recognize whether he/she will be allowed to be an active participant. I learned a belated but valuable lesson from a former African American male colleague, who warned against attending every meeting a department and university will have. He always said, "You have to protect your research time."

Cooper and Stevens (2000) state, "You may be tempted to hide at home, but try to resist that temptation. There is always the danger of being judged as someone who is not a team player" (p. 228). The advice is valuable, but may have limited utility for minority faculty. Endless meetings only prevented me from working on what really mattered. If people know you are in the office, you will seldom be able to work on your own activities. I found that, if people knew I was in the office, I had constant interruptions. I answered questions for students who couldn't meet with their own professor, attended meetings, and helped walk-ins, and answered endless questions like "do you know when Dr. So-and-so will be in?" Eight hours later, I had done other people's busy work, not my own projects. I have found that my most productive times in the office are Fridays, evenings, and weekends when many people are not at work.

Furthermore, I used to go to all of the meetings, only to discover that I was not allowed on the team the way my White colleagues were. As a minority, my views were frequently rejected. Even when I could substantiate them with relevant research I would have to discuss information with extreme detail to get colleagues to recognize my view points.

Be careful about what classes you agree to teach. For the first year and a half I worked in the department, my classes were held at professional development schools in neighboring towns. As a result, I spent an hour or more of time traveling to and from the field practicum placements. The loss of an hour or two daily is no small matter for a novice researcher.

Use time away from the office productively, also. Designate sufficient time daily for research and grant-writing opportunities. Uchiyama and Simone (1999) advise that the research writing should occur in a comfortable place conducive to productivity. They further add that writers should set aside two hours for each writing session along with writing a note to oneself documenting what areas to refer back to when writing on the next occasion.

Preserve your home time. Either have a private home telephone number or caller identification. Many desperate calls come from students who simply do not locate answers themselves. Even if I have not given my home telephone number out, students will find the number and call, even late. Interestingly enough, the student who told her parent I was harassing her all semester thought nothing of calling me late at night about how to cite references using APA style. Other students have called to ask when an assignment is due, even though the due dates are printed on the assignments or assignment schedule.

I will rarely give a student my home number unless I believe the student sincerely needs help that could not be accommodated during the day. For example, the White male instructor who felt I had no input in the students' grades incorrectly informed two minority students how to write lesson plans for their thematic unit (the assignment with the highest amount of points for their fieldwork grade). I was livid when I realized that he confused the students and gave them totally incorrect information, suspecting that he did it on purpose. In that instance, I gave the students my home number since they had a major assignment which was due the next day. Even if I don't disseminate the number, students will find it and call even when I have written in the syllabus to call me at the office.

Clock Advancer #2: Become very organized and detailed regarding teaching responsibilities. It is natural for novice professors to be anxious about their class preparation and to have considerable uncertainty about whether they have prepared adequately. Given my experiences, I would highly recommend that assistant professors have a detailed syllabus which includes the following components: (a) specific assignments with the number of points to be received, (b) the policy for handling disagreement over grades, (c) policies for absences and tardies, and (d) expectations for assignments including type of font, paper color, and margin specifications.

When I first began teaching at the university, I assumed that students would know expectations for submitting assignments. I thought that students knew they should submit take-home assignments on white paper in black ink. I was surprised when students submitted assignments on pink paper, purple paper, in pink type, or green ink. I have had students not report for tests, yet expect to take a make-up exam at their leisure. I do not want to appear negative towards the students. Some are not aware of academic norms and professional standards; however, because they are becoming teachers, they have to model appropriate language and writing for the K–8 students they will teach. Expectations for assignments from my syllabus are included, verbatim, as a sample of the policies and procedures to include in the syllabus. (See Appendix 1.)

Having a detailed syllabus reduces attempts by students to undermine the professor or circumvent commonsense expectations. If you are using an old syllabus and are the professor of record for the course, update the syllabus for each class and select assignments that are relevant to your course content. If you are not the professor of record, tactfully communicate with the individual to determine possible updates. Sometimes professors will have assignments in the syllabus that have nothing to do with the class, the objectives of the course, or the course content.

After teaching a group of students who complained that my test grading was subjective and after excessive attempts by students to pressure me into lowering my grading standards, I made changes to my assessment procedures. The College of Education at my university awards the highest percentage of A's with the College of Engineering awarding the fewest number. At the 2002 spring graduation, the College of Education had the highest amount of cum laude distinctions. Clearly, I was out of step with students' expectations. As a result, I decided to give a multiple-choice exam as a final each semester. Administering a multiple-choice final has been one of the best teaching decisions I have ever made. With the final, students don't argue about the grading, since it is not subjective. The decision also greatly reduced the number of complaints about test content, since I give them a study guide with concepts to study that correlate with every single question on the test. We also discuss each concept thoroughly in class, along with opportunities for questions. As a result, under-prepared students only have themselves to blame. Multiple-choice exams are also enormous time-savers. Scoring the exams is done mechanically; my only responsibility is dropping off the scan sheets and picking up the grade reports.

I always provide detailed instructions describing all assignments and assessments at the beginning of the semester or on the first day of class. I also inform the students they will be graded for punctuation, grammar, spelling, thoroughness, and accuracy. I learned that if students received a B in my class, I could expect tears, complaints, accusations of unfairness, and lamentations about me to other professors. When I administer essay assignments on some course objectives with detailed handouts regarding directions, inevitably, a student or two will complain the grading is unfair. One semester, a student continually told me, on two different assignments, "This is 'A' work." When the student became teary-eyed and defensive, I told her I would allow two other instructors to grade the papers and use their average with my score as the final grade. The two instructors (White, non-doctorate) whom I asked to grade the paper gave the student a lower score on both assignments than I did. The student accepted the lowered grade they gave without tears and complaints. If a student becomes too emotional, I would request a trustworthy witness to be present or tape-record the conversation.

On every assignment, I put "date disseminated on" with a blank for students to fill in the date they received the assignment. Many students who perform poorly will claim that I did not give them accurate directions for the assignments, so recording the date will prove that either they did not listen or they were absent.

In the syllabus, include points for "attitude, participation, and professionalism." The terms relate to the NCATE terminology of knowledge, disposition, and performances. Having attitude, participation, and professionalism criteria built into the grading structure allows the professor to deduct points for a number of behaviors that relate to teaching. Areas can be obtained from the list of criteria typically found on employee recommendation forms from school districts (punctuality, integrity, reliability, etc.). It is also important to refer to the university policy on student misconduct in the syllabus.

Clock Advancer #3: Learn the culture of your organization and recognize your boundaries and limitations. Clock Advancer #3 can pertain to a variety of experiences including how one is allowed to interact with the group, how one grades students, and how an individual is viewed by the department. At least seven of the professors in my department have terminal degrees from our university including the department head and assistant dean. The practice of an university hiring its own graduates is commonly referred to as intellectual incest. I do not want to suggest that having a degree from the university is problematic, that a university should never hire its own graduates, that I am criticizing a specific individual, or that there is a problem with a specific individual; but I feel that having several professors who are graduates of the university may encourage cliques and unintentionally limit outsider input.

Clock Advancer #4: Maintain professionalism, tact, and composure under stress. In other words, be assertive not aggressive. Cooper and Stevens (2002) also recommend that professors should "acknowledge that the personal, professional, and political are interwoven in the academy" (p. 226). It is crucial for minority faculty members to advocate for themselves firmly, yet with control. Listen first, obtain the details regarding a situation, think about a productive plan of action, and document any instances that are suspect. It is natural during an emotional confrontation to become angry or mention an incident to one's superior. Yet hastily responding to offensive acts or frequently seeking the department head's assistance may not resolve an issue. It is preferable to have a calculated plan for how to handle inappropriate acts, a plan that requires documentation, awareness of any outside factors, communication with relevant stakeholders, and articulation of concerns in writing. It's very important to think before acting.

Clock Advancer #5: Through communication, subtle eavesdropping, and feedback from colleagues and administrators, know expectations and options regarding promotion, tenure, and the annual review process. Be very detailed, organized, and specific regarding information you will include in the annual review, since it is the device used to evaluate faculty annually. Each year, the novice professor should establish a file folder called "promotion and tenure" to house descriptions or copies of any and every activity directly or tangentially related to the job. Update the review document throughout the year. Try to subtly or directly find out what other professors are putting in the annual review. After overhearing a few comments about other professors submitting annual review boxes and another colleague with a four-inch, three-ring binder labeled "annual review," I learned to be obsessive-compulsive about the evaluation.

Ascertain the divisions/components of the annual review well in advance of the actual meeting with the department head. Because my university is a land-grant institution, public and community service are important. I learned, through communication with another colleague, to write faith-based and even sorority activities on the annual review. As a result of being detailed, I noticed an increase in my annual review ratings for all sections (teaching, research, service, and advising). One of the themes was to "understand the nature of your institution and its tenure process" (Cooper & Stevens, 2002, p. 226). Also include supporting documentation with the annual review as if you were constructing a professional portfolio. Submit an annual review with supporting documentation (like a portfolio).

Because of the substantial amount of advising I was having to complete, I made a matrix where I could write the student's name and a tally mark for each time I communicate with each individual student whether via phone, email, or in person. For instance, from June 2002 to September 30, 2002, a four-month period, I completed approximately 203 advising contacts with only 52 of my undergraduate advisees via e-mail, via telephone, or in person. (See Appendix 2 for sample documentation to include on the annual review.)

Components of the annual review will vary by university. Some units have a standard form on which professors list accomplishments and accolades. Determine what your university says it values and what it actually values. Sometimes your superior will claim that he/she is looking only for certain information. The minority faculty member should include above and beyond what others may submit. The annual reviews can limit or facilitate promotions and raises, so the advantages of having a very detailed annual review are obvious.

Cooper and Stevens (2002) further comment that professors should "listen, document, and clarify in writing all statements made by your chair, your dean, and promotion and tenure committees about the process and expectations for you in particular" (p. 226). In other words, learn the name of the game and how to play the game.

Clock Advancer #6: Select and utilize support mechanisms. On a personal level, mentors, my spirituality, friends, and attending and becoming active in the American Educational Research Association (AERA) have helped me endure the first years in the professorate. I encourage minority faculty to find activities that sustain them and participate in those activities for respite. Two Black women faculty members have helped me learn how to navigate the university as well as have shared policies and procedures with me that have been invaluable. Additionally, White male and female faculty and staff have helped me succeed professionally.

Attending the annual conference of AERA has helped tremendously and has been rewarding. Communicating with successful, intelligent, and articulate Black professors has been very motivational. For a novice Black professor, the opportunity to meet with or attend a presentation by the Black elite of academe is comparable to a teenager's meeting a famous athlete or entertainer. Learning from and communicating with the nation's leading researchers is very affirming. Within AERA, I have learned a lot from attending the Research Focus on Black Education (RFBE) Special Interest Group (SIG) meetings/symposia/roundtables and interacting with the RFBE members and officers. Also, there have been Black professors and majority professors who have who have been supportive and encouraging to novice faculty. Lastly, AERA members of various races have conducted workshops for new faculty and dissertators. The AERA Web site has a very useful document, "Publishing Educational Research: Guidelines and Tips," which has been helpful. The document was available at www.aera.net/epubs/howtopubl/index.htm at the time the chapter was written.

Davidson's and Foster-Johnson's (2001) research of minority graduate students of color concludes that mentoring helps students become integrated into the core of the department, develop networks, complete research requirements, and make the transition from graduate school to the work force. Additionally, they assert that cross-race mentoring should embody the components of knowledge and action. By knowledge, the authors imply the mentor should know himself or herself, know the mentee, and understand cultural diversity in the organization. By action, the authors encourage the university to develop a model for cultural identity, develop a mentoring program, focus on the diversity climate of the department, and sponsor formal events to promote diversity including change of individual faculty members. The suggestions can also extend to mentoring faculty of color.

Clock Advancer #7: Be positive, strive to be successful in all that you do, learn from your mistakes, and continuously reflect. To be successful in the university, you have to evaluate your strengths and weakness, do your part, and develop genuine competency in your job.

If you are a minority faculty member, you are truly "the proud, the chosen, and the few." Success will not come easily. Obstacles will temporarily divert you from success. You will have to devise a plan for success. Eliminate or reduce clock stoppers. Lastly and most importantly, conceptualize a list of additional clock advancers beyond those provided in the chapter. Work hard and good luck.

Acknowledgments

Dan Webb, my former colleague, was very successful in grant writing and publications. Pamela Barber-Freeman (a former professor at my university, now at Prairie View A&M) and Linda Cornelious (an educational technology professor at my university) apprised me of many university policies that have helped me negotiate with my supervisors and colleagues. These two women, along with a Black female instructor (Algeria Crump) have been wonderful mentors, also reinforcing the spiritual strength that comes from faith in God, prayer, and spiritual readings. Additionally, majority faculty and staff including Nancy Verhoek-Miller and Mindy Wolfe have been very supportive.

I appreciate professors like William Tate and Jean Madsen, who often give novice professors supportive comments and suggestions. I also appreciate the willingness of those like Paul Bredeson, Mary Louise Gomez, Carl Grant, Carolyn Kelley, and Kent Peterson to serve as professional references.

Appendix 1
Components of the Syllabus: Class Policies and Procedures

Assessment of assignments will be based on the criteria established by the instructor (e.g., rubrics, checklists). All assignments are due on the established date. For each day an assignment is late, 10% of the total number of points for the assignment will be deducted.

1. Any final grade average (including content and field experience) below a C will constitute failure for recommendation to student teaching. Make-up examinations will be given only for death of family members or illness (at the discretion of the professor). Appropriate documentation from a medical doctor will be required for make-up exams. Make-up examinations will be essay.

2. For any assignments using outside references and resources, the materials must be appropriately cited on the assignment. Please follow the format provided in the 5th edition of the *American Psychological Association Manual.*

3. In order to align with national initiatives, all students must have an e-mail account. University accounts are available to all students.

4. All take-home essay/paper/journal assignments must be submitted typed, double-spaced on white paper with one-inch margins (top, bottom, left, and right) in black ink. The font should be size 10 or 12 only in Times New Roman or Arial. Points will be deducted (at the discretion of the professor) for any assignments not adhering to this guideline. All assignments should be submitted with correct grammar, punctuation, and spelling. Points will be deducted for grammar, punctuation, and spelling errors.

5. If a teacher candidate disagrees with how the instructor graded any assignment, he/she will have the option of having the assignment graded by another instructor familiar with the assignment/course content. The original assignment grade will be added to the second graded assignment and divided by the number 2 to determine the average. The average of the two graded assignments will be the grade for the teacher candidate (whether higher than the grade on the original paper or lower than the grade on the original paper). If the teacher candidate still objects to how the assignment was graded, he/she may contact the head of the Curriculum and Instruction Department. The three grades will be averaged to determine the final grade.

6. Teacher candidates should read the required readings in order to be prepared for the lectures and examinations.

7. For communication with the instructor outside of the class's scheduled meeting times, please contact the instructor at the contact information listed on page 1 of the syllabus. For unscheduled appointments, please visit the instructor's office to view the instructor's office hours.

8. All assignments should be completed by the teacher candidate submitting them. Assignments should be actually written and conceptualized by the actual teacher candidate. For violations of the policy, academic misconduct proceedings will be pursued in accordance with the university policy.

Appendix 2
Possible Annual Review Components

- Listing of roles and duties on any university, college, and departmental committees and subcommittees you serve on
- Copies of selected student evaluations
- The yearly average of student evaluation scores
- Letters/e-mails from students requesting you as the advisor
- Awards received from local entities
- Letters/e-mails of thanks from students
- A listing of offices held or membership with the university/community/national/professional/civic organizations
- Professional development workshops and consultations conducted with local school districts
- Number of advisees and number of advising contacts made with students
- Grants applied for and received
- Publications (the cultural capital of most universities)
- Special materials and innovations developed for classes
- Any judging/volunteering you have done for local schools
- Any times you are featured in the newspapers
- Any reviewing you have done for journals, conferences, or national organizations

Notes

1. First professional degrees are those beyond the bachelor's level in dentistry, medicine, pharmacy, law, and theology. U.S. Department of Education, 2001c.
2. Four of the Black faculty are administrators, not faculty. The College of Education (COE) NECATE Committee Institutional Report of my university states:"The success of the efforts to recruit and retain diverse faculty and candidates is demonstrated by the increased percentages of minority representation in both groups over the five-year span [1996–2001] (COE NCATEF, 2001, p. 57). I find this statement misleading. In actuality, the numbers have decreased from the 1999–2000 school year to the 2000–2001 school year. For the past five years, the number of minority faculty, including both teachers and administrators, have been 12, 11, 13, 14, and 13. In other words, there has not been a significant change. Since 2001–2002, one Black faculty member left the university, another was nonrenewed, and a third retired.
3. The University of Wisconsin's Departments of Educational Administration and Curriculum and Instruction are often ranked no. 1 or 2 in *U.S. News and World Report*'s annual ratings issue. I do not wish to ignore the prestige of other schools. One colleague has a degree from Michigan State University, and another graduated from Berkeley. I do not mention the ratings to be haughty, arrogant, or elitist, but it underscores the fact that minorities are frequently not valued at my institution regardless of their proven level of competence.

4. I am certainly an advocate for meeting the needs of students with disabilities and discussed this situation with my supervisor. She advised me that the policy exists to help prevent fraudulent claims and that I should not make any exceptions until the student followed the university's policy and received an assessment from Student Support Services.

References

Allen, W. R., Epps, E. G., Guillory, E. A., Suh, S. A., & Bonous-Hammarth, M. (Winter/Spring 2000). The Black academic: Faculty status among African Americans in U.S. higher education. *Journal of Negro Education, 60*(1–2), 112–127.

College of Education NCATE (National Council for the Accreditation of Teacher Education) Committee. (2002). *Institutional report.* Mississippi State, MS: College of Education.

Cooper, J. E., & Stevens, D. E. (Eds.). (2002). *Tenure in the sacred grove: Issues and strategies for women and minority faculty.* New York: State University of New York Press.

Cress, C. M., & Hart, J. L. (2002). *The hue of campus climate: How faculty of color and White faculty view the institution.* Paper presented at the American Psychological Association annual meeting, New Orleans.

Davidson, M. N., & Foster-Johnson, L. (2001, Winter). Mentoring in the preparation of graduate researchers of color. *Review of Educational Research, 71*(4), 575–611.

Hobson-Horton, L. D. (2002). EDE 2511: Intro to Elementary Education Syllabus Components.

Lee, S. M. (2002, Fall). Do Asian American faculty face a glass ceiling in higher education? *American Educational Research Journal, 39*(3), 695–724.

Solarzano, D., Ceja, M., & Yosso, T. (2000, Winter/Spring). Critical race theory, racial micro-aggressions, and campus racial climate: The experiences of African American college students. *Journal of Negro Education, 69*(1–2), 60–73.

Uchiyama, K., & Simone, G. (1999, Fall). *Publishing educational research: Guidelines and tips.* American Educational Research Association. Retrieved in January 2003 from www.aera.net/epubs/howtopub/index.htm.

U.S. Department of Education. (1999). *National study of postsecondary faculty data analysis system.* Washington, DC: U.S. Department of Education, National Center for Education Statistics.

U.S. Department of Education. (2001a). *Background characteristics, work activities, and compensation of faculty and instructional staff in postsecondary institutions: Fall 1998.* Washington, DC: U.S. Department of Education, National Center for Education Statistics.

U.S. Department of Education. (2001b). *Digest of education statistics, 2000.* Washington, DC: U.S. Department of Education, National Center for Education Statistics.

U.S. Department of Education. (2001c). *Projections of education statistics to 2011.* Washington, DC: U.S. Department of Education, National Center for Education Statistics.

ASSERTIVENESS OR THE DRIVE TO SUCCEED?: SURVIVING AT A PREDOMINANTLY WHITE UNIVERSITY

Explanations about why African Americans remain unrepresented or underrepresented among faculties in higher education typically fall into one of two categories: "either past discriminatory policies or demographic realities that are directly devoid of any racial intent" (Jackson, 1991, p. 136). When African American women work at predominantly White institutions, they are more likely to be assistant professors and instructors than full or associate professors. Moses (1997) found that African American female faculty experience racial and gender discrimination in subtle and not so subtle ways that include but are not limited to stereotyping, disrespect, isolation, hostility, and lack of support networks. Alfred (2001) adds: "Black women experience problems in White institutions because institutional leaders and other members do not recognize and acknowledge the cultural evolution taking place with the inclusion of Black professionals in their White institutions" (p. 110). Instead, the expectation is that African American women and men must assimilate or flirt with failure. This dynamic influences the types of strategies adopted in what is often perceived to be a hostile climate.

The halls of the academy are made hostile because of racist comments and practices. Many scholars characterize the Black presence as contested space. These spaces at predominantly White institutions are contested because European American colleagues question whether African Americans' presence in the academy is the result of affirmative action, thereby undermining the quality of our research and teaching. Such responses to our presence in the academy are fueled by long-held beliefs about Black inferiority. How could we have possibly "earned" a place in the academy if it weren't for our race? This assumption implies that European Americans "legitimately" earned their place, despite the fact that racial homogeny stems from practices that privilege Whiteness in the faculty selection process.

bell hooks (1981) observed that, when African American women faculty voice their concerns about the racism they experience, European American women, for the most part, pose as their allies and attempt to construct a "sisterhood." However,

> From [African American women's] peripheral role in the movement, we saw that the potential radicalism of feminist ideology was being undermined by women, who, while paying lip service to revolutionary goals, were primarily concerned with gaining entrance into the capitalist, patriarchal power structure. (p. 502)

Consequently, even those posing as our allies can be guilty of "racist verbal expressions" (McKay, 1997, p. 14).

Lois Benjamin (1997) and others point out that the message of "you don't belong" is conveyed in a myriad of ways. Our academic scholarship is invalidated or relegated to research on "Black stuff"; our accomplishments are either undervalued or begrudgingly recognized; and when African American women do receive acknowledgment, their colleagues are more likely to praise their attractiveness than their scholarly achievements (Benjamin, 1997, p. 29). While the demands of academe are taxing for all faculty, "styles of thinking, acting, speaking, and behaving" reflect European cultural practices, making departmental climates less hostile toward European American faculty (Alfred 2001, p. 115). Caldwell (2000) likens the impact of this climate on African Americans to a toxin. Thus arises the need for African American faculty to create what bell hooks (1981) calls a "homeplace." This space enables African Americans to reaffirm one another, healing our wounds in order to become whole again. It is within this context that we share our stories as faculty at a predominantly White Southern institution ("Southern University") in the United States.

An African American Woman Faculty Member

As I review the research on the experiences of African American faculty at predominantly White institutions, I have flashbacks of my own experiences. While I have benefitted immensely from having supportive mentors and administrators, both in my institution and outside of it, the loudest messages were often the unfriendly ones. Consequently, reading the scholarship on the African American experience in the academy is at once supportive and disheartening because it validates my perceptions of my experiences as a faculty member at Southern University.

I was the first African American in my department. Naively, I believed that I would experience less discrimination in the academy than I had in the rest of the world because I thought my degree meant that I "had arrived." "Education will make your life easier," my mother said to me throughout my life. This dreamlike state quickly dissolved during the first month on the faculty at Southern University.

"You only got your job because you are Black," he said. I paused, leveled my head, and with the stereotyped "Black female" neck movement, I replied, "Since I am the first African American in this department, obviously you got your job because you are White!" The posture was my defense against assaults about my ability triggered by attitudes about my race. After all, given this perception, the only way that someone who is African American can prove his or her worth is to cease to be Black or to be White. "You only got your job because you are White" is never assumed. After that experience, I found myself hoping that I would experience fewer of these assaults.

Two months into the semester, Mr. "You only got your job" refused to work with me. We had been asked to develop the course for which we were both responsible. "Standardize the curriculum for the course," said Mr. Department Head. However, Mr. "You only got your job" met with a senior faculty member to discuss the history of the course without me. When I asked why he didn't tell me about the meeting, he said, "I'm smarter than you. They know that." And I thought we were supposed to work collaboratively to develop the course.

The tenor of our professional relationship made it very difficult for me to socialize with my cohort, because Mr. "You only got your job" was part of that cohort. However, instead of my cohort's supporting me after I confided in them the things that he said to me, they excluded me from the social events. How did I know? They passed around photographs from their get-togethers. Was it an accident that I was allowed to see them or not? At one point, the host commented, "I didn't invite them over. They just keep showing up. I didn't want you to feel uncomfortable around Mr. 'You only got your job.'" The result, however, was that I socialized with my cohort only when Mr. "You only got your job" was not present. Since that rarely happened, it became difficult to maintain ties with my colleagues outside office hours, an important consideration in acclimating new faculty into any academic department. I felt completely marginalized.

In another conversation with one of my mentors, I again felt the lack of inclusiveness, support, or confidence in me. When I started working at Southern University, my dissertation defense date was set for one month into the semester. Two months into my employment at Southern University, Dr. "Mentor," one of the three members in the department who has always mentored me, asked, "Didn't you defend your dissertation last month?" I said, "Yeah. I'm just working on the last few revisions." Dr. "Mentor" said, "I thought so. I don't know why Dr. "So-and-So" said he didn't think you would ever finish. I told him I thought you were finished." These and similar experiences reinforced my need to develop a social network outside the department because the most overt messages conveyed were that I didn't belong, I wasn't really welcome, and I was less than. . . . This network, which included my departmental mentors, saved me during my first year at Southern University. I became a social butterfly in the real world. I spoke to people in the grocery store, went to church, and found a place away from the city of Southern to dance my burdens away. My "homeplace" was my saving grace.

Mr. "You only got your job" ended his term at Southern University in one year. Ironically, I chaired the search committee that selected his replacement and ended up with a very compatible colleague who became part of my "homeplace" at the work place. We could process and defuse all the racist comments and general departmental politics together. That is how I remained sane. Dr. "Homeplace" and I were always together. Yet she occupied an interesting place in the workplace. She wasn't African American, so her challenges were different. She seemed to benefit from every battle we faced in the department and I didn't. This was most evident when it came to serving on student committees.

Serving on student committees are required if you want to achieve graduate faculty level two status. My cohort and I raised the issue in our departmental meeting during my first year. We needed to serve on committees to gain level two status. After that meeting, the members of my cohort discussed the response of the senior faculty members to the conversation. Each of them had been asked to serve on at least one student's dissertation committee—that is, everyone except me. At the end of that first year, I raised the issue in my annual review. Mr. "Department Head" suggested that I have individual discussions with senior faculty members. I cannot adequately describe how awkward it was for me to have to schedule meetings with senior faculty members to ask, "Do you have any student committees on which I might serve?" To my knowledge, nobody else in my cohort had to resort to such a measure. After meeting with two senior faculty members and hearing, "I don't have anyone doing anything of interest to you," I pondered the response. Neither of them had ever asked me about my areas of expertise or research interests. However, the response "I don't have anybody doing anything on Black students" made the message clear.

When Dr. "Homeplace" arrived, she seemed to be the buffer for them. She and I raised the issue of serving on student committees in the departmental meeting midway during my second year, Dr. "Homeplace's" first year. She was pulled onto committees after the meeting and received apologies for the oversight. When it was discovered that a member of my cohort was advising all the master's students, whether they were his or not, expressions of outrage were made to Dr. "Homeplace." No one could believe he would do something so unethical.

When I chaired a second search committee, she heard complaints that expressed less concern about the quality of the program than about getting someone people liked. Dr. "Homeplace" became part of a racial hierarchy that painted me as the "bitch" and her as the "cute little Indian girl." While I knew in my heart that Dr. "Homeplace" was my ally, there were times when her higher place on the racial ladder negatively influenced our relationship. I felt as if she adopted an "I'm better than you are" attitude on a couple of occasions. These instances led to discussions and apologies, but they always stood as a reminder to me of the cost associated with existing in a hostile environment. "Who are your allies" emerges as the most crucial question that must be answered if one is to succeed in such a place with one's self-esteem intact.

Then, on the road to promotion and tenure, the plot thickened. My experiences drastically changed when Dr.-Mr. "Homeplace," the department's first African American man, joined the faculty during my third year. I'm sure he had his own challenges. However, by the time he arrived, I was always on the defensive at work because the discriminatory encounters in the hallway were becoming more frequent. The message was clear: Assimilate to the departmental climate or get out. I should have anticipated this hostility because I was at a crucial point in my career. It is during the third-year review that progress towards tenure is assessed.

My contributions to the department were ignored, undermined, and/or undervalued. I came to prefer being ignored. I suspect that my third-year review letter was one of the longest in the history of the department. I had allies in the department who valued my work and my contributions to the discussion, while others did not. My letter became very ambiguous because someone attempted to praise my contributions to the department while defining what "collegiality" meant in the context of the tenure and promotion process. It was Somebody's attempt to say, "We don't like her," contradicted by Somebody Else saying, "You don't have to like her for her to be successful here." One of my mentors said, "I guess I thought everyone valued your input as much as I do. I was wrong." I suppose my experiences in the department prepared me for this sort of assessment of my work in ways for which my mentors were not prepared.

Meanwhile, public comments by some of the senior faculty members to junior faculty members reinforced the "go along to get along" message. At the departmental holiday party, a junior faculty member gave a senior faculty member an engraved gold coffee mug. The senior faculty member quipped, "So you really do want to get tenure!" Lots of people laughed. The members of my homeplace did not. We recognized that this wasn't really a joke despite the senior faculty member's tone. I'd already had another senior faculty member open my office door without knocking, come in, sit down, and tell me, "You need to learn to get along here." I got the distinct impression that it never crossed anyone's mind that diversity in the department would require any change in the departmental climate. Instead, the responsibility was all on me: I could adopt the departmental climate or else. I don't think this expectation is any different for a faculty member of another race, just that the greater the cultural distance between the department and that individual, the harder it is to achieve the adaptation.

In sharing my experiences, I want to be clear about the challenges I faced as a faculty member at Southern University. I had a problem only with those parts of the departmental culture that worked to silence me and to undermine my success. I mistakenly believed that hiring me meant that I was automatically included in discussions about departmental activities. I believed that we should hold everyone to the same standards. I believed that we should be vigilant about the quality of what we do. I also believed that my contributions would improve the quality of the departmental activities. Instead, the most overt messages were that I should contribute but be silent. If I spoke up, I wasn't "going along to get along."

In many respects, the messages about the departmental culture required me to sacrifice what I have worked so hard for during my entire life—to make places better for those of us on the margins. Wouldn't everyone benefit from being in a place that values the opinion of the person perceived to be most different from the others? The most outspoken members of the department didn't think so and their voices always seemed to muffle the voices of the margin. So it is up to the individual to decide how to respond. I felt it was necessary to assert myself in ways that would ensure my success because acquiescence was not an option for me. Whether an individual feels naturally assertive or not, I strongly believe that, to be successful, YOU HAVE TO STAND UP FOR YOU. Otherwise, you will never become one of the few African Americans who survive in the academy with your self-esteem intact. I felt that I completed my B.A., M.A., and Ph.D. in spite of the departmental climate, not because of it. I felt exactly the same way about achieving promotion and tenure. Dr. Mae Jemison, the first African American female astronaut, in a talk at Southern University shared the same sentiment. She said, "Sometimes I feel like I've succeeded despite the system."

Challenges to African American Success

As my colleague has articulated, there is a great need for African Americans and other people of color in institutions of higher education. In the recent past, a central theme in American higher education has been diversity and multicultural education. Many universities and colleges have made genuine efforts to integrate courses focusing on cultural diversity into their curriculum. There has also been an increase of diversity at faculty and administrative levels. Aside from the obvious attacks against affirmative action scholarships, most colleges have continued their outreach attempts toward racial minorities and women (Marable, 2002).

However, the higher up the academic hierarchy one goes, the Whiter the institution or scholarly society becomes (Marable, 2002). A 2001 survey of the 27 highest ranking research universities in the United States showed that 3.6% of the faculty were African American. Thus, African American educators remain underrepresented in the upper levels of academic administration. Often those who are counted among "faculty" are actually adjunct professors, instructors, administrators who are counted as instructors, and faculty working on limited, term contracts. Therefore, the numbers of African American faculty are usually inflated, obscuring how White higher education really is. For example, a recent study published by Trower and Chait (2002) reported that 94% of full professors in science and engineering are White, and 90% are male. At research universities, 91% of the full professors are White, and 75% are male. In the United States as a whole, 87% of the full-time professorate are White, and 64% are male. Only 5% of the full professors in the United States are African, Hispanic, and Native American.

The proportion of African American faculty at predominantly White colleges and universities—2.3%—is virtually the same as in 1979. Even in fields with a relatively ample supply of scholars from diverse racial backgrounds, such as education and psychology, the proportion of African and Hispanic American faculty at predominantly White institutions barely approximates the percentages of people in these groups who hold doctorates or professional degrees in those fields (Trower & Chait, 2002). The American Academy of Arts and Letters (AAAS), perhaps the nation's most prestigious academic society, has only 160 African American members out of a membership of more than 3,700—approximately 1.6%. Among the African Americans in the AAAS are John Hope Franklin, William Julius Wilson, Johnnetta Cole, and Cornel West (Marable 2002). Manning Marable (2002), professor of history and political science at Columbia University, stated: "With these and other exceptions, when one considers the hundreds of outstanding African American scholars who are today redefining the shape of academic disciplines throughout the humanities and social sciences, their lack of representation in the AAAS is indefensible and outrageous" (p. 6).

While education has been viewed as a major path for historically disadvantaged persons to expand their opportunities, data show that the number of African American students in graduate school has remained unchanged, while Asian Americans and Hispanics have made the largest gains in college admission and attainment of graduate degrees (Kulis, Chong, & Shaw, 1999). Tierney (1997) argues that student admissions and the employment of faculty in colleges and university are directly linked. If the student body is not diverse enough, the institution has difficulty attracting culturally diverse faculty members. If professors of color are not visible, students of color are less likely to enroll. Yet as more graduate students of color are admitted to programs, the pool of potential faculty grows and thus the number of faculty of color increases to mentor more students of color in the future. However, barriers exist in the recruitment, hiring, and promotion practices of many colleges and universities.

Kulis, Chong, and Shaw (1999) characterized "institutional discrimination" as a situation in which "the dominant status groups continue to maintain their privileged position in the workplace" (p. 118). Such privileges become part of organizational norms and result in the silencing and marginalization of some and the acceptance of others (Cohen, 1998). Being White and male remain a candidate's most positive factors when interviewing for a faculty position. Conversely, because of the conscious and unconscious but pervasive systemic racism that pollutes our society, the instinctive reaction of many White faculty members to a non-White candidate is to find something—anything—to justify disqualification. According to Shareef (2002), quoting from an article in the *Chronicle of Higher Education*, "If left [on] their own, White male professors will simply replicate themselves" (p. 2). Whether it be a candidate's accent, possible problems with immigration, or a perception that the candidate "just won't fit in," European American faculty typically seek to hire people who look just like them.

Resistance from faculty is only one battle many African American faculty members confront. The other form of resistance is the one we get from students. In a collegiate environment in which well over half of the menial or service positions are occupied by African Americans but only 8.7% of the faculty are from underrepresented racial/ethnic groups, the stereotypical image of a gray-haired European American male professor dominates student perceptions (Hamilton, 2002).

This situation poses two dilemmas from the very beginning. First, in a collegiate environment I am not part of the group that performs menial or service jobs, I am part of the 8.7% underrepresented faculty. I am in charge of facilitating discussion, assigning reading materials, starting and adjourning class, evaluating students, and distributing grades. Second, I am neither European American nor gray-haired. I am an African American man in my mid-thirties, bald, with an earring. Therefore, if most of our students at Southern University buy into the stereotype of a professor and have been exposed only to the 90% of the teaching force that is White and middle-class (Sleeter, 1993), then my presence in the classroom is surprising, even shocking, to many of my students.

Studies have shown that faculty of color are measured by a set of unspoken and covertly racist standards that carry their own confusing punishments and rewards. Well known is the "Brown-to-Brown Research Taboo" which communicates to people of color doing research on people of color that their teaching and their research are not taken seriously (Hamilton, 2002). If students do not take faculty seriously, controlling the classroom or establishing a standard of civil behavior can become a problem for any faculty member. Adding race to the equation means that the faculty member has an even greater struggle in trying to maintain a learning environment. However, when European American faculty review student evaluations, they fail to take into consideration the challenges that African Americans or other racially diverse faculty face when teaching at a predominantly White institution.

During my first year of teaching, an African American man, "Dr. Brotha," at another institution received some negative student evaluations. A senior White male professor—"Dr. Control"—gave him some advice on how to maintain discipline in his classroom. "Dr. Brotha" responded: "With all due respect, sir, when you try to take control of your class, the students accept it. Maybe they're grateful for it. When I try to take control of my classes, I get student evaluations that say 'I'm mean,' 'I'm intimidating,' 'I make them uncomfortable,' 'I force my opinions on them' or 'I'm racist.'" With this type of resistance, many students avoid all challenges to some of their core values and assumptions. Consequently, African American faculty are marginalized both by their colleagues and by students resistant to having racist views challenged in the classroom.

Being perceived as marginal, like my colleague, has never seemed unusual to me. I was armed with confidence during my early upbringing, always encouraged by my parents and relatives to venture into unfamiliar territory. I was always told that I had to be "twice as good." I realize now that this meant I had to learn to be successful in two worlds: the academic arena and my social/community life. For many women faculty and faculty members of color, these two worlds are polar opposites that seldom if ever intersect. I was always told that education encompasses a broad spectrum of learning experiences and that engaging with different cultures, philosophies, and ideologies was part of learning. Therefore, I was eager to learn from whatever situation present itself.

Nevertheless, as an African American man on the faculty at a predominantly White university, I harbor some of the same fears as other faculty members of color who are fortunate enough to land a position in the academy. I am often confronted by students who have no hesitation in announcing that they have never associated with, lived near, or been taught by a person of color. Some students flatly refuse to begin their journey toward a better understanding of "difference" and withdraw from the course. Some even switch their career paths. Fortunately, others make a concerted effort to learn and appreciate the education that can be gained from reading materials that force them to critically examine and create their teaching philosophy. In addition, the student learns to value the exchange of ideas among peoples of diverse cultures.

Conclusion: Lessons We've Learned along the Way

Clearly, the experiences of African American faculty members at predominantly White institutions are complex. Knowing the ropes and learning how to play institutional politics are critical to the success of faculty in tenure-track positions. The significant point of this essay is that issues of diversity go much deeper than hiring faculty members from racially diverse backgrounds. Since the market for African American academics has narrowed (Kulis, Chong, & Shaw, 1999), no institution can afford to ignore the issues of retention, promotion and tenure when it comes to diversity among its faculty. However, being successful in the academy is as challenging as gaining access to it. Once inside, African Americans face a myriad of challenges different from those of European American faculty in similar situations.

The presence of an African American faculty member creates a greater degree of cultural dissonance. The departmental/institutional culture will typically convey the message, "Go along to get along," yet that behavior often requires such a degree of assimilation that African Americans may find it intolerable. The options are then to assimilate or struggle to transform the culture so that it is less hostile for oneself and for future faculty of color.

Based on our experiences, regardless of the choice made, it is paramount that African American faculty create a "homeplace" both within and outside of the institution. Creating a "homeplace" requires extra effort. Most important to creating a "homeplace" within the academy is the ability to identify mentors, people who have the ability to give good advice regarding the campus culture, and to help the new faculty member plan a strategy for coping in that climate. It is also important to develop mentoring relationships with colleagues who will provide feedback on manuscripts, since publication at a research institution is an absolute requirement. Some of these mentors may present themselves readily while others must be sought.

Another challenge is that the social climate in predominantly White institutions is typically not welcoming to African American faculty. Therefore, it is important to establish a "homeplace" outside of the institution, away from the challenges at work. We found these "homeplaces" among other African Americans at Southern University; within institutional organizations designed to promote, further, and protect the interest of African American staff and faculty on campus; at church; in the Black communities surrounding the university; and in the sanctuary of our homes. These "homeplaces" continue to keep us sane and give us the energy to engage in the activities that contribute to our success at a predominantly White institution like Southern University.

References

Alfred, M. V. (2001). Expanding theories of career development: Adding the voices of African American women in the White Academy. *Adult Education Quarterly, 51*(2), 108–127.

Benjamin, L. (Ed.). *Black women in the academy: Promises and perils.* Gainesville: University Press of Florida, 1997.

Caldwell, L. (2000). The psychology of Black men. In L. Jones (Ed.), *Brothers of the academy: Up and coming Black scholars earning our way in higher education* (pp. 130–138). Sterling, VA: Stylus Publishing.

Cohen, R. M. (1998). Class consciousness and its consequences: The impact of an elite education on mature, working-class women. *American Educational Research Journal, 35*(2), 353–375.

Hamilton, K. (2002, March 14). Race in the college classroom: Minority faculty often face student resistance when teaching about race. *Black Issues in Higher Education, 19*(2), 32–36.

hooks, b. (1981). *Ain't I a woman: Black women and feminism.* Boston: South End Press.

Jackson, K. (1991). Black faculty in academia. In P. Altbach & K. Lomotey (Eds.), *The racial crisis in American higher education* (pp. 135–148). Albany, NY: SUNY Press.

Kulis, S., Chong, Y., & Shaw, H. (1999). Discriminatory organizational contexts and Black scientists on postsecondary faculties. *Research in Higher Education, 40*(2), 115–148.

Marable, M. (2002, July). *Black in higher education: An endangered species?* Retrieved November 8, 2002, from http://manningmarable.net

McKay, N. Y. (1997). A troubled peace: Black women in the halls of the White academy. In L. Benjamin (Ed.), *Black women in the academy: Promises and perils* (pp. 11–22). Gainesville: University Press of Florida.

Moses, Y. (1997). Black women in academe: Issues and strategies. In L. Benjamin (Ed.), *Black women in the academy: Promises and perils* (pp. 23–38). Gainesville: University Press of Florida.

Shareef, R. (2002, July). Virginia Tech's egocentric faculty culture. *Roanoke.com.* Retrieved November 8, 2002, from http://www1.roanoke.com/columnist/shareef/6064.html.

Sleeter, C. (1993). How White teachers construct race. In C. McCarthy & W. Critchlow (Eds.), *Race, identity, and representation in education* (pp. 157–171). New York: Routledge.

Tierney, W. G. (1997). The parameters of affirmative action: Equity and excellence in the academy. *Review of Educational Research, 67*(2), 165–196.

Trower, C. A., & Chait, R. P. (2002). Faculty Diversity: Too little too long. *Harvard Magazine, 104*, 33–45.

Gloria Kersey-Matusiak

11

THE POWER OF ONE VOICE: WHY FACULTY OF COLOR SHOULD STAY IN SMALL, PRIVATE, PREDOMINANTLY WHITE INSTITUTIONS

Colleges and universities, like other institutions, are microcosms of our society, sociopolitical arenas in which a variety of people from various backgrounds and disciplines must interact. Despite that fact, the racial and ethnic background of faculty within these institutions does not always reflect the diversity of our nation. In small, private, predominantly White institutions (PWIs), this difference is even more pronounced; and while increasing numbers of minority students are emerging on these campuses, faculty of color remain few. In these settings, minority faculty members often serve as the single representative—or one of few—of the Asian, Black, Hispanic, Native American, or in some cases, minority perspective on campus.

Faculty members of color, while few in our nation's institutions of higher learning, are not a monolithic group. Rather, they are a small collective of a variety of educators and scholars striving to find and maintain their places at their respective colleges and universities. Like other professors, the nature of their work depends largely on the type of institution they serve. And, while each faculty member shares such common concerns as tenure and scholarship with academicians everywhere, their road to success is often paved with challenges and cluttered with barriers not experienced by their White counterparts. These barriers set them apart from their White peers by forcing them to confront and resolve a myriad of conflicts to survive on their journey to the professorate. Like their White peers in the academy, faculty of color must meet the demands of their professional roles as teacher, researcher, scientist, or scholar, etc., as defined by their institution. At the same time, they must also contend with perplexities and dilemmas that result from being "other" in a largely homogeneous environment.

In these settings, as "other" they are forced to confront issues of identity and acceptance and the complex nature of their relationship with White and minority students. They must also identify and overcome the barriers and conflicts that are inherent in the sociopolitical context in which they find themselves and which threaten their own survival as members of the academy.

As one of a few or even the only voice representing a minority perspective, faculty of color must also confront the greatest barrier to their success, the great wall of indifference toward issues of diversity still maintained and supported by some faculty, administrators, and students in these settings. Despite the emphasis on diversity and multiculturalism today in higher education, indifference is a wall difficult to penetrate as it is often concealed behind a façade of political correctness and civility. This is particularly true in settings that have sustained long histories of exclusiveness toward minority groups.

Some faculty in these institutions, who may hold tenure or who may have the respect of their peers, consider issues of diversity irrelevant or threatening. Therefore, if they consider such issues at all, they give them low priority among other institutional considerations. Such faculty are the advocates for the status quo. As a result, at times of important decision making, they stonewall meaningful dialogue on diversity, stifle creative planning toward diversity initiatives, and vehemently oppose multicultural curricular change.

Faculty in small, private, predominantly White colleges and universities that emphasize teaching are much less pressured to compete for tenure, do arduous research, write grants, or publish or perish. However faculty of color must still contend with a number of obstacles influencing their success on these campuses. Of course, they may choose to ignore any or all of these obstacles, try to rise above them, or succumb to their pitfalls in their journey to the professorate.

This paper describes the conflicts and barriers faculty members of color face in serving small, predominantly White institutions; the choices they make to overcome them, the influence of these choices on their collegial and student-faculty relationships, and the impact of such choices on the faculty member's success in the academy.

Issues of Identity and Acceptance

In light of their minority status on campus, individual faculty members of color may truly wish to "represent" the Asian, Black, Hispanic, Native American, or even, minority voice on campus; however, a major conflict lies in recognizing the impossibility of speaking on behalf of every African American (or person of color) and feeling compelled to try. This conflict becomes part of the "psychological dilemma involving issues of identity, ideology, and legitimacy" that Akbar (2002, p. 32) says must be reckoned with if we are to survive as academicians.

For African Americans and other faculty of color, it is because of our ethnicity and the value we place on that group membership, as well as our longing to give back, which make it nearly impossible to leave these values at the door as we enter the academy. Yet being "other" makes it difficult for these faculty members to gain credibility among their peers and students alike.

It would certainly be much easier to simply assume the position and role that the academy dictates and the "prefabricated identity" of professor, researcher, scientist, philosopher" (Akbar, 2002, p. 33). It becomes possible, then, to ignore the sociopolitical climate on campus, to disregard the deafening silence of the minority voice, and to avoid being placed at the center of any controversy. After all, without a critical mass of persons of color among the faculty or staff on campus, there is no social network from which to draw sociocultural collegial support for the effort.

For most of us, being the only representative of any group, or one of few, forces us to seriously consider who we really are in these settings. For a novice in the academy, particularly when one is isolated from networks of support, it becomes critical to acknowledge a self-identity that goes beyond the designated role of teacher, researcher, or scholar.

Without answering the question of who we are, Akbar (2002) warns us that "academicians risk living a life of adolescent indecision, drifting back and forth between dependency on the despotic rulings of others or forging a comfortable self-definition" (p. 33). We may, as minority group members, define ourselves or be defined by the predetermined assumptions of others. Akbar also encourages academicians to determine an identity that is "reality-based" (p. 34) and which incorporates race as an important dimension.

For students of color in small predominantly White institutions, establishing a personal identity that integrates racial awareness can sometimes foster a sense of sociocultural isolation and alienation from members of the dominant group (Kraft, 1991; Saddlemire, 1996; Stage, 1989; Stewart, Jackson, & Jackson, 1990; Tinto, 1975; Watson, 1996). Numerous scholars discuss this sociocultural alienation as a factor that interferes with the academic success of students in colleges and universities. For faculty of color in these same settings, perceptions of being "other" can be equally frustrating and demoralizing. Feelings of alienation from one's peer group may lead some minority faculty, in an effort to "fit in," to remain passive, erroneously denying the significance of race in their personal self-definitions and denying the relevance of race in daily campus life.

However, viewing ourselves through the same lens used by our White peers in these settings affords us an opportunity to see ourselves realistically within the context of our respective institutional cultures. At the same time, it is important for us as minority members of these academic communities to remember that, as microcosms of our society, these institutions reflect the same racism, sexism, classism, and other -isms inherent in our society. By developing an awareness of self in that context, we are much better able to determine the "behavioral imperatives" described by Akbar (2002, p. 34) that ultimately lend direction to our purpose and actions as members of that community.

As a new African American instructor in a small, predominantly White, liberal arts college, I became aware early of the issues of identity and acceptance that affect faculty of color on these campuses. As a woman I was also struck by the significant role of gender in defining who we are within the academy. I recognized the importance of including gender considerations in any serious attempt at self-definition. This consideration is particularly true for those of us who are women of color. Undeniably, both men and women minority professors can each make strong separate cases for how we have been undervalued and given less status than our White counterparts (Myers, 2002). However, because of our numbers, minority faculty must continue to develop coalitions to address our shared issues, interests, and concerns in the academy. But how does one accomplish this in settings where there is no network?

Myers (2002) identified interaction with other faculty as a key factor in the career longevity and success of African American women in the academy; however, as Atwater (1995) reminds us: "We cannot entirely depend on White faculty. Self worth and self-reliance must be internally generated; support networks in and outside of the university setting are needed" (p. 11).

In my own experience as an African American woman in the academy, it has been helpful to nurture relationships with other African Americans outside of my institution. Many of them were men who offered encouragement, advice, and support. These relationships were established through contacts made during workshops and conferences that fostered a sharing of mutual interests and concerns. It was not only morale boosting to learn of the achievements of other African Americans in the academy but also reaffirming to learn of the tremendous obstacles that many of them were able to overcome. Following these networking experiences, I always returned to my own campus, inspired and rejuvenated by my interactions with my brothers and sisters in the academy.

Choosing to Make a Difference

Faculty of color who are able to view themselves realistically can decide to be silent and invisible members of this so-called elite society or to be keepers of the flame of hope on these campuses. In recalling my own experiences as an African American female faculty member, it is the latter group to whom I wish to communicate.

I was struck by the irony of lessons learned during my first years as a junior faculty member at a small liberal arts PWI. In the beginning, faculty within my own department extended warmth and kindness easily to me; and it was not until I became comfortable enough as a member of the group to challenge my peers on matters of principle that the honeymoon abruptly ended. On two separate occasions at the start of my career I experienced the isolating and traumatizing feeling of being "other." These two events, though psychologically damaging, became defining moments for me as a faculty member at a PWI.

The first occurred following a teaching workshop for our department that I had attended with my colleagues. During the workshop, I raised a question that was answered thoughtfully by the presenter. Following the meeting, one of my colleagues commented that I had asked a really good question. She expressed wonderment that "one of us didn't think of that." I responded that one of us had. Despite her effort to compliment me, I was stung by the reality of how I was perceived as "other" despite being a member of the faculty.

On another occasion some time later, I attended a meeting within our department. Prior to the meeting, three other faculty members, whose friendships I valued, and I decided to broach an unpleasant topic about faculty-student relationships during the meeting. It was the proverbial hot potato that clearly no one wanted to address. I had agreed to act as spokesperson for my small group of colleagues during the scheduled meeting. Everyone denied that the problem existed. Everyone pretended not to understand what I was talking about. No one, not even those I had considered allies, or those who had encouraged me to speak, came to my aid. It was my first experience as a victim of stonewalling. The depth of my feelings of alienation was indescribable.

Following the meeting, individuals from the group privately apologized for what had happened and told me that they really felt bad about it. They acted as if they had really had no control over their previous behavior, apparently seeing themselves as mere victims of mob behavior. I was confused and hurt when one individual said she felt that her integrity was in question during the meeting because my questions threatened to reveal inappropriate behaviors on the part of people she valued as friends. It became clear to me that she had not really considered me among her friends. I countered that I had not mentioned any names, speaking only in general terms. I wondered if this was not a gender issue, since all of my colleagues in this situation were female. Were women more passive and less able to stand up for their beliefs and values when it was an unpopular position? I also wondered why I had been misled into believing that we were all one big happy family who could sift through our problems together.

I learned from this experience that, as "other" in the social sense, I was superficially accepted by the group but that I had no legitimate authority to challenge any other member. While it was all right to be a silent or affirming member of the group, it was unacceptable to go against the norm. I would be much better off staying in my place, on the periphery. I began to see how my colleagues saw me— not as an integral member of the group but as someone with only a shallow and perfunctory attachment to it. I was indeed the token Black.

Although I was easily recognized on campus and could maintain friendly relationships with peers in my department, I found no real network of faculty of color with whom to debrief about shared feelings of sociocultural isolation. There was really no one with whom I felt comfortable speaking about my classroom experiences where some White students challenged my every word or about the plight of minority students who were struggling for both academic and sociocultural survival on our campus.

In retrospect I realize that it was my own recognition and acknowledgement of myself as a spiritually strong, intelligent, and competent African American educator that kept me grounded. I was certain that, even as "other," I was quite capable of making a meaningful contribution that might enhance the learning environment for all of my students. Viewing myself as "other" in this context helped me to determine my personal goals, based on my own abilities and motivation. I could determine the roles for which I was best suited. That determination has remained a source of inspiration and strength, sustaining me even amid some of the most challenging experiences of my career.

The Complex Nature of Our Relationships with Students

Faculty members in institutions of higher learning assume a variety of roles in relating to college students. These roles include those of teacher, role model, mentor, counselor, and advocate. In addition to these roles, faculty of color, in their interactions with minority students, must often become the persons to whom the minority students looks for sociocultural support, particularly when they perceive this aspect of their college life as missing.

Many minority students who are the first generation seeking higher education in these colleges have no role models at home and few, if any, at school to assist them with their acculturation to college life. On predominantly White campuses where there is no critical mass of students of color with whom individual students of color might network, many minority students attempt to connect with the institution's few faculty of color. This natural tendency can place an enormous burden on faculty of color, especially novice faculty, who are themselves struggling with issues of identity, acceptance, and acculturation to the college environment. As an African American faculty member in a predominantly White institution, it was imperative for me to decide early whose needs and interests I would be serving.

Clearly, my own personal need for professional growth was as important to me as my obligation to my employer to meet my institutional commitments and responsibilities. I also felt a strong moral obligation to address the learning needs of all of my students regardless of their backgrounds. Preparing all students to assume their roles as members of a multicultural society and workplace became for me one of the most important challenges of my role as faculty member.

Students of color as well as White students across disciplines who felt estranged from the mainstream for reasons of age, background, or other demographic differences sought me out, expressing their need for camaraderie with someone with whom they believed they could relate. Initially, we formed a support group called the Rainbow Connection. As club moderator, I learned that, by identifying with and attempting to address these students' perceptions of sociocultural isolation, I was also addressing my own. Together we had established a mechanism by which these students could become visible members of the student government association and could learn to view themselves as integral members of the college community. The group's membership has waxed and waned over the last several years, but the organization continues to serve those students who are seeking a network of support.

Through my discussions with faculty about the needs of these students, I was able to identify a small but growing group who shared my interests in diversity. We held informal meetings about our concerns. As others and I studied the demographic predictions of the 1980s and 1990s, we recognized the need to work toward making our predominantly White campus more culturally sensitive and inclusive. I spearheaded efforts that included an assessment of our campus environment by administration, faculty, and students.

We learned through these assessments that many White students were threatened by the prospects of more faculty of color "Will they be prepared?" they commented. They also expressed reluctance to recruit more students of color. "Where will they come from and how will they afford this school?" During a forum intended to allow open discussions about race, White students expressed both anger and frustration at the mere thought of minority students being offered any incentives to attend the college. After all, they themselves were working class, employed part-time, and some full-time, to meet their own expenses. "These minorities are looking for handouts," they argued. The undercurrent of racial tension was palpable as we listened to the articulation of these racist assumptions. Many of these White students came from families with long traditions of racial bigotry toward the minorities in the inner cities, whom they had presumably escaped in making their way to the cloistered White middle- and working-class community that was the enclave from which we drew most of our students.

Meanwhile, students of color continued to express their own need for more students of color on campus with whom to study or socialize. The "cafeteria syndrome" of selective segregation was alive and well in our institution. My office became a locale where many minority and international students would hang out or stop by to discuss the problem of the day. And although this drop-in atmosphere sometimes interfered with my own planned activities, I found these conversations to be some of the most appreciated and gratifying experiences in my role as professor.

I felt a growing personal need to address students' issues cross-culturally. I wanted to assist White students in uncovering and examining their racist attitudes and in developing an appreciation of the benefits of diversity that would serve them well in the multicultural workplaces where they would be employed. The increased diversity I envisioned could benefit all groups on campus only if there were institutional structures in place to support administration, faculty, and students' development to prepare them as role models as we sought to bridge the gap between culturally diverse groups on our campus. Those supportive structures would need to include many considerations that would meaningfully impact our campus environment, our curriculum, and the attitudes of our entire staff.

Increasingly more faculty rallied behind us. The college president appointed our small faculty interest group to serve as a body in developing a plan to articulate the value we placed on a multicultural learning environment that would have an impact on each area of our institution. I was appointed Coordinator for Diversity and currently chair a representative committee that works collaboratively with others on campus in implementing our charge. After many surveys and discussions with administrators, faculty, and students, we concluded that, while there were many who supported the changes that were needed to make our campus more inclusive, many did not. Despite our ability to raise the consciousness of faculty who had straddled the fence on issues of diversity, others were clearly not interested or were resistant. As affirmative action lost momentum in colleges across the country, many faculty conceptualized diversity as efforts that exclusively served minority students who were generally perceived as underprepared.

Some White students and faculty questioned the fairness of recruiting and providing services for disadvantaged students of color when we had limited resources to support the students who were already on campus. I believed that such supports might be garnered through grant writing and through the establishment of mentoring and tutoring programs. With administrative and faculty support within my department, we explored avenues for strengthening support services, not just for students of color who needed them, but for all students considered at-risk. This process is still continuing.

Within my department, faculty listened seriously to the results of my dissertation, "Black Students' Perceptions of Factors Influencing Their Success in a Small Predominantly White, Private, and Religious Institution" (Kersey-Matusiak, 1999). I discussed the need for both the academic and the sociocultural integration of students of color if they were to succeed on our campus. Faculty recognized that change was needed in our teaching methods if we were to change our success rates for students of color who were having difficulty in our program.

Today after many years of being the designated cheerleader for diversity on our campus, I recognize that much remains to be done. My colleagues and I continue to work collaboratively within my department to build bridges among our 29% students of color and the White students. While I claim no major victories at this point, I am certain that my presence at this institution has, in many ways, influenced the attitudes of some faculty regarding issues of diversity. More importantly, it has provided a place to turn for many students who would otherwise have had no one with whom to share their feelings of isolation and alienation.

On the other hand, despite my enthusiasm, despite the increased awareness among the members of our campus community about the need for diversity initiatives, and despite the authority given our group by the college president to implement multicultural change, there remains a subtle but deep and powerful resistance deep within our organizational structure that emanates from the hearts and minds of many well-respected members of our faculty. It is perhaps the most challenging of obstacles that faculty of color in predominantly White institutions must overcome.

Confronting the Great Wall of Indifference

In light of the discourse about diversity today in colleges and universities across the nation, most faculty generally acknowledge the need for diversity initiatives that seek to address issues like the recruitment and retention of minority students and faculty and the need for all students to be prepared to work in a multicultural work place. Thus, most faculty members seem to support minority student recruitment activities, consciousness-raising, and other non-threatening diversity efforts on their campuses. Faculty in a small, private PWI, whose faculty, staff, and student populations have remained bastions of exclusiveness, are much less enthusiastic about more aggressive efforts such as actively recruiting students and faculty of color and implementing significant multicultural curricular change.

Such settings also see a strong and pervasive resistance to exploring the complex issues of diversity, a resistance that is often masked by apparent civility and political correctness. Moreover, some faculty hold with clenched fists to old models of teaching and learning, despite their proven ineffectiveness in teaching culturally diverse populations, and to the traditional "canons" of their disciplines. In this atmosphere, meaningful dialogue that might strengthen relationships among diverse groups is stifled. Multicultural curricular change is impeded and the status quo is maintained. I view such resistance as a powerful barrier, springing from some faculty's negative attitudes toward multicultural change. These attitudes are concealed under a veil of polite indifference that, on the one hand, seems to acknowledge the need for change but, on the other, silently discourages any serious steps in that direction.

For example, in my own institution, many administrators, faculty, and staff readily participate in cultural celebrations or in faculty and student recognition days that celebrate individual contributions in support of diversity. However, discussions about ways to enhance our curriculum to give our students a multicultural perspective or about ways to actively attract minority students or more faculty of color to our campus are usually met with silence. Yet these same individuals can quote verbatim the college mission and its affirmation of the oneness of the human family, the dignity of all human persons, and so on. I am reminded of Paulo Freire's (1993) *Pedagogy of the Oppressed:* "To affirm that men and women are persons and as persons should be free, and yet do nothing tangible to make this affirmation a reality, is a farce" (p. 50).

Perhaps the silence of some faculty about these issues reflects the same fears expressed by White students in contemplating an increase in the numbers of students of color on campus. Perhaps these faculty members share the students' anxiety about being "displaced" by those who are perceived to be less prepared and who will come seeking, but not deserving, a host of incentives that will certainly be reallocated from the pie of institutional resources that has been exclusively their own. They, like the students, are misguided in their thinking because of the underlying assumptions they make based on stereotypical notions about all people of color. Unfortunately, as a result, they are unable to see the benefits of diversity or multiculturalism for the common good because they are blinded by their own self-interest and fear of change. Consequently, in situations where it matters most, these faculty, administrators, and staff become part of a silent but powerful united front, co-conspirators in an effort that renders impotent the ideals of their college mission statement. Members of the college community who are hesitant to respond to the institutional need for inclusion because they are uncertain about what diversity will mean to them personally are most concerned about what they may be personally giving up. They are unable to appreciate the great benefits they withhold from all students and ultimately from a society so dependent upon them for intervention.

Despite all of these considerations, there are many ways in which faculty of color can make meaningful contributions in predominantly White, private institutions of higher learning that can greatly enhance the learning environment for all students. This is not to suggest that all faculty of color should immerse themselves in the challenging and politically charged task of promoting diversity and multiculturalism on their campuses, although some must. Rather, each faculty member of color should support such efforts as they are able.

In our struggle to survive as members of predominantly White college communities, we faculty of color must first define our role in the institution according to the dictates of our own values and beliefs systems. In defining ourselves in these institutions, faculty of color should be forever mindful of the legacy of those who have gone before us, the challenges facing those who will follow, and the sanctity of the values, beliefs, and dreams of those we represent.

During my sixteen years in academe, I have come to believe that there is much that faculty of color can do in these settings to assist in promoting diversity and multiculturalism on their campuses. Through their contacts with White and minority students, they can provide opportunities for meaningful discussions that promote intercultural interaction and enhanced understanding between culturally diverse groups. They can conduct or support learning activities and research both in and out of the classroom that allow all students to critically examine issues of race, class, and gender from a multicultural perspective. They can also advocate for a more inclusive campus environment and, within their own departments, support hiring individuals of color for administrative, faculty, and staff positions. They can serve as role models for all students in demonstrating an appreciation for diversity and an intolerance of that which undermines, or threatens to undermine, inclusion on campus.

A major barrier to inclusion on these campuses is the wall of indifference that blocks the recruitment and retention of a critical mass of minority students and faculty and that inhibits significant curricular change. This barrier continues to be maintained by those who benefit most from the status quo.

The journey to the professorate is a long and tortuous one, complicated by many barriers that faculty of color must overcome. As a single, or as one of few minority representatives on small, predominantly White campuses, it is sometimes difficult to appreciate the various roles we can play in these settings. It is even more difficult for us to view ourselves as effective agents of change. Though challenges exist, the growing fellowship of Black and other minority scholars can be a source of inspiration for others within the academy. Energized by the legacy of their heritage, faculty of color can make a significant contribution to higher education by making a serious commitment to stay on these campuses and to begin dismantling that wall of indifference that exists, even if that means removing one brick at a time.

References

Akbar, N. (2002). The psychological dilemma of African-American academicians. In L. Jones (Ed.), *Making it on broken promises: Leading African American scholars confront the culture of higher education* (pp. 31–41). Sterling, VA: Stylus Publishing.

Friere, P. (2000). *Pedagogy of the oppressed*. Trans. Myra Bergman Ramos. New York: Continuum. Originally published in 1970.

Kersey-Matusiak, G. (1999). *Black students' perceptions of factors related to their academic success in a predominantly White undergraduate nursing program at a private Catholic college*. Unpublished doctoral dissertation, Temple University, Philadelphia.

Kraft, C. L. (1991). What makes a successful Black student on a predominantly White campus? *American Educational Research Journal, 28*(2), 423–443.

Myers, W. L. (2002). *A broken silence: Voices of African American women in the academy*. Westport, CT: Bergin and Garvey.

Saddlemire, J. R. (1996). Qualitative study of White second semester undergraduates' attitudes toward Black American undergraduates at a predominantly White university. *Journal of College Student Development, 28*, 484–495.

Stage, F. K. (1989). Motivation, academic and social integration, and the early dropout. *American Educational Research Journal, 26*(3), 385–402.

Stewart, R. J., Jackson, M. R., & Jackson, J. D. (1990). Alienation and interactional styles in a predominantly White environment: A study of successful Black students. *Journal of College Student Development, 31*, 509–515.

Tinto, V. (1975). Dropout from higher education: A theoretical synthesis of recent research. *Review of Educational Research, 45*(1), 89–125.

Watson, L. W., & Kuh, G. D. (1996). The influence of dominant race environments on student involvement, perceptions and education gains: A look at historically Black and predominantly White liberal arts institutions. *Journal of College Student Development, 37*(4), 415–423.

12

FROM DISBELIEF, PRESUMPTION, AND DISRESPECT TO MEMBERSHIP IN THE LEGACY OF COMPETENCE: TEACHING EXPERIENCES AT THE HBCU AND THE PWI

A student stops by the main office of the College of Education and asks if Dr. Sekayi is around. The response is "yes" and the student is given directions to my office. The student arrives at room 1434. My nameplate is directly under the office number. I am sitting at my desk, alone in my office, working on a paper. The student looks at my nameplate, looks at me, looks back at my nameplate, and then asks, "Will Dr. Sekayi be back soon?"

When I first began my tenure-track appointment at age 28, I believed that the combination of race/culture, age, and gender would impact this professional experience just as it had impacted others. Now at age 35, I've discovered two things: (a) that this combination of personal characteristics does in fact impact my professional experiences; however (b) what matters far more than the response I get from students and some colleagues is my response to their response. This is where the issue of personal transformation comes into play. In the first portion of this chapter, I will address my experiences with students which I will categorize as disbelief, presumption, and disrespect at predominantly White institutions (PWI) and membership in the legacy of competence at historically Black colleges and universities (HBCU).

In the second portion of this paper, I will make five acknowledgments that have been a central part of my personal transformation and have facilitated my professional growth, specifically in my role as a teacher.

Experiencing Multiple Identities at a PWI and an HBCU

My informal observations suggest that young, Black, female faculty facing pre-dominantly White student populations often struggle with issues that I have cate-gorized as "disbelief, presumption, and disrespect." Unfortunately, the greater part of the work done on the relationships between teachers and students of differ-ent races/cultures focuses on White teachers and students who do not share their culture (Gregory, 1999). Very little has been done with regard to the experiences of educators of African descent with students who do not share their culture. In my experience, this phenomenon can be described using the concept of "matter-out-of-place" put forth by British social anthropologist Mary Douglas (qtd. in Media Education Foundation, 1996). She posits that when we see dirt in the gar-den, we are comfortable and, in fact, take its presence for granted. However, when we see dirt in the bedroom, we react negatively. The African presence as intellec-tual authority among predominantly White students often evokes a matter-out-of-place response.

Frequently we face challenges from students motivated by their lack of experi-ence with African American faculty. That lack of experience combined with racism, sexism, and ageism can manifest as disbelief that they are expected to accept the in-tellectual leadership of this individual, presumption that this person is not truly qualified, regardless of academic credentials and experience, and finally disrespect in the form of constant challenges to that intellectual leadership.

Even those ostensibly successful or well-acclimated faculty experience psychic trauma in predominantly White institutions (Frierson, 1990). I find this point of critical import because faculty classified as well acclimated are often held up as "proof" that there is no race problem in the school, college, or department. There-fore, no further work is deemed necessary to support faculty from oppressed or underrepresented groups.

In contrast, my experience at a historically Black institution as a professor has been exclusively with graduate students who have, for the most part, spent their undergraduate years at HBCUs. In the words of Na'im Akbar (1998), these stu-dents have been exposed to the "legacy of competence." They are accustomed to intellectuals who share their culture. Excellence is commonplace and respect is abundant. Having an African-descended faculty member is not a novelty, an ex-periment, or a source of strife.

One of the major differences between students at HBCUs and students at PWIs is that level of comfort. African people are underrepresented in the ranks of college and university faculty. Further, those who have chosen a career in academe are heavily concentrated in HBCUs (Fields, 2000). So, students at predominantly White institutions have typically had little experience with Black faculty. Although the achievement ideology is generally accepted by Americans, including those who have not experienced success within this society, it is often not extended to the Black professor in the PWI. The ideology suggests that one's level of success is a di-rect result of effort and ability. However, several assumptions typically modify this assumption for the Black professor in the classroom. One set of assumptions seems common in the context of the historically Black institution, while another set is typical in the predominantly White institution. Those varying assumptions as supported by my experiences and the literature, will be the focus of this essay.

bell hooks (1994) writes about teaching as a performative act. Surely, the actor must be believable in the role if the audience is to become engaged in the performance. Apparently, for many students at the PWI, I was simply not right for the part of the professor. This disbelief from students can potentially cripple the professional development of the professor. In Black institutions, race for an African-descended person does not inspire suspicion. In my experience, age has had a greater impact, but in a much different way than at a predominantly White institution.

Personal accounts of ageism are often shared by flight attendants, actresses, models, athletes, and men and women forced to seek new careers in their fifties and beyond. People in American society (my only substantive experience) are constantly being told that they are too old. This message resounds in the media as well as in the workplace and often within families. On the contrary, as a young professor I experience ageism as well. Probably because of the way old age is viewed in our country, I am often told that I should be flattered when people mistake me for a student. I am often told that I will appreciate mistakes of that nature when I am older. Students are often surprised to hear that I taught children prior to a career in academe. They are surprised to know that I worked in corporate America prior to a career in academe. They ask when I had time to do that considering my age. Students have refused to address me as "Doctor" because of my age. On more occasions than I can count, I've been asked, "What should we call you?", a question that isn't as regularly asked of my older colleagues.

At the HBCU, age has taken on a different meaning for me. Most of my colleagues are much older than I am. Many students have commented to me that they've never had such a young professor and are refreshed by it. They seem to see themselves in me and have expressed themselves as being inspired by my youth. No one has ever asked me what I should be called, even on the occasions when they have been my age-mates or my elders. This is certainly representative of the intersection of culture and age. They insist on calling me "Doctor." Where the conflation of multiple identities was generally problematic in my PWI experience, it actually serves me well in my HBCU experience.

To continue this discussion of raced-gendered age, I will address the second thread which connects my experiences in my earliest years in academe: presumption. Presumption deals in large part with the issue of authority, which means different things to different groups of people. Aisenberg and Harrington (1988), write about the voice of authority as it relates primarily to White women in academe. In their discussions the struggle for voice is not between professor and student but between colleagues.

My struggle with voice and authority has involved colleagues in many instances and included episodes such as the citation of literature on the experiences of African Americans to minimize a personal experience I had shared or the attempt to silence me in discussion of race when those discussions included racism. Student challenges to me in the PWI were slightly different and tended to focus on my intellectual authority primarily as it related to assigning grades. It seemed that I was believable enough as a lecturer/facilitator; but as a judge of their academic achievement, I received consistent resistance, sometimes passive, sometimes active. My teaching evaluations were generally positive; and, over time, I felt that I was able to connect with the student body. This is a statement that any effective teacher could make. The difference, as I see it, is that I was not initially given the benefit of the doubt. This "gift" is immeasurable in value and its importance is often overlooked. The benefit of the doubt is often granted based on race (Whiteness) and gender (maleness) (MacIntosh, 1988). It is also granted based on age (perceived experience). I didn't possess any of these qualities upon my initial appointment, and my students frequently withheld that "gift" as manifest by their looks of doubt, the nature of their questions, and the tone of voice used (particularly in discussions of course requirements). In the end, I usually felt vindicated. The students usually discovered that I did know the course content, that my credentials were earned legitimately, that, in fact, I was worthy of their respect. Although this final resolution is great, it would be nice to have begun with these assumptions. That is generally the case at the HBCU.

At some point I began to realize that there was very little I could do about students' negative perceptions of me based on that combination of race, gender, and age. I was not willing or even interested in "proving myself" to people, students included. That was a new discovery for me. After tirelessly seeking the approval of students to "make up for" being younger than the average professor, I decided that this was an exercise in futility. I will teach. I will tell them what I know, I will tell them what I think, I will encourage them to express their knowledge and thoughts, and I will attempt to create an environment where we can all be learners and feel comfortable in that role. I came to this philosophy as I moved further into my own personal process of transformation and away from my lifetime of miseducation (Woodson, 1933).

Personal-Cultural Transformation

The concept of personal transformation has been discussed by scholars in a variety of contexts. Fanon (1963) writes about the three phases involved in the evolution to national consciousness of what he terms the native intellectual. In the first phase, the native intellectual demonstrates that he or she has assimilated the culture of the occupying power. Fanon labels this first phase "unqualified assimilation." In the second phase, the native intellectual is disturbed and decides to remember who he or she is. In the third and final phase, which Fanon labels the fighting phase, the native intellectual becomes an awakener of the people and the "mouthpiece of a new reality in action" (p. 223).

Paulo Freire (1970) describes a process in which an individual moves from semiintransitivity of consciousness to the critical transitivity of consciousness. The categories trace an individual's development from a consciousness that is concerned only with things that are biologically necessary for survival to a stage where other problems are recognized, but oversimplified, to the final stage where problems and situations of all sorts are acknowledged and considered seriously and critically.

Both Fanon and Freire provide valuable descriptions; however, Asante (1988) describes a progression toward a critical consciousness and a transformation that is specific to the African American experience. This five-stage process consists of skin recognition, environmental recognition, personality awareness, interest-concern, and Afrocentric awareness, the culminating stage. He defines this awareness as the point at which a person becomes totally changed at a conscious level, aware of the struggle to liberate his or her own mind. Only when this happens can we say that a person is aware of the collective conscious will.

I can speak only for myself when I say I am in a constant state of becoming. I want to be in this state. It keeps me in perpetual analysis of my character, my attitudes, and my actions. This constant state of becoming also prohibits me from adopting labels. I find labels confining and constricting. Individuals who believe they have made the complete transformation to Afrocentric awareness can sometimes, in my experience, be merciless in their critique of those of us who consider ourselves in that constant state of becoming. In contrast, I have found that maintaining the process of becoming is critical, not only in my personal development, but also in my professional development, particularly in my role as teacher.

Black Women Faculty

Much of the literature on Black faculty addresses issues of collegial relationships, tenure and promotion, and affirmative action. Most of it is focused on Black faculty in general without paying specific attention to issues of gender (women) and age (youth). Additionally, relationships with students tend not to be addressed in this literature. Anderson (1988) writes about racism perpetrated against students by faculty and against faculty by administration and other faculty. Collins (1990) challenged me with her writings on Black feminist thought and enlightened me with the "outsider within stance," which "functions to create a new angle of vision" and is "essential to Black women's activism" (p. 11). This description certainly speaks to my experience in academe. Cook's (1997) analysis of Black women's survival in White academia focuses on collegial relationships, while Cose (1993), writing about middle-class African Americans in general, includes the experiences of a law professor with her colleagues. Benjamin (1997) presents a very comprehensive look at Black women in academe. While sections of chapters address faculty-student relationships, it is not the focus of the text.

Smith (1999) gets very close to my interest in student-faculty relationships in writing about the challenge of being an "authority" and a "minority" in the academic setting. She focuses on breaking down the barriers caused by multiple identities, identifying student "isms" as a major source of the problem. Although I connect with many of the experiences she describes, I would argue that we must use our own process of internal development as a starting point for dealing with in-class tensions. This approach is meant in no way to minimize the existence of racism, sexism, ageism, or homophobia in academe. These biases are there, are pervasive, and unfortunately will remain there. My approach is simply meant to acknowledge that, in addition to activities meant to transform academe and society as a whole, I must refine myself as a manager of those issues in the meantime so that standing before students who are not respectful becomes less of an arduous task and more of a learning experience.

Personal Transformation and the Professor:
Five Acknowledgments

Having considered various theories of cultural transformation and the experiences of Black faculty in institutions of higher education in the United States, I wish to explicate my own theory of personal transformation as it relates to professional life in academe, particularly the aspect of teaching. Here I offer five acknowledgments that have facilitated my well-being:

1. I acknowledge that professional omniscience is impossible and undesirable.
2. I acknowledge my self as a learner in all situations, including the classroom where I am the professor.
3. I acknowledge that my place in the process of personal transformation impacts how I perceive myself and how others, especially students, perceive me professionally.
4. I acknowledge that, in the final analysis, even if I have done my best, I will not be accepted or even respected by all students and that unanimous acceptance and/or respect is neither possible nor desirable.
5. I acknowledge that at some point in my personal transformation I should make critical professional discoveries which will make my life in academe easier to manage. (Sekayi, 2000)

These five acknowledgments resulting from my personal and professional transformation served me well in the predominantly White setting and continue to serve me in an historically Black institution. The intersection of multiple identities is not, in and of itself, problematic. Based on my experiences, the meaning of my multiple identities is in many ways contextual. While my personal development allows me to maintain a stable self-definition, I must acknowledge that students, among others, will attempt to define me based on my existence as a relatively young, African-descended woman. Those definitions might be manifest as disbelief, presumption, and disrespect, or as admission to membership in the legacy of competence.

References

Aisenberg, N., & Harrington, M. (1988). *Women of academe: Outsiders in the sacred grove.* Amherst: University of Massachusetts Press.

Akbar, N. (1998). *Know thy self.* Tallahassee, FL: Mind Productions and Associates.

Anderson, T. (1988). Black encounter of racism and elitism in White Academe: A critique of the system. *Journal of Black Studies, 18*(3), 259–272.

Asante, M. (1988). *Afrocentricity.* Trenton, NJ: Africa World Press.

Benjamin, L. (Ed.). (1997). *Black women in the academy: Promises and perils.* Gainesville: University Press of Florida.

Collins, P. H. (1990). *Black feminist thought: Knowledge consciousness and the politics of empowerment.* Boston: Unwin Hyman.

Cose, E. (1993). *The rage of a privileged class.* New York: Harper Collins.

Cook, D. (1997). *The art of survival in White academia: Black women faculty finding where they belong.* In M. Fine, L. Weis, L. Powell, & L. Wong (Eds.), *Off White: Readings on race, power, and society* (pp. 100–109). New York: Routledge.

Fanon, F. (1963). *The wretched of the earth.* New York: Grove Press.

Fields, C. (2000). Can HBCUs compete for Black faculty? *Black Issues in Higher Education, 17*(20), 39–41.

Freire, P. (1970). *Pedagogy of the oppressed.* New York: Herder and Herder.

Frierson, H. T. (1990). The situation of Black educational researchers: Continuation of a crisis. *Educational Researcher, 19*(2), 12–17.

Gregory, S. T. (1999). *Black women in the academy: The secrets to success and achievement.* New York: University Press of America.

hooks, b. (1995). *Teaching to transgress: Education as the practice of freedom.* New York: Routledge.

MacIntosh, P. (1988). *White privilege, male privilege: A personal account of coming to see correspondences through work in women's studies.* Working Paper No. 189. Wellesley College, Center for Research on Women.

Media Education Foundation (Producer). (1996). *Race: The floating signifier.* Videorecording featuring Stuart Hall. North Hampton, MA.

Richards, P. M. (1998, Autumn). A stranger in the village: A Black professor at a White college. *Journal of Blacks in Higher Education,* no. 21, 88–93.

Sekayi, D. (2000). Personal transformation and the professor: Five lessons. *Teachers College Record,* published 10/15/00. Available from http://www.tcrecord.org. ID Number: 10593.

Smith, R. (1999). Walking on eggshells: The experience of a Black woman professor. *ADE Bulletin, 122,* 68–72.

Woodson, C. G. (1933). *The miseducation of the Negro.* Trenton, NJ: Africa World Press.

Part III

TEACHING RACE IN A
PREDOMINANTLY
WHITE UNIVERSITY

13

James E. Osler II

THE CRISIS: CLASSROOM CULTURE: IDENTIFYING AND ANALYZING SEVEN FACTORS THAT DISABLE AN EFFECTIVE COLLEGIATE TEACHING METHODOLOGY

The Rationale

Often in academia African American scholars are the "silent shadow," a large and talented pool of people who are often misunderstood, unheard, ignored, and unfelt. These scholars have been nurtured with rigor, fashioned with expertise, and driven to overcome many methods of attrition. Thus, there is an undying hunger in these individuals to share their vast pool of experiences and wealth of knowledge to learners with an unbridled passion.

However, despite often having overcome almost unbelievable odds to attain their academic successes, these academicians must once again face difficult factors in the classroom that have often been left by a legacy of injustice and prejudice. It is my aim in this chapter to expose the outcomes of a "negative mind-thought culture" that can disable and ultimately harm the learning environment. Many African American professors, instructors, and educators experience these seven factors. I have experienced each of these factors first hand and have carefully synthesized and defined them so that one may have a clear picture of the harm that they can cause and how they may be overcome.

Throughout academia, teachers, educators, and all manner of instructors have typically encountered student-based factors in the classroom that have inhibited the process of learning. The aforementioned factors can be detrimental to the student's ability to progress and are counter-productive to the learning environment as a whole. The purpose of this chapter is to collectively and carefully illustrate seven major student-based factors I have encountered that disrupt the collegiate teaching environment and inhibit learning in general. Following the analysis of the seven factors, I will discuss classroom management styles to provide a basis for understand how channels of communication can break down, causing conflict to develop between students and their teachers.

I gleaned illustrations and examples of each of the seven factors from a qualitative approach which took into account personal experiences, in-depth observations, and conversations with other university faculty members. Within this chapter, the seven factors will be comprehensively identified, critiqued, and analyzed. Classroom management styles will be given the same detailed analysis. The goal is to bring to light behaviors that can cause faculty and students to become tense, negative, antisocial, and embittered. When faculty and students are affected in this manner they create an anti-productive classroom environment that is the antithesis of the process of learning. By disseminating this information, it is my hope that a new level of awareness may develop between faculty and students that will allow them to build rapport and remain cognizant of detrimental attitudes and behaviors that can surface in the classroom.

Learning: The Mutual Human Interactive Interaction Exchange

The interaction between the teacher and the student is of primary importance in any arena of learning. In the university setting, the teacher (i.e., professor) serves as the primary conduit of knowledge, and the learner must become a willing receptacle of content and information. If each person remains true to his or her duties then the learning environment hopefully can evolve into a mutual learning exchange. However, there is an added level of awareness that the teacher or instructor is responsible for. As the primary conduit of knowledge the teacher must always be aware of keeping the flow of content delivery as open as possible. Any obstacle to the exchange between the instructor and the student becomes a barrier to the delivery of content and thus inhibits any possibility of the student's future success.

There is a fine and delicate balance that must be maintained in the learning environment by both sides of the equation. Both instructor and student play vital roles in the learning process. The teacher has many responsibilities in executing and maintaining the vitality of the pedagogy (or androgogy) and the student must be willing and open to learn.

In the collegiate setting, there are many required prerequisite skills, skill sets, and behavioral patterns that the instructor and institution expect the student to already possess. These values and knowledge are critical and vital. In addition, the student must become a willing receptacle to the information that the instructor is delivering. A lack of this genuine openness is detrimental to the student's success; without an openness to learn new ideas and knowledge a student cannot truly excel.

This is the very essence of the process of teaching and learning: content delivery by the instructor and a need to learn new knowledge and content by the learner. Thus, an analogy of the learning environment as an equation applies; there must exist a balanced, shared, coexisting level of understanding between the teacher and the student. Within the classroom an attitude of mutual respect must be established and maintained. By doing so both the teacher and the student carefully focus their efforts on attempting to comprehend, understand, and appreciate one another. In this manner, mutual respect is established; and as a result, course content, relevant data, and a plethora of information readily flows.

The onus is now placed squarely on the shoulders of the teacher as the primary custodian of the realm of classroom interaction. The teacher must be at a constant state of readiness and be prepared to mediate any and all situations that can rapidly develop into conflict. He or she must be a consistent scout, constantly aware of the red flags or warning signs that are the signals for a breakdown in communication and interaction.

There are several other areas that a teacher must be aware of to create a trouble-free communicative environment in the classroom. Instructors must be ever vigilant and intuitively cognizant of polluting the learning process and the classroom with their own prejudices and biases. This is an added responsibility of teachers that includes an ongoing watchfulness toward the overall effects of how they go about content delivery and teaching.

As the primary content deliverer, those instructing students must remain keenly aware of the effects of and reactions to their method of delivery. The aforementioned are just a few of the great responsibilities that teachers willingly accept when they enter the classroom. Yet we must not forget that, on the opposite pole, students must be dedicated and able to persevere in their learning of new and different ideas.

Both students and teachers as each side of the learning exchange must remain constantly aware of personal wants, needs, and desires that are all inhibitors of the interaction between the teacher and the learner. If unreasonable or left unchecked, the preferred wants, needs, and desires of an entire class or a single individual can detract or obstruct content delivery. Thus, the entire learning environment is endangered. As a result, the process of gaining new knowledge takes a back seat to newly emerged emotions. The conflict now becomes a stifling barrier to communication between the teacher and the student, creating an uncomfortable environment that may become belligerent, hostile, and completely unmanageable.

The Seven Factors That Can Prevent a Student from Learning and That Can Destabilize the Learning Environment

This chapter is concerned with identifying common barriers to the process of learning. A question may emerge as one teaches in the classroom setting and experiences difficulty in the exchange, dialogue, and/or communication process with students. The question is this: How can we as teachers (whether we are administrators, educators, professors, or instructors) identify certain key traits or commonly observed behaviors by students that emerge in the classroom and obstruct or prevent the process of learning?

I have experienced and directly observed seven factors that are student-based behaviors that emerge and cause difficulty in the classroom setting. I list them below.

The seven factors are as follows:

1. Disbelief
2. A lack of respect
3. The question of age
4. The need to constantly challenge
5. Cultural tension and shock
6. Misperceptions of rigor
7. Lack of faith

Disbelief

Disbelief in the instructor or the content is not an uncommon occurrence in any classroom. Disbelief most often manifests itself as silence, awe, and resistance to the instructor and the learning environment. Students may ask questions such as, "You're my instructor?" or exclaim, "I can't believe you're teaching this course!" Disbelief may disappear once a level of familiarity is established between teachers and students. It is most often annoying, distracting, and an inhibitor to key relationship building that is vital to building a rapport between the instructor and the student.

The best way to diffuse this factor is to address it head on. Students cannot begin the process of learning course material if they are full of questions and not open to the instructor who is delivering the course content. Methods of addressing disbelief include: early and open conversations to create a familiarity between the teacher and student, directly addressing any questions regarding unfamiliarity and confusion, and discoursing directly on course content to avoid any and all distractions.

A Lack of Respect

A lack of respect is typically shown or indicated by the mannerisms that students convey in their behavior and actions towards their instructor. There are many ways in which a lack of respect is often manifested. Examples include: abrupt interruptions while a teacher is speaking, conversations during vital course topics or discussions, unscheduled debates or arguments over course-related topics, and students walking out of classrooms for emotional or personal reasons.

The best way to deal with a lack of respect is to address the student privately and directly when the behavior is manifested. If this fails to provide a solution to the issue, the teacher may be forced to refer to official class or university policies regarding student attitudes and behavior. The main objective is to maintain class stability, which can be easily disturbed by the random unchecked acts of a single individual. Establishing course ground rules for respect through contacts on set and established classroom policies at the start of the course is an effective way of protecting the integrity of teaching and the classroom environment.

The Question of Age

Age has always been a point of contention between younger and newer faculty and students who are of a similar age or older. Questions on the age of a teacher can lead to a misunderstanding and in some cases be viewed as a direct insult. Often resistance to the instructor because of age can lead to a lack of belief in the instructor's ability to perform the professional duties required in the academic setting.

The most harmless way to address this factor is greatly dependent upon the individual and the set of circumstances in which the question was asked. Some may choose not to address the question directly and may professionally remind students to return to the course subject matter. Others may choose to address the question if the students are not belligerent and are genuinely curious.

The Need to Constantly Challenge

The need to constantly challenge often emerges as a result of the learning environment. This often depends upon the course content that is actually being addressed and the student's level of confidence with the aforementioned subject matter. University classrooms are the breeding ground for active discourse and debate. However, the teacher in the collegiate setting must be aware of the difference between a challenging question and an insult directed at his or her competence and knowledge of the subject matter.

Methods of addressing constant challenges in the classroom can vary depending upon the circumstances. In some cases, a private meeting between the instructor and the student may be required to straighten out differences. If the challenges persist, it may become necessary to refer to university policies regarding student behavior in the classroom.

Cultural Tension and Shock

Cultural shock, or tension as a result of an adjustment to differing ideals, can become a liability rather than an asset in the classroom. This can become an open problem when diversity, gender, and ethnicity emerge as result of the learning environment or become major topics of discussion in the course. Individuals may become angry or confused when forced to come to terms with different points of view from others with different ethnic perceptions, experiences, and backgrounds.

Maintaining the peace and providing the ability for all students to openly express themselves is the key toward providing a viable solution to this particular factor. Class participants must learn to respect the varied viewpoints of others. Keeping a respectful discourse among students becomes the major duty of the instructor. Students must come to the understanding that, despite differing viewpoints, experiences, and origins, mutual respect is the vital component that they must work at maintaining. If they are successful, they can create a communicative, manageable, and productive diverse learning environment.

Misperceptions of Rigor

Students in the collegiate setting often believe that they are being "hazed" by receiving what they view as too much work. Rigorous study is the hallmark of collegiate learning. Complaints and complaining by students about workload are a core component of misperceptions of rigor.

This factor is best addressed by referring students to course duties and requirements covered in course syllabi, university catalogs, organizational standards, and requirements for their particular field of study. A reminder to students of their rationale for being in the university setting, backed by positive reinforcement, may aid in building their confidence. In addition, it may help to suggest that students manage their time wisely and confer with their academic advisor if they are feeling overwhelmed.

Lack of Faith

Fear best describes this factor. Students who are afraid that they cannot meet the challenge of academia fall within this factor. Feelings of being lost and hopelessness are common. The teacher who has a student who is experiencing a lack of faith in the classroom must address it immediately because it can become contagious and contaminate other students who may be vulnerable but who are not openly expressing their true feelings regarding the course.

Consistency becomes the mainstay when addressing the needs of a student who is actively dealing with feelings that exemplify this factor. Positive reinforcement and strong guidance through academic advisement or counseling may help a student with a lack of faith. Encouragement will go a long way towards building the self-esteem of the student, which is extremely vulnerable when he or she is experiencing feelings of desperation or despair.

Student-Teacher Conflict with the Classroom Management Style

Classroom management styles can often mean the difference between student success and student failure. How students view their teacher is often determined by how the teacher interacts with students as they deliver their content in the classroom. The following four classroom management styles are behaviors I have identified that are typically shown by teachers in their respective classrooms. The descriptions that follow are basic and followed by a brief description of how students may react to the particular style and how conflict and misunderstandings may develop. The four classroom management styles are:

1. The dictatorial classroom management style
2. The mentoring classroom management style
3. The existentialist classroom management style
4. The apathetic classroom management style

The Dictatorial Management Style

A dictatorial teacher is unshakeable and firm. This classroom management style prefers to have specific limits and constant control in the classroom. Students immediately learn that this type of teacher operates from a rigid and straightforward methodology. If tasks are assigned, then expectations are high that they are completed. This teacher operates from a "no nonsense" communication style. Directness is the key.

Typically one may adopt this style of classroom management when content delivery is at the forefront and time is of the essence. For example, methods courses and classes that require that a multitude of information must be committed to memory in a short amount of time may require this management style. Often the teacher prefers not to be interrupted. Verbal exchange and discussion are not encouraged; communication skills are often not at the center of importance in the classroom.

A teacher adopting this style will want his or her students to display vigorous discipline. Students will often be expected to follow directions and not to challenge or ask why. This may be where the teacher begins to develop a conflict with students. Due to the way that this management style operates, students may mistakenly believe that a teacher utilizing this style has little interest or care for their learning or overall well-being. This is dangerous in the classroom because it may lead to students feeling overwhelmed, powerless, angry, and confused.

Thus, a teacher with this style must change and adopt the style to incorporate methods for increasing achievement, empowerment, and motivation, through positive reinforcement and through encouraging students to set personal achievable goals.

The Mentoring Management Style

A teacher who adopts the mentoring classroom management style places emphasis on personal growth and development and simultaneously encourages independence. This teacher often explains the reasons behind the rules and decisions. Interactions between the student and teacher are vital to the success of this management style.

A mentoring management style requires a large amount of time. The teacher and the student must interact on a regular basis. A rapport must be built between the two over time. Both teacher and student must be prepared to interact verbally, with the student being open to regular critique and criticism. The ability to communicate is heightened by the interaction, and the student may learn much by watching his or her teacher perform in his or her duties and interactions.

The key with this management style is the maintenance of a careful interactive balance with the student. The teacher must not become overly dominant, demanding, or intimidating. If this happens, then some form of conflict will develop between the teacher and the student. Such conflict may surface as anger, argument, and open resentment.

Positive reinforcement through ongoing praise and encouragement are vital to the growth and development of the mentoring classroom management style and development of the student/teacher relationship. Careful student guidance by the mentoring teacher is the key to success. If guidance with corresponding positive reinforcement is steady and maintained, then the student will eventually become self-motivated, self-reliant, and successful.

The Existentialist Management Style

The teacher who uses the existentialist management style places few demands on his or her students. This classroom management style can be best described by the French phrase *laissez-faire* (literally meaning "Let us alone"). In the classroom a teaching methodology is adopted that is best described as independently motivated learning. The learning environment and classroom structure are unhampered and relaxed in their structure. A teacher with this classroom management style allows the student to learn via pursuits that are relevant to student interests.

Difficulty may emerge when the teacher who uses this classroom management style strives to be aware of all student feelings and has major difficulty saying no or enforcing classroom policies, procedures, and rules. Further difficulty may occur when there are opportunities for discourse and discussion. Frequent interruption and a lack of respect toward the teacher and peers may occur if a student with an aggressive personality attempts to assert his or her values or ideas.

The key toward success with this management style is the placement of a high emphasis on academic concerns and the correct mode of behavior in the classroom. The teacher who uses this style must keep his or her students abreast of mutual respect in the classroom. This will protect the class social climate and thereby provide the instructor with the opportunity to encourage self-motivation in the learning environment. This is not always easy and may be extremely difficult when students view their teacher as permissive and the overall classroom climate as easy and free-floating. Additionally, if the teacher chooses to place very few rigorous demands on students, there is a danger that some students who are not intrinsically motivated may have little (if any) desire to achieve academically.

The Apathetic Management Style

The apathetic classroom management style can best be described as focused independent learning. A teacher using this style may often be perceived as indifferent and is not very involved with his or her students or actively present in the classroom. Distance and timely engagement via scheduled meetings are traits unique to this form of classroom management. A teacher who uses this style places few demands on the students and appears to be aloof, distant, or generally uninterested. A teacher who adopts this management style wants his or her students to learn on their own and be totally self-directed in their learning.

An apathetic teacher does not impose on students. Although the teacher may be present, students are expected to be self-initiating, self-motivated, and eager to learn independently. In addition, teaching by proctor or another agent (i.e., graduate student, etc.) is not out of the question with this management style. Constant contact and interaction between teacher and student are not deemed a priority or necessary. As a result of this, teacher and student may not meet until a scheduled appointment time or until relevant course content, assignments, and assessments are due.

Often with this management style, students may sense and may openly reflect what they perceive as an attitude of indifference from their teacher. The danger of this particular classroom management style is that, without the teacher as an active agent in rewarding students and correcting their mistakes, very little learning may actually occur. An aura of aloofness may develop over time. This aloofness is dangerous, as both teacher and student are vulnerable to this lack of concern. As a result, students may miss valuable opportunities to observe and practice much needed and often required skills. The teacher using this management style may be unwilling or unavailable to offer expertise through guidance and active criticism. If any kind of student/teacher interaction is lacking, the student does not receive guidance, learn to meet required demands, and receive ongoing active encouragement. Thus, students are likely to be unsuccessful in their academic pursuits and may decide to give up altogether.

Building an Ongoing and Engaging Rapport with Students and Maintaining Balance in the Classroom

To summarize, often a teacher faces a great challenge when attempting to build rapport with students. Several factors may emerge that provide difficulty in building bridges and channels that can create a positive and dynamic learning environment. As noted above, seven factors that can inhibit this process are:

1. Disbelief
2. A lack of respect
3. The question of age
4. The need to constantly challenge
5. Cultural tension and shock
6. Misperceptions of rigor
7. Lack of faith

The challenge may become further difficult if the teacher has not addressed his or her own classroom management style. As summarized, four common classroom management styles are:

1. The dictatorial classroom management style
2. The mentoring classroom management style
3. The existentialist classroom management style
4. The apathetic classroom management style

Methods for addressing the seven factors and conflicts with classroom management styles involve a committed resolution by the collegiate teacher to become a positive agent of change. Tools such as consistency, positive reinforcement, and strong guidance may help a student to become motivated and may aid in unleashing his or her true potential. In addition, encouragement will go a long way toward building the self-esteem of the student and help him or her to set achievable goals and objectives. Thus, by encountering and adapting to the seven factors and conflicts with his or her classroom management styles, a teacher in the university setting improves his or her students and aids in building a better and more productive learning environment.

Summary

Earlier in this chapter African American scholars were described as the "silent shadow." However, now the shadow is no longer silent and speaks with a resounding voice. African American faculty and scholars are in possession of a unique set of experiences that allow them to express diversity and relate to all people. The key to unlocking this golden harvest of vast knowledge, unlimited potential, and unique experiences is a single and yet powerful component. That component is respect.

Respect for African American faculty must be fostered and maintained both in and out of the classroom. Respect for these individuals must be modeled by institutions, shown by colleagues, and delivered by peers. Respect must be consistent and expected, especially from students in the classroom. It is only with true honor and respect that the seven factors no longer become methods that can inhibit learning.

Ultimately, if respect is given and delivered to African American faculty, the learning environment will grow. As a result of this growth, the process of learning will gain best practices and new learning strategies, greater techniques and methodologies, new models, and ideal classroom management styles. In this manner, the process of learning will continue to develop and students will continue to prosper and grow.

14

Cyrus Marcellus Ellis

"I SHALL NOT BE MOVED": TEACHING
RACE IN A MULTIETHNIC CLASSROOM

> *To engage in a serious discussion of race in America, we must begin not with the problems of black people but with the flaws of the American society—flaws rooted in historic inequalities and longstanding cultural stereotypes.*
> CORNEL WEST, 1999

Although there are major differences in the racial climate of the United States, discussing race in political arenas, academic arenas, and social arenas still brings about major debate and repressed volatile emotions in many Americans. The topic of race is not a singular topic germane to a sect of people in present-day America; rather it is a topic of multidimensional factors concerning the historical understanding and social contexts of the people under examination (West, 1999).

The world of higher education has not been immune to the difficulties encountered when discussing race. Higher education is a dimension of the American fabric; thus, the inequalities of our society find themselves in the fabric of our institutions of higher learning. If the academic setting is purported to be a place of academic freedom where questions can be asked and human phenomena can be investigated, what makes discussions of race difficult and controversial? Further, what is an African American academician to do when he or she attempts to teach and discuss race in an unreceptive classroom? This essay will explore the difficulty of teaching race, culture, and ethnicity as an African American faculty member, focusing in particular on the educative value of exploring the important role race has in forming the American identity, African American identity in the professorate, and the ability to discuss racial and cultural differences in higher education. Additionally, this essay offers a symbol to communicate that the bearer recognizes the impact of race in our society and that he or she is committed to discussing racial issues in an open and respectful manner, free from divisive and destructive "party lines" and dysfunctional rhetoric.

Race and the American Identity

When the founders of the United States formed their view of a more perfect union they began that reality with explicit and implicit differences between men, women, and race. From the formation of the nation, differences between European settlers, Native Americans, and Africans as slaves began to weave the American fabric. The resulting battles, both political and military, shaped a confusing and dichotomous American identity. Racial issues in America have resulted in the extinction of Native American tribes, the slaughter of African people, and the death and destruction of hundreds of thousands of people who fought brother against brother. Amid political battles as well as on earthen battlefields across the nation, race grew as an issue that confounds America to this day. Decisions made in that time, along with the inability of most Whites to see former slaves as equal participants in society, set in motion a succession of events that furthered the racial divide that still exists in our present-day society.

Race permeates our national policies concerning health, welfare reform, education, housing, employment, justice, and political representation. This commentary addresses the resulting thoughts, attitudes, feelings, and beliefs of academicians still anchored in a history that subconsciously prevents necessary discussion concerning racial and ethnic differences. Thus, African American academicians who recognize the need to confront issues involving race, not multiculturalism, find that the sanctity of academic freedom in the classroom is threatened by unresponsive students as well as by some colleagues.

African Americans in the Professorate

One need only look at the data on Black men with doctoral degrees to understand the paucity of information concerning race and ethnicity in the classroom. Harvey (2002) provides keen insight into the numbers of African American men and women obtaining doctoral degrees as compared with other non-White populations and Caucasians. I urge you to seek out Harvey's collection of data.

African American faculty who have experienced the voiced, irrational beliefs of colleagues, administrators, search committees, and students about the impact that race plays in American society understand the restrictive climate that exists when issues of racial disharmony are presented and discussed in higher education settings.

As part of my on-going qualitative research, I have spoken with African American professors, both men and women, who teach diversity and other courses on predominantly White campuses. For the nontenured professor, issues revolving around race and racial attitudes are seen as "lacking scientific value" in comparison with other arenas of academic pursuit. Often, subtle and not-so-subtle reminders to the budding professor reinforce the fact that departmental colleagues judge the appropriateness of their scholarly work, thereby placing strict parameters on the saliency of one's academic output. Na'im Akbar (2002) states the dilemma for African American academicians this way: "The dilemma of the Black academician probably reaches its most critical expression around the issue of *legitimacy*. Legitimacy has to do with the issue of who is the audience for your academic enterprise and who can authenticate your work" (p. 36). Akbar adds that the institution and those who carry out its mandates have a great deal of influence over the selection, retention, and tenure of its personnel. Consequently, the African American professor must not only contend with addressing racial issues but also contend with how their colleagues perceive their disposition and the issues they find relevant to investigate.

The Ability to Discuss Racial and Cultural Differences

"Any brother in the Academy must start with awareness of the African excellence tradition, ancient and modern, in higher education, which predates slavery, colonization apartheid, and White supremacy ideology."
HILLIARD, 2002, p. 51

If we are to engage in a conversation discussing the importance of African American academicians remaining steadfast in their mission of discussing race and racial issues to educate our students, we must begin the conversation by discussing the importance of Black academicians' preparation for such duty. Particular attention must be paid to how the prospective professor organizes his or her academic and personal preparation for the world of higher education. Charlie Nelms (2002) speaks to the issue in this manner:

> The most significant requirement for effective leadership is preparation. The preparation of which I speak must occur on at least three levels. The first of these entails obtaining the basic academic credentials . . . [second] experience—experience as a teacher and a scholar . . . [third] crafting for oneself a rationale for pursuing such work. (pp. 191–192).

African American professors entering hostile academic environments when it comes to racial issues must prepare themselves in ways that include complete knowledge (not merely personal opinion), understanding, and pedagogical skill. Black academicians, already facing questions concerning their intellectual ability, must recognize that the terminal degree is not always equated with intelligence in the minds of one's colleagues. There is a common perception that African Americans scholars investigating Black issues are more emotional than scholarly (Watkins, 2002). To counter such perceptions, African American scholars need to ensure that their knowledge sets and pedagogy encompass best practices in the classroom. Therefore, Black professors need to train themselves to provoke the thought process of their students, while synthesizing additional information from a "universal" position on oppressive regimes. This tactic calls for expanding reading materials to include a variety of authors and to arrive at a holistic view of all people from various disciplines. This level of intensity presents a formidable challenge in the classroom. While this strategy does not guarantee that resistant students or colleagues will validate your work (or validate the unique experience of African people in this nation), it does provide the African American faculty member with the ability to introduce credible information on racial issues with a high degree of scholarly merit from a interdisciplinary posture.

Equally important is the individual's paradigm, or personal method of operation. Lincoln and Guba (1985) define a paradigm as a person's worldview, a way of extrapolating meaning from the multiple layers of the world (p. 15). As tenuous as it is to address oppressive racial matters in a variety of settings, the individual providing educative information bears the responsibility of critically appraising the information disseminated to be sure that it meets the systematic criteria for both external review (who is the author, what is the document's purpose, when was it written, and what is its origin) and internal review (determining if the information is factually correct) (Fraenkel & Wallen, 1993). While this review is important in building effective pedagogical skills, their remains a final piece necessary for preparing to teach race in the multiethnic classroom.

W. E. B. DuBois (Akbar, 2002) reminds us of our continuing dilemma. In his landmark text, *The Souls of Black Folk,* DuBois posits the nagging problem of our existence when he states that the American Negro possesses two souls, two thoughts, and two unresolved strivings existing in one body. From this dual position, the Black academician has an internal need to shout from every academic building the plight of an oppressed people—then, now, and for the future.

Often our frustrations can get the better of us when we encounter ideologies that diminish the status of African American people in America. Emotional responses are often interpreted as hostile and threatening, a perception that impacts the view of our academic position. In addition to preparing properly for the academy, I add a symbolic icon that indicates the displayer's/bearer's ability to discuss racial issues with a passion but without fear and without assigning blame. This symbol can be displayed, much like the inverted rainbow triangle, to communicate to students and colleagues alike that the free expression of information concerning race is acceptable. This icon is called "The Four Points of a Circle."* "The Four Points of a Circle" communicates that the bearer can *respect* others while *listening* to their views, thus ensuring *equity* among all those engaged in the dialogue to promote their *healing.*

Address queries about the "Four Points of the Circle" sticker to the author at c-ellis@govst.edu.

RESPECT

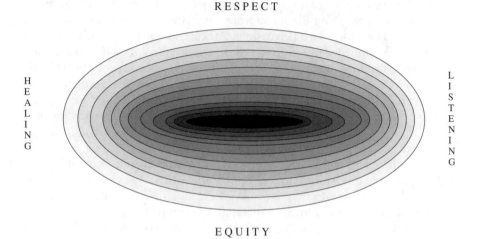

HEALING

LISTENING

EQUITY

The Four Points of a Circle

Whether it is one's paradigm or one's personal, emotional response, it is incumbent upon the one committed to educating others about race to be attentive to one's teaching stance and to provide information to students and colleagues while ensuring that the method of delivery is credible for all persons involved. Kotler and Brown (2000) observe that the self serves as an instrument through which teachers can understand and influence others.

Conclusion

Teaching race in the multiethnic classroom is a difficult task that tests the soul and professional stamina of African American faculty in the academy. Black academicians who provide instruction on racial issues on campus face a variety of challenges from students and colleagues. African American professors need to ensure that they can face those challenges effectively by preparing their professional identity and acquiring sound pedagological skills to disseminate racial information solidly and systematically to unsure audiences. Through the use of the Four Points of a Circle icon, African American professors can communicate their willingness to invite conversation on race and racial issues to any and all persons. Keep the faith!

References

Akbar, N. (2002). The psychological dilemma of African American academicians. In L. Jones (Ed.), *Making it on broken promises: Black men confront the culture of higher education* (pp. 31–42). Alexandria, VA: Stylus Publishing.

Fraenkel, J. R., & Wallen, N. E. (1993). *How to design and evaluate research in education* (2nd ed.). New York: McGraw-Hill.

Harvey, W. B. (2002). The data speak: No rest for the weary. In L. Jones (Ed.), *Making it on broken promises: Black men confront the culture of higher education* (pp. 15–30). Alexandria, VA: Stylus Publishing.

Hilliard, A. G., III (2002). One by one, or one: Africans and the academy. In L. Jones (Ed.), *Making it on broken promises: Black men confront the culture of higher education* (pp. 43–60). Alexandria, VA: Stylus Publishing.

Kotler, J. A., & Brown, R. W. (2000). *Introduction to therapeutic counseling: Voices from the field* (4th Ed.). California: Brooks/Cole Publishing.

Lincoln, Y. S., & Guba, E. G. (1985). *Naturalistic inquiry.* Newbury Park, CA: Sage.

Nelms, C. (2002). The prerequisites for academic leadership. In L. Jones (Ed.), *Making it on broken promises: Black men confront the culture of higher education* (pp. 189–194). Alexandria, VA: Stylus Publishing.

Watkins, W. H. (2002). Understanding the socialization process. In L. Jones (Ed.), *Making it on broken promises: Black men confront the culture of higher education* (pp. 99–106). Alexandria, VA: Stylus Publishing.

West, C. (1999). *The Cornel West reader.* New York: Civitas Books.

15

Denise M. Taliaferro Baszile

"WHO DOES SHE THINK SHE IS?" GROWING UP NATIONALIST AND ENDING UP TEACHING RACE IN WHITE SPACE

At age nine, as I sat and listened to my parents, grandparents, aunts, and uncles talking about George, I became upset. From what I could gather, George was an old man who had been a janitor for some big company in Detroit. Much to my family's dismay, he had recently been fired because he was accused of "stealing" a trash bag from work. I remember asking my mother to explain; but no matter how many times she repeated the details, I was perplexed. How could an old man lose his job over a trash bag? This was the first time I heard my God-fearing grandmother say something I would hear her repeat time and again, "If he was a White man, this wouldn't be happenin' to him." Although at age nine, I did not understand the full extent of my grandmother's refrain, I understood enough to be sufficiently annoyed that I sat down and wrote a letter to the *Detroit Free Press* expressing my outrage at George's situation. I was convinced, then, that the whole matter could be cleared up, if only they knew how unfair it really was. I never received an answer to my letter; and as far as I know, George never got his job back.

This was my first act of political activism, and it changed me forever. It marks the point in my life where I started to be attentive to the racial inequality that constructed the spaces in which I lived and learned and became more aware of my family's understanding of and responses to racial injustice. Because I grew up in the segregated city of Detroit in a family active in Black national politics, my understanding of race and racism has always been highly politicized. Many of my family members were key in the establishment of the Republic of New Afrika, a revolutionary nationalist organization which fights for, among other nationalist desires, a separate and sovereign Black nation and reparations. The incorporation of RNA rhetoric within my family politics (which also represented a unique Black Catholicism) has inevitably and significantly influenced my thinking on race and racism in American society. Though I have had those moments in my life where I would have liked nothing more than to shed my family politics and their burdensome seriousness about this race thing, I was never able to stray too far for too long.

My struggle with my family politics has been, no doubt, related to the images Black nationalism usually evokes in academic circles—images of violence, hatred, or just plain wrongheadedness. Although my inclination is to pose a serious critique of modernist and postmodernist essentialization of Black nationalist politics, that is truly another paper. Here I will only agree with Giroux (1996) who insists that "the linkage between national identity and nationalism is not bound by any particular politics. And nationalism is not by definition intrinsically oppressive" (p. 191). Thus, while many imagine Black nationalism as an expression of some "infamous" organizations and movements set on undoing the America that we know, little attention has been given to how Black people—affiliated or not with nationalist movements—articulate nationalist ideas in the politics of everyday life. How can we not? Living the realities of (racial) marginality requires one—to some extent—to engage a struggle against what Charles Taylor (1994) identifies as non- and misrecognition. In his essay, "The Politics of Recognition," Taylor explains that

> our identity is partly shaped by recognition or its absence, often by the misrecognition of others, and so a person or group of people can suffer real damage, real distortion, if the people or society around them mirror back to them a confining or demeaning or contemptible picture of themselves. Nonrecognition or misrecognition can inflict harm, can be a form of oppression, imprisoning someone in a false, distorted, and reduced mode of being. (p. 75)

From this perspective, Black nationalism is not simply a political agenda that is exclusive and radical; it is a way of thinking about race and racism from the point of view of the oppressed, and it is in this sense not a totalizing discourse but one strand in many that make up people's everyday politics of survival and transcendence. Thus, I revisit my family politics, not only as a commitment to a certain political agenda, but also as a struggle to name ourselves in the midst of national, local, and school politics that are working to reimagine and rearrange us so that we will fit quietly and neatly within the paradigm of unquestioned American patriotism.

There is always gonna be racism. Certainly, I cannot remember a time when this was explicitly stated, but it was always implied, for why else were we seeking a sovereign Black nation? Yet equally as significant as the idea that racism is a permanent part of our global capitalist economy was the understanding that we must commit to the struggle against racism. In this sense, struggle was never a temporary or sometime thing; it was not just about money troubles or family squabbles.

Struggle was a paradigm for living, a conscious commitment not simply to survive but to make moves for justice. In the bosom of my family's politics, I came to understand the praxis of struggle and its significance in the construction of my worldview. Through their personal and political endeavors, my family taught me that liberation was not a singular gift but an enduring process mediated through struggle. It is only by way of reflection on my family's commitment to the struggle that I intimately understand what Freire (1970) means when he defines the struggle as an act of love. He contends that the oppressed

> will not gain liberation by chance but through the praxis of their quest for it—through their recognition of the necessity to fight for it. And this fight, because of the purpose given it by the oppressed, will actually constitute an act of love opposing the lovelessness which lies at the heart of the oppressors' violence. (p. 45)

My family loved me (and loves me still) deeply and powerfully, for they saw to it that I not only learned the significance of the struggle to our literal and spiritual survival but that I also learned to embrace it and to love it. At home, my education was rooted squarely in positive images of Africa, knowledge of the history of African Americans, and a commitment to community action as well as an ethic of self-determination and faith. In school, however, my home knowledge was barely mentioned, rarely confirmed, and often contradicted. I sprouted, at a young age, dialectical selves—the home-grown me and the schooled me. Struggling amidst this tenuous dialect all my life, I am oftentimes barricaded behind self-doubt and accosted by confusion. Yet I am steadfast in my conviction that my ability to think critically and compassionately about the "revolutionary not yet" (West, 1983) and to struggle onward has its roots in my family's efforts at counter-educating me.

Today, as a professor who teaches about the relationship between race and education, I often reflect on what I have learned as a result of my family's struggles to be. I contemplate, often in amazement, how significantly their understanding of racism and resistance to it has infused my worldview and guided my life's work as teacher-activist/scholar.

Teaching as Giving Back

Always give back. Community action was one of the most critical commitments one can make in struggle. At least that was the message I got each time I tagged along with my aunt to a RNA meeting, became annoyed by mother's presence at my school to challenge some rule or another, or marveled at my uncle's willingness to defend the civil rights of numerous nonpaying clients.

Teaching has always been my best way of giving back. Ever since I can remember, I have wanted to be a teacher. Yet only since I have gotten older have I been able to understand it as my way of giving back, my calling, my desire to bring more people into the thinking and working possibility of the revolutionary-not-yet. Some of my earliest teaching experiences were in Saturday schools and recreation programs where teaching/learning was empowering, because it was absolutely connected to a paradigm of liberation which encouraged—above all else—self-understanding. Since I have left these environments to pursue teaching in school contexts, I have struggled with systemic dissent to teaching as intellectual and activist work.

Almost since the beginning of my teaching career, I felt that neither conservative nor liberal paradigms of teaching encompassed a critical sense of social justice. Conservative paradigms were consumed with relaying information and liberal ones were focused on downplaying power. I was interested in struggle, struggling against the rules, ideas, codes, mis- and non-recognitions that were eating us alive. Eventually I decided that the academy was the best place for my radical teaching sensibilities. I was excited when I secured my first position as assistant professor of education. Yet, at the same time, I was terribly anxious and unsure of what it would mean for me to teach at a an elite college where 85% of the student body and 90% of the faculty were White. Although both my undergraduate and graduate experiences were in predominantly White institutions, this was different. The root of my anxiety could be summed up in one haunting question: How was I, whose teaching exuded a love of Blackness as political resistance, going to teach White students about race?

As it has turned out, my work—teaching, research, and service—has been some of the most challenging yet insightful work I have thus far done. Without question, inviting students to imagine the revolutionary-not-yet meant challenging the existing paradigms, which currently dominate teaching in the academy. There was/is definitely no manual and rarely any direct instruction as to how to proceed; therefore, I was forced to and free to rely on my own proclivities. In this sense, my pedagogical struggle was and is a constant process of theorizing—theorizing that, in its liberatory quest, cannot be, as bell hooks (1994) recognizes, separated from practice:

> When our lived experience of theorizing is fundamentally linked to processes of self-recovery, of collective liberation, no gap exists between theory and practice. Indeed, what such experience makes more evident is the bond between the two—that ultimately reciprocal process wherein one enables the other. (61)

I have theorized much in the course of teaching/learning with sometimes critical, open, and respectful and other times hostile, frustrated, and resistant students. In the following sections, I share some teaching/learning experiences and the theorizing which works to rethink many of the ideas about teaching for social justice in the academy.

Teacher as Counter Hegemonic Text

Another consistent message in my family politics was that White people were not like us. They were different. Thus, in my worldview, White people were in every way the Other. I was never taught to dislike or hate White people; but within the course of everyday activities and conversations around my family, in school, and in the neighborhood, I understood that White folks were just different. When I was taught how to teach, however, no one took this into consideration. The literature on multicultural teaching focused almost exclusively on the ability of White teachers to teach students of color. There was no attention given to the challenges teachers of color might face in teaching White students.

The first time I engaged the discourse of race in the classroom, many people said I was brave for broaching such subject matter. Yet looking back, my bravery reflected the same kind of naiveté that characterized my letter to the *Detroit Free Press*. I had no idea what would unfold in my classroom. I ventured into the lesson with the assumption that open and honest dialogue would lead to understanding—and it did, but not at all in the way I had imagined. I was teaching 11th grade honors English to a group of mostly White, working-class students in the deep South. We were focusing on the racial discourse in Mark Twain's *Huckleberry Finn,* and one of our initial lessons involved a discussion on the use of the word "nigger" and the perception of some students that Jim was, in fact, a happy slave.

As I questioned and challenged the students on their ideas, the class became increasingly restless and agitated because I was trying to make "a big deal outta nothin'." By the end of the day, the rumors mythologizing me as a racist were running wild. During the next five and half weeks, the students were angry with me for "forcing" them to consider the text and context of race in the writing and reading of the novel. I was also angry with them because I felt that their mythologization of me as racist was an indirect and somewhat successful attempt at silencing me.

Though many things ailed me about this six-week lesson, what sticks in the back of my mind most is the students' reaction to my dysconscious use of the word "we" when referring to enslaved Africans. In their journals, they complained that it was wrong of me to say "we," because I was not and never had been a slave. Although I was, at first, taken aback, I did come to realize that my use of "we" in relationship to enslaved Africans positioned the students as a "them" in relation to slave masters. I remember this distinctly because I was troubled by the idea that I would have to give up my "we"—a we that was, for me, culturally significant. Growing up, I learned that Black people were a "we" here and now, dead and gone. The students, however, were clearly annoyed by my "we" and clearly resisted the imposition of the "them."

Do I give up my "we?" Do I ignore their discomfort? Do I explain my use of the "we?" Do I challenge their tendencies to use "we" in relation to historical text? Working through the "we" dilemma signifies a point in my teaching career and consciousness that was far more complicated than just determining what to do at that moment with that group of students. More importantly, it was about my deciding if teaching this subject matter, especially to White students, was in fact a commitment I wanted to make, one I wanted to endure. At some point, I obviously decided yes, despite my suspicions that the "we" dilemma would never go away. And after four years of teaching against and within the discourse of race at a predominantly White institution, I can absolutely say that it never has, in fact, gone away. Though the "we" dilemma is not exactly the same as it was then, the essence of the problem remains virtually unchanged. How do I facilitate discussions that emerge as "us" and "them" discourse where I am explicitly or presumptively located as either an "us" or a "them"? In confronting such situations, I have had to contemplate my positionality: What does it mean to be a Black woman with radical politics engaging the discourse of race and racism within the racial/spatial order of the college at large and my classrooms in particular?

Again turning back to my family politics, my teaching has always been activist work in the struggle for Black liberation, a discourse in which White people—not people of color—held the othered status. Admittedly, then, the idea of engaging White students in discussions of race and racism was an uncomfortable one, hence the haunting question: How was I going to teach White students about race? When I accepted the job at Colgate University, my dilemma was not at all resolved; the question lingered, expanded, fractured, doubled, and eventually generated a plethora of other questions: How do I create a "safe" space for the few students of color to speak their experiences without simultaneously creating an "unsafe" space for White students? How do I talk race to (White) students who do not see themselves as racialized beings? How do I share my experiences with students without overemphasizing that I am more understanding of the experiences of Black students than other ones?

In her essay, "On Race and Voice in Liberal Education," Chandra Mohanty (1990) contends that education is far more complex than engaging disciplinary knowledges: it is a "central terrain where power and politics operate out of the lived culture of individuals and groups situated in asymmetrical social and political positions" (558). To this end, she rightly adds: "There are much larger questions at stake in the academy these days, not the least of which are questions of self, collective knowledges of marginal peoples and the recovery of alternative oppositional histories of domination and struggle" (558), which must not only be addressed within our scholarship; they must also be defined pedagogically as questions of strategy and practice (559). Mohanty's point is imperative, because it not only requires that we see education in an untraditional sense, but she also implies that doing so insists that we see teaching/teacher as oppositional text as well.

Given my background and its influence on my current thinking, I must deal with the reality that, at times, my presence as the "authority" figure in the classroom is uncomfortable and/or intimidating to students, particularly White students. I admit without reluctance or reservation that I intentionally work to decenter the classroom, contesting and negotiating the "culture of power" and reconfiguring the racial/spatial order. How can I not? My very presence is, in and of itself, counter-hegemonic. My experiences as Black child/woman have been on and of the margins, framing my consciousness in ways that are often in tension with and in resistance to the center, which in this case is constructed by Whiteness, maleness, and liberalness. Thus, it is no surprise that I will evoke feelings of discomfort among some students.

As some one who has studied teaching, I see that herein lies an inevitable contradiction. In recent teaching literature, increasing attention has been paid to relating better to students and making them feel "comfortable" in their learning spaces. I understand the importance of making students comfortable enough to be open to learning; yet I also know that, when I am teaching about race and racism, they must be, at the same time, uncomfortable enough to be open to learning. In other words, I must negotiate the fine line between their comfort and discomfort.

Moreover, when I am teaching controversial subject matter, comfort is often linked to teacher objectivity/neutrality. This is problematic because, as a Black woman teaching about race, I am imbued, from the students' perspective, with the authority of experience. Whether I refer to my experiences or not, students are making their own assumptions about the relevance of those experiences to the subject matter. Thus, regardless of my credentials—my studied learning of race—students are more taken with the ways in which I am visibly marked as qualified to teach a course on race. As one student succinctly put it, "A White professor just can't teach this course effectively."

Although I disagreed with this student's comment, it did cause me to think more seriously about how my experiences were informing my teaching strategy. I could choose not to incorporate them as part of the curriculum—to, in other words, feign an objective stance. But if I chose to do so, I would be working against one of the basic premises of the course: that racism is not only an institutional phenomena but also an inter/intra personal one. To act as if my experiences are irrelevant is to allow many students to remain too comfortable, to obfuscate my complexity as a person, and to reinforce the idea that race and racism is simply about respecting difference.

The question for me, then, is not whether to include my experiences, but how to engage them critically and responsibly. Knowing that I am the first, and for many the only, encounter with a Black female professor, I have come to understand that I am myself a counter-hegemonic text, a living oppositional framework, and as such a subject of study by the students.

Safe Place, Contested Space

When I crossed Eight-Mile Road, leaving the chaotic comfort of inner-city Detroit to attend high school in the mostly White suburbs, my grandmother cautioned me that things would be different now that I was going to school with White folks. I had to be careful. What was she talking about? Everybody knows that the White suburbs are supposedly a lot safer than where we lived. Although once again unsure of what my grandmother meant, I remember the distinct feeling that my elders knew something I did not about the other side of Eight-Mile Road.

What my grandmother was communicating to me, I presume, was the terror of Whiteness/White space (hooks, 1992) that had very much defined her life. When she warned me about crossing Eight-Mile, she knew that the threat was not necessarily physical but mental, being in the right frame of mind to deal with White folk. In reflection, I am convinced that my grandmother was not at all warning me about evil White people so much as she was simply saying that, where difference is evident and structured by unequal distributions of power, there are no safe places.

When confronting identity and difference, safety is allusive. Mica became defensive when Halle, who began to cry, challenged her Whiteness. Kianna was so mad she could not speak. Jada was tired of African American students assuming that Caribbean students have no differences from them. Annie and Justin wanted to know why Asian Americans are left out of discussions of racism. And Lea's bottom lip quivered as she tried, without tears, to express her invisibleness as a Native American student. The classroom is not a safe place.

In her essay "There are No Safe Places: Pedagogy as Powerful and Dangerous Terrain," Annette Henry (1993) critiques the idea that the classroom is a safe place. Presumptively, the classroom is a place where students can share their experiences and as such feel "empowered." In disagreement, Henry recognizes the notion of safety as one which has emerged out of liberal feminist discourse and is subsequently rooted in class and race privilege. Agreeing with Henry, I would add that the vision of a safe classroom is also linked to particular pedagogical practices, specifically behaviors that avoid conflict. In the classes that I teach, these privileges are all the time being disrupted by the polemics inherent in the discourse of race and by my choice of pedagogical practice. Wanting students to not only understand the institutional politics of race but also the way these politics are mapped onto our bodies and lived as configurations of the self, we engage theory and experience, self-knowledge and other knowledge in the classroom.

In theory, then, no one is safe, because as Henry goes on to point out:

> Teaching and learning about race/ethnicity, culture, religion, language background, socio-economic background, gender, sexuality, and able bodiedness are difficult. Learning about these issues by examining our own lives, by tracing and exposing our personal and social histories is dangerous. (2)

What exactly does "being safe" imply anyway? Does it mean that everyone will respect everyone else's opinion? Does it mean that students' opinions will not be challenged? Does it mean that we do not raise our voices? Does it mean that the things said should not make people cry or make them furious? Does it mean we can tell the truth — really tell the truth — without grave consequences? Safety, in my opinion, is unrealistic in a room where everybody is under surveillance. I am watching the students, the students are watching me, the students are watching each other, we are watching ourselves, and we are all being watched by outsiders.

Another not-talked-about reality that makes safety illusive is the way in which classrooms are not simply reflections of the present moment; they are also historically situated, as is everyone in them. The history of American racial ideology lingers like an invisible cloud in the classroom. One of my White students, who wanted to work with some of the Black students at an urban community center, told me that she felt her fellow Black students did not trust her intentions. I assured her that they probably did not but that it had little to do with her as a person and more to do with the history of Whiteness in which and because of which she stands. Was that a safe thing to say?

I cannot and do not imagine the classroom as a safe place. I envision it, instead, as contested space, a site of cultural struggle, where we are situated in complicated, historically grounded relations of power. In much of the current discourse on diversity, this issue of power is avoided, submerged in politically correct conversations about tolerance and sublime pleas of "can't we all just get along?" Many of the students I work with remember diversity as powwows, Cinco de Mayo celebrations, and Black History Month. White students do not want to think about how their privilege is tied to power, nor do many students of color want to critically engage an understanding of their power in liminal spaces. Yet some understanding of discourses of power is necessary, for they undergird the effects of American racial ideology and mediate any critical discussion of it. Thus, through discussions, activities, and assignments, I try to negotiate a space that is always contestable, a place where paradigms and power are always shifting as I draw them back to the basic questions: Whose interests are being served? Whose authority is affecting other people's life chances? Who has defined reality?

Silence as Refuge, Silence as Weapon

My uncle refused to shake the university president's hand when he walked across the stage. My aunt was kicked out of law school for leading a protest. Another aunt glared at the store employee as she made it clear that she did not at all appreciate his following us through the store. My parents, especially Momma, never hesitated to confront any injustice they thought we might be facing at school. The Taliaferro family—both the men and the women—were ardent about speaking up, especially where injustice was concerned.

Yet I was a quiet child, an anomaly in a family of activists. That all changed when I left for college. It was ironic indeed, because leaving for college was one of those moments in my life that signified my wanting to escape my family politics. Thinking about race all the time was tiring. Throughout my freshman year, I did manage to be sufficiently apolitical (or shallow, as I imagined it). I just did my work and had fun. No rallies, no protests, no riots, and my group of friends looked like the Rainbow Coalition. Things took a drastic turn in my sophomore year. Several incidents and events occurred on campus that called me back to the politics of home. I remember talking with a group of angry students, who were preparing a protest on behalf of a Black professor who did not receive tenure. One of the more vocal group members insisted, "Y'all know this wouldna happened if he was White." I took that as a message from my grandmother, and the rest is history.

Finding my voice in college was not as intense as using it in graduate school, where I always felt this ever-intense rage when having conversations about race with my White peers. I would experience hot flashes, pink face, and watery eyes. One day I finally broke out in a rash that covered my entire body. I imagined that each ugly little red spot was a silenced thought, and there were hundreds of them speckled from my neck to my ankles. My peers did not want to hear about race, and they especially did not want to hear anything I had to say about it.

Eventually I grew weary, left with many disheartening moments of silence and a barrage of self-doubt about my abilities to be "reasonable" about race. The horror and humiliation of that kind of silencing has helped me and haunted me in complicated ways. My skin has grown thicker. I have become more observant of the unavoidable dynamics of interracial discussions about race. I have come to realize the inevitability of silencing in the context of such discussions. I have come to learn that honest and open discussion about race is painful and does not necessarily render the intended and imagined results. Silencing is real, inevitable, and sometimes necessary for one's sanity.

Though I sought refuge in silence, seeking cover from the war raging in my classrooms and in my head, silence can also be used as a weapon in the war (Ladson-Billings, 1996). The dialogue-silence dialectic is forever the impending crisis in my classroom. Daily, I toil with the effect of my presence on the (un)willingness of White students to actively participate in classroom dialogue. I have considered fear. They are perhaps afraid of offending, afraid of rejection, afraid of displaying their uncomfortableness. While I can certainly relate, I am troubled by a more complicated possibility, one that does not dismiss fear but factors in resistance—not just resistance to the teacher and/or the knowledge, as Ladson-Billings (1996) discusses in her essay "Silences as Weapons: Dilemmas of a Black Professor Teaching White Students," but also resistance to visibility.

When White students are challenged on their silence, they often respond with, as one student assured me, "I have nothing to contribute to the conversation. My experiences are not relevant." Such a comment taken at face value might be justifiable in courses where the discourse on race and racism focuses exclusively on the experiences of underrepresented groups. However, in my course, I intentionally incorporate readings on Whiteness and encourage dialogue on a variety of experiences (educational, familial, etc.) which are applicable to all students. In this context, students of color and I are consistently giving up our stories and our testimonies, thus situating ourselves as vulnerable and seeking validation of our experiences. The majority of White students, however, opt for silence, thus maintaining their invisibility in the discourse of race.

The more White students use silence, the more frustrated the students of color become, until they too eventually opt for silence. The frustration of the students of color is itself a complex phenomenon. On one hand, they implore the White students to share their experiences. Yet, on the other, when they don't, the students of color tend to assume that the silence of the White students is indicative of racist thoughts. In other words, my students of color believe that, if White students are afraid to speak, it is because they want to make racist comments. Although this belief is rarely, if ever explicitly, verbalized, it is communicated nonetheless through reactionary body language and under-their-breath comments. The silence of the White students essentially denies the students of color the opportunity to resist the imposition of their assumed racist thoughts. Ironically though, the few White students who do participate in dialogue only rarely challenge the thinking or the tone set by students of color. Essentially, then, what unfolds in the classroom is what typically is the case in conversations about race in American culture. Patricia Williams (1997) explains:

> Perhaps one reason that conversations about race are so often doomed to frustration is that the notion of whiteness as "race" is almost never implicated. One of the more difficult legacies of slavery and of colonialism is the degree which racism's tenacious hold is manifested not merely in the divided demographics of neighborhood or education or class but also in the process of what media expert John Fiske calls the "exnomination" of whiteness as racial identity. Whiteness is unnamed, suppressed, beyond the realm of race. Exnomination permits whites to entertain the notion that race lives "over there" on the other side of the tracks, in black bodies and inner-city neighborhoods, in a dark netherworlds where whites are not involved. (p. 7)

To this end, despite attempts to nominate Whiteness, the dialogue is reified in a White normalcy-other consumption dialectic, where the discourse of race remains deviant. Through the silence of White students, Whiteness remains invisible and maintains a position of normalcy. However, White normalcy is not just undergirded by the silence of White students, but also by the testimonies and other contributions of students of color and me, whose experiences are visibilized through the discourse of race and are thus situated as deviant and problematic but good for shock value. In the conversation, then, while White students are situated as voyeurs, students of color and I are fixed in the voyeurs' line of vision, a disturbing dilemma.

In real time, of course, the students are dysconscious of the ways in which their behaviors reconstitute racial hegemony and how the consequences of this reconstitution are often played out in terms of the learning curve. On one hand, White students' learning is maximized. They are exposed to the theory, to the experiences of students of color, and to a critical analysis of their own experiences through journal work. In contrast, though the students of color are also exposed to theory, they are not privy to the experiences of White students, which could present fundamental challenges and which would in turn assist them in developing their own critical analyses of self and other in the context of race.

The paradox, however, is that while silence takes its toll, talking also takes its toll. The ways in which we envision open and honest dialogue is itself problematic because what we expect from these situations is that everybody will "understand" everybody else, which requires eradicating difference—which is inevitably impossible. So what I have learned is that the most meaningful dialogues require that we confront the impossible so that we can see what is, in fact, possible. And in this sense, what is impossible is avoiding silence and silencing. Instead of overworrying about whom I or others may be silencing, I engage silence and silencing as subjects of study in the classroom. In essence, I find myself working on the dialogue-silence dialectic every semester and have to decide to ask the students to do the same. In other words, I do not hesitate to ask them to analyze the raced, gendered, and classed dynamics of our dialogues and how they contribute or not to meaningful learning.

The Possibility

Contempt. In contempt. Jail time. Expulsion. Harassment. Death threats. Dreams not deferred but stolen—all indicative of the radical political activism that surrounded me. Real? Indeed. Scary? Absolutely. Daunting even. I learned that being afraid was okay but that indefinitely giving up on the struggle was not. When I think about the people of Birmingham who walked for 381 days, the Black children who survived the trek to Central High School in Arkansas, the Black Panthers who stared down the White police forces throughout the country, the Black children of Soweto who risked their lives for freedom, and every one and anyone who faced down the system to change the world in some way—I remember that impossibility is constructed by possibility.

I would be remiss if I did not admit that some days I do indeed feel pessimistic about race and racism in America, and particularly about teaching as a viable front in the struggle against oppression. I question, until now secretly, how my pedagogical practices, which are intended on some level to challenge racism and other social injustices, has in fact fortified the obstacles to some extent. As I work through that haunting question, more questions arise: Is my pedagogy a disservice to students of color? Is there some way to give both groups of students what they need? Although for me these questions are almost paralyzing, I am more afraid of not having such questions than of having them. Certainly, not having them means I am not seeing something I need to see.

It is all very paradoxical indeed, and there is no room for me to deny or forget this as I am, on most days, in the midst of a struggle for the future, by teaching young participants, perpetrators, and victims of American social injustice. Yet this essay is not about being pessimistic in any fixed sense. It is about exploring the impossible in an effort to reach the possible. As a Black woman who grew up nationalist and ended up teaching about race and racism in a predominantly White space, I must contend with my own peculiar position inside of these paradoxes.

While naming my nationalist nuances opens me to being mythologized as essentializing, radical, and even racist, doing so, it turns out, is absolutely critical to my ability to problematize what and how and whether I teach about race and racism in American education. Such intense self-reflection has helped me recognize the enormous importance of my agency despite the well-documented obstacles faced by many Black women who have committed themselves, in and through the academy, to teaching and researching for social justice (Benjamin, 1997; Mabokela & Green, 2001).

To this end, I close these thoughts by reminding myself, as I often have to, of my favorite line in Annette Henry's essay, "For me as a Black woman, my pedagogy is not only a political act, but an act of courage" (2).

References

Benjamin, L. (Ed). (1997). *Black women in the academy: Promises and perils.* Gainsville: University Press of Florida.

Freire, P. (1970). *Pedagogy of the oppressed.* Trans. Myra Bergman Ramos. New York: Continuum.

Giroux, H. (1996). *Fugitive cultures: Race, violence, and youth.* New York: Routledge.

Henry, A. (1993). There are no safe places: Pedagogy as powerful and dangerous terrain. *Action in Teacher Education, 15*(4), 1-4.

hooks, b. (1992). *Black looks: Race and representation.* Boston, MA: South End Press.

hooks, b. (1994). *Teaching to transgress: Education as the practice of freedom.* New York: Routledge.

Ladson-Billings, G. (1996). Silence as weapons: Challenges of a Black professor teaching White students. *Theory into Practice, 35*(2), 79-85.

Mabokela, R., & Green, A. (Eds.). (2001). *Sisters of the academy: emergent Black women scholars in higher education.* Sterling, VA: Stylus Publishing.

Mohanty, C. (1990). On race and voice: Challenges for liberal education in the 1990's. In A. Halsey et al. (Eds.), *Education: Culture, economy and society* (pp. 557-571). New York: Oxford University Press.

Taylor, C. (1994). The politics of recognition. In D. Goldberg (Ed.), *Multiculturalism: A reader.* Cambridge, MA: Blackwell.

West, C. (1983). Philosophy, politics and power: An Afro-American perspective. In L. Harris (Ed.), *Philosophy born of struggle,* pp. 51-59. Dubuque, IA: Kendall Publishing.

Williams, P. (1997). *Seeing a color blind future: The paradox of race.* New York: Noonday Press.

16

BLACK FACULTY COPING WITH RACIAL BATTLE FATIGUE: THE CAMPUS RACIAL CLIMATE IN A POST–CIVIL RIGHTS ERA

Introduction

If you can think of the mind as having 100 ergs of energy, and the average man uses 50 percent of this energy dealing with the everyday problems of the world—just general kinds of things—then he has 50 percent more to do creative kinds of things that he wants to do. Now, that's a White person. Now, a Black person also has 100 ergs. He uses 50 percent the same way a white man does, dealing with what the white man has [to deal with], so he has 50 percent left. But he uses 25 percent fighting being Black, [with] all the problems being Black and what it means.
SENIOR BLACK MALE PROFESSOR

African Americans spend countless amounts of energy, personal and familial, dealing with White racism and patterns of institutionalized racism (Clark, Anderson, Clark, & Williams, 1999). Unfortunately, we still hear reports of African Americans being the first Black to be hired to certain jobs, the first to earn a particular degree from an academic program, the first to play for a specific professional sports team, the first to be hired as a coach at a predominantly white school, or the first to own a National Basketball Association franchise (Spears, 2003). Therefore, America is still replete with White spaces to which African Americans have historically been denied access. Even in places where there has been a history of employing

African Americans, usually the superiors are White; and Blacks are evaluated by Whites who typically have little or no experience with Blacks as friends, colleagues, or superiors (Feagin & Sikes, 1994). Institutions tend to be microcosms of the larger society. Sadly, in the new millennium, untoward racial accounts are very common on America's college and university campuses. Some researchers might argue that White campuses are far more hostile for Black students and faculty than in the larger society (Feagin, 2002).

In this essay, I lay out a pattern of exclusion that was part and parcel of the racial climate on historically White campuses in the pre-civil rights era. These historic patterns of racial exclusion and justification have emerged in contemporary attitudes and excuses toward the Black faculty experience and experiences on predominantly White campuses. By the time Black faculty were being hired in these institutions, a climate of hostility was part of the foundation of the university.

Today, new foot soldiers (White students) matriculate every year in institutions of higher education, bringing with them sharply honed skills of stereotypical beliefs and attitudes about African Americans and Blacks as professors ranging from subtle to hostile. Most of these students have never seen a Black person face to face, lived near African Americans, or attended religious institutions with them (Kinder & Sanders, 1996). For reasons I outline in this chapter, many White students resist taking African American studies classes or classes that focus on race and diversity (Smith, 1998). Consequently, being confronted with a constant barrage of varying attitudes and stereotypes about Blacks, Black professors, African and African American history and contributions to society, as well as basic discussion on racial inequities, can place tremendous stress on African American faculty, resulting in deleterious health consequences. A theoretical concept for understanding the kind of stress that African American faculty are dealing with is developed here with suggestions for adaptive coping strategies.

The Racial Climate in the Pre–Civil Rights Era

The struggle for African American scholars participation in American higher education has been a dubious racist battle since the beginning of U.S. colleges and universities (Anderson, 2002). Descendants of enslaved Africans in America emerged from slavery, not as believers that Blacks were intellectually inferior to Whites (Brigham, 1923), but with an expressed intent of becoming literate and highly functioning and contributing citizens (Anderson, 1988). In fact, ex-slaves believed that full emancipation was commensurate with being able to read and write. There is one sin that slavery committed against me, one ex-slave maintained, which I will never forgive. It robbed me of my education (qtd. in Anderson, 1988, p. 5). American higher education, since the founding of its first institution, Harvard, in 1636, developed a parallel system of racial exclusion that merged White racial supremacy and meritocracy into a single objective more racially restrictive than in American society at large (Anderson, 1993, 2002; Smedley, 1993).

On October 24, 1992, in Boston, James D. Anderson (1993), an American educational historian and social historian of Black education, delivered his presidential address at the annual meeting of the History of Education Society. In his presentation of archival research, Anderson meticulously demonstrated how universities failed to follow their own mantra of using meritocractic and egalitarian hiring practices when it came to employing African American scholars. Anderson identified a strategic campaign on the eve of World War II, conducted by agents of the Julius Rosenwald Fund, to integrate African American scholars into northern White universities. Fred G. Wale, the funds director of education, sent a letter to about 600 university and college presidents inquiring if they would hire qualified applicants who happened to be African American. Wale mailed a supplemental list of approximately 150 outstanding African American scholars[1] to each of the college and university presidents. Most of these Black scholars were trained at elite northern universities (e.g., University of Chicago, 20, Harvard University, 15, Columbia University, 10, the University of Michigan, 6, and the University of Pennsylvania, 5, or in Europe (e.g., Oxford). Only 200 of the 600 presidents responded. The majority who responded displayed lukewarm enthusiasm toward any suggestion of hiring African American scholars.

The overwhelming majority of northern college presidents had no African American scholars in an official part-time or full-time faculty appointment before, during, and after the immediate World War II era. Between 1900 and 1940, there was an enormous need to hire new faculty members. According to Anderson (1993), American higher education enrollment surged 529 percent during this period. Additionally, the nation's total population increased by 73%, individuals between the ages of 18 to 21 increased by 63%, and, in the six years preceding World War II, more than 30,000 African Americans graduated with college and professional degrees. By the mid-1940s, approximately 3,000 African Americans held master's degrees and more than 550 possessed doctoral degrees. However, in an effort to disregard the need to hire more faculty from the available pool of African Americans and the opportunity to break the color bar in academe, college and university presidents and administrators consistently made subtle to overt racist excuses to exclude African Americans from employment. One university president in New York exclaimed, "I do not know whether they [the department heads] will feel that the educational needs of our students now warrant our making any special effort to employ Negro teachers or to discriminate against White applicants" (qtd. in Anderson, 1993, p. 169). Somehow, these northern university presidents, their boards, and department chairs rationalized to themselves and others that the virtual exclusion of African American faculty members was not a racially discriminatory hiring practice; yet any special effort to hire Blacks was discrimination against Whites. Similar arguments developed during this early period would become popular during the post–civil rights era.

Racial Priming in a Post–Civil Rights Era

Today race is more commonly explained as a socially constructed category, invented and maintained by Whites, rather than a biological one. Despite acknowledging its social construction and political-material usage, our understanding of Whites' racial views and behaviors in a post–civil rights era is vitiated with confusion (Bonilla-Silva, 2001). Some scholars have described Whites' race-related belief as dysconscious racism (King, 1991), modern racism (McConahay, Hardee, & Batts, 1981), symbolic racism (Kinder & Sears, 1981), laissez-faire racism (Tuch & Martin, 1997) or color-blind racism (Kinder & Sanders, 1996). One thing is sure: White racial attitudes are not static; they respond to changing social, demographic, economic, and political dynamics, interracial contestations, as well as class and gender dimensions within the dominant race (Bonilla-Silva, 2001; Feagin, 2000; Tuch & Martin, 1997). Therefore, it is terribly disingenuous to think that just because Whites' responses in survey questions developed during the Jim Crow era have improved that this is not an overestimation of their tolerance toward Blacks and other folks of color (Bonilla-Silva, 2001). Furthermore, anti-Black attitudes are maintained and backed by a system of power and privilege parceled out and remunerated by elite Whites, disproportionately benefiting all Whites. Yet discussions of race and the present-day effects of the legacies of racism and White supremacy remain very sensitive and volatile issues on the American racial fault lines.

According to a White majority, we are living in a post-racist era which has put away its attitudes of racial indifference, bigotry, hatred, discrimination, and misunderstandings. Racism is considered to be a historical artifact; and (so goes the reasoning), it is only one's personal or group ineptitude that provides adequate explanations for modern racial inequities (Bobo & Kluegel, 1993; Kluegel & Smith, 1983, 1986; Reddy, 2002). This belief system is an example of being *racially primed* not to see racism or oneself as racist, while one thinks, speaks, and acts in racist ways towards Blacks and other people of color. Racial priming is a cumulative socialization process by which Whites systematically internalize racist attitudes, stereotypes, assumptions, fears, resentments, discourses, images, and fictitious racial scripts which fit into a dominant White worldview and rhetoric. This socialization has evolved into an outgrowth that involves the inculcation of a well-structured, highly developed, racially conservative, race-neutral or color-blind reactionary belief system in which White children actually learn race-specific stereotypes about African Americans and other race/ethnic groups (Smith, 1996, 1998, 2003; Van Ausdale & Feagin, 2000); as they get older, they continue to receive both involuntary and voluntary corroborating messages of anti-Black stereotypes from adults, friends, games, folklore, music, television, popular media, and the hidden curriculum (Bonilla-Silva & Forman, 2000; Holmes, 1995; Smith, 1996, 2003; Van Ausdale & Feagin, 2001). Left unchallenged, these racial priming lessons become increasingly strengthened components of White youths' internalized self-identity during adulthood and may be invoked as overt, reactionary, or flippantly racist responses (Bowman & Smith, 2002; Smith, 1998).

Racial priming is not new. In fact, it has been part and parcel of the American system of racist relations. Since the 19th century, European and non-European immigrants have reached America only to be judged and stratified within a system of White-on-Black oppression (Feagin, 2000; Jordan, 1968; Myrdal, 1944). According to Joe Feagin (2000):

> Each new immigrant group is usually placed, principally by the dominant whites, somewhere on a *white-to-black continuum,* the commonplace measuring stick of social acceptability. This socioracial continuum has long been imbedded in white minds, writings, and practices, as well as in the developing consciousness of many in the new immigrant groups. Generally speaking, the racist continuum runs from white to black, from civilized whites to uncivilized blacks, from high intelligence to low intelligence, from privilege and desirability to lack of privilege and undesirability. (p. 210)

This socio-racial continuum was firmly in place by the Reconstruction period. Before this period, a modern sociology of race was embedded in the minds of Americans as it was in most of the world, especially as it related to Black people (Schuerich & Young, 2002; Watkins, 2001). Racist stereotypes, scholarship, and discourse about Africans in America had been popular in writings prior to Thomas Jefferson's famous 1781 manuscript, *Notes on the State of Virginia,* and definitely before Carl Campbell Brigham's influential *A Study of American Intelligence* (1920). However, Marimba Ani (1994) and William H. Watkins (2001) proclaim that, while little public knowledge circulates regarding Arthur de Gobineau of France, he is one of the earliest and most significant intellectual racists to relegate Blacks to the lowest rungs of the human family. In fact, Gobineau's views were the foundation that further promoted and secured anti-Black stereotypes, merging into the later racist pseudo-scientific scholarship:

> The Negroid variety is the lowest, and stands at the foot of the ladder. The animal character, that appears in the shape of the pelvis, is stamped on the Negro from birth, and foreshadows his destiny. His intellect will always move within a very narrow circle. . . . If his mental faculties are dull or even non-existent, he often has an intensity of desire, and so of will, which may be called terrible. Many of his senses, especially taste and smell, are developed to an extent unknown to the other two races.
> The very strength of his sensations is the most striking proof of inferiority. All food is good in his eyes, nothing disgusts or repels him. What he desires to eat, to eat furiously, and to excess; no carrion is too revolting to be swallowed by him. It is the same with odours; his inordinate desires are satisfied with all, however coarse or even horrible. To these qualities may be added an instability and capriciousness of feeling, that cannot be tied down to any single object, and which, so far as he is concerned, do away with all distinctions of good and evil. We might even say that the violence with which he pursues the object that has aroused his senses and inflamed his desires is a guarantee of the desires being soon satisfied and the object forgotten. Finally, he is equally careless of his own life and that of others; he kills willingly, for the sake of killing; and this human sacrifice, in whom it is so easy to arouse emotion, shows, in face of suffering, either a monstrous indifference or a cowardice that seeks a voluntary refuge in death. (qtd. in Biddiss, 1970, p. 135)

According to Winthrop Jordan (1968), individuals like Jefferson, Gobineau, Brigham, and many of their predecessors and contemporaries influenced the development of anti-Black ideologies and they helped to create an ideology where White and Black connoted, respectively, purity and filthiness, virginity and sin, virtue and baseness, beauty and ugliness, beneficence and evil, God and the devil. These beliefs aided in justifying White dominion over Black people in America while relegating them to the lowest socioeconomic strata. Alfred Milner, who was billionaire Cecil Rhodes's special agent in South Africa and America, in an address to the Municipal Congress of Johannesburg in 1903 stated:

> The white man must rule, because he is elevated by many, many steps above the black man; steps which it will take the latter centuries to climb, and which it is quite possible that the vast bulk of the black population may never be able to climb at all. But then, if we justify, what I believe we all hold to, the necessity of the rule of the white man by his superior civilization, what does that involve? Does it involve an attempt to keep a black man always at the very low level of civilization at which he is today? I believe you will all reject such an idea. One of the strongest arguments why the white man must rule is because that is the only possible means of gradually raising the black man, not to our level of civilization—which it is doubtful whether he would ever attain—but up to a much higher level than that which he at present occupies. (qtd. in Copland, 1990, p. 37)

Racist ideologies and stereotypes like these have persisted into present times and are the sources of many decisions Whites and other non-Blacks make in assessing their disdain, relationships with, acceptance of, and intimacy with and toward African Americans.

As an example of the impact of racial priming, George Yancey (2003) reported data from several studies based on the Lilly Survey of American Attitudes and Friendship (1999–2000) on racial beliefs, preferences, and practices among European Americans, Latinas/os, and Asian Americans. He found that non-Black groups believed that no other U.S. racial group had been more discriminated against than African Americans. However, these same groups indicated that, if their children married someone outside of their own race, they preferred marriage into any other racial/ethnic group rather than marriage with an African American.

In a supportive large multiracial study of more than 4,000 Los Angeles residents, Zubrinsky-Charles (2000) assessed residential preferences for African American, Asian American, European American, and Latina/o neighbors. She found that with the exception of African Americans respondents, respondents of all other races, answering a question about what their ideal multiracial neighborhood would look like, described a multiracial utopia in which Blacks were only a small peripheral minority. European Americans indicated that only 16.15% of their ideal neighborhood would be African American, while 18.91% of the White respondents preferred a Black-free neighborhood. Latinas/os were slightly more exclusive about Blacks as neighbors (13.76%) than Whites, while 31.66% of the Latina/o respondents did not want any African Americans in their neighborhood.

Asian Americans were the most likely to have an African American restriction in their neighborhood. Of this group, only 11.05% wanted Black neighbors in contrast to the 39.94% who preferred no Black neighbors. In fact, no other racial/ethnic group was excluded in its totality by Asian Americans and Latinas/os more than African Americans. African Americans were also the last preference as neighbors for Asian Americans, Latinas/os, and European Americans, respectively. While African Americans were the least racially restrictive and desired a more balanced multiracial/ethnic neighborhood (African Americans = 37.41%, European Americans = 23.67%, Latinas/os = 21.32%, and Asian Americans = 17.77%). This racial imbalance is also true for U.S. higher education (Bowman & Smith, 2002; Smith, 1996, 1998; Smith, Altbach, Lomotey, 2002).

Racially Primed Students in a Post–Civil Rights Era

White racial ideologies, based upon defective notions of individualism and merit (Sturm & Guinier, 1996), make classroom discussions about the impact of systemic racism and White supremacy against African Americans very contentious (Bowman & Smith, 2002; Feagin, Vera, & Imani, 1996). Systemic racism encompasses the White prejudices, racial priming, and institutions the economy, politics, education, religion, the family that are integral to the long-term domination and stereotyping of African Americans and other people of color (Feagin, 2000). Most White pre-collegians are racially primed with racist stereotypes and are ready to oppose affirmative action, special minority admissions, diversity-required courses and programs, African and African American contributions to society, and discussions about contemporary racial inequities (Smith, 1996, 1998; Tusmith & Reddy, 2002). Educators must understand *how* White students have been racially primed throughout their lives to view African Americans in stereotypical ways. If they understand the process of racial priming, they will be better able to distinguish white students' attempts to defend positions of Whiteness instead of considering the claims of people of color. Understanding and defusing racial priming in a White dominant society is not an easy task. According to Christine Sleeter (1994), with precious few exceptions, White people do not talk about White racism. Instead, we talk about group differences, very often in ways that simplify and devalue others while rendering Whiteness itself as invisible, or normal (p. 6). Moreover, it is far too weighty to be placed on one teacher or one discipline such as African American studies.

In a large 1996 multiracial study of undergraduates attending a major Midwestern university (Smith, 1996), I found that college students from different racial and ethnic backgrounds do indeed tend to bring distinct race-related ideologies and policy attitudes to the campus community. A statistically significant difference emerged from the views of the four race/ethnic groups (i.e., European Americans, Asian Americans, Latinas/os, and African Americans) about African Americans. Asian Americans and Whites, respectively, were most likely to agree that African

Americans tend to be violence-prone rather than peace loving, prefer to live off welfare rather than to be self-supporting, are lazy rather than hard working, and are unintelligent rather than intelligent. Latinas/os emerged as a third group who held significantly different ideologies than African Americans but were clearly less stereotypical than Asian Americans or Whites. African Americans, as expected, held the least stereotypical ideologies about Blacks. Based on this campus study, in conjunction with national studies like the National Opinion Research Center (NORC) and the Anti-Defamation League surveys, many Whites, in particular, still stereotype African Americans in ways that keep Jefferson's, Gobineau's, and Milner's arguments, among many others, vital in updated formats.

In an extension to the 1996 study, I found that White college students, overall, held the lowest levels of support for race-targeted programming and efforts at diversifying the curriculum (Smith 1998). The second study showed that White students held the lowest endorsement of efforts aimed at developing special minority admissions policies, special minority scholarships, special minority academic support programs, special minority facilities, required multicultural courses, expanding women's studies in the curriculum, and expanding African American Studies in the curriculum. Mean levels of support for White students ranged between 2.42 and 3.53. Asian American support ranged between 3.01 and 3.94, while Latinas/o support was between 3.70 and 4.39. African Americans maintained the highest levels of support for all race-targeted programming and curriculum diversity efforts (4.29 to 4.71). Parallel findings can be found in cross-sectional studies on other adult White populations on affirmative action and beliefs about inequalities (Bobo, 2000; Bobo & Kluegel, 1993; Kinder & Sanders, 1996; Kluegel & Smith, 1983, 1986; Tuch & Martin, 1997). In these studies, racially primed opponents of affirmative action and diversity efforts claimed to be the true champions of a color-blind system, advancing the values that America was built upon. The same race/ethnic pattern emerged with Whites and Asians being the most oppositional and Latinas/os representing a middle group. African Americans were the most supportive of diversity and recompense efforts. Consequently, racially primed Whites will ascribe the position of the have-nots to Blacks' personal failings, culture, or circumstances but fail to consider how systemic White racism in institutional, societal, and civilizational manifestations is a major contributing discriminatory factor for Blacks in their daily lives (Kinder & Sanders, 1996; Scheurich & Young, 2002).

Racial stereotypes and prejudices become useful explanations, for White college students, about why Blacks do not have as much nor do as well as Whites in several areas of society. Racially primed students believe that African Americans have an inferior culture and racial ethic, thus explaining why there are mammoth racial inequalities in a society that claims to be based upon egalitarian principles (Bobo 2000; Bobo & Kluegel, 1993; Bonilla-Silva & Forman, 2000; Feagin, Vera, & Batur, 2001; Kluegel & Smith, 1986). Therefore, any special effort to redress racial inequalities perpetrated against African Americans is seen as a discrimination against Whites. This racist paradox has been played out on the nation's college and university campuses since 1636 in faculty-hiring preferences, classroom grading practices, admissions decisions, student housing assignments, Greek-letter fraternity and sorority membership practices, student government elections, faculty tenure and promotion decisions, and more recently since the latter part of the 1990s, in forms of campus violence echoing the 1960s, 1970s, and 1980s. In short, White racial animus, exclusion, and discrimination have always been part of the experience of Black students and faculty at historically White colleges and universities.

Black Professors and Racial Battle Fatigue

Too often, academics who teach race-based classes, as well as ethnic studies professors, treat White students as if they are racial *tabulae rasae*. They underestimate the degree to which White students enter their classrooms with sophisticated racial scripts, which they have inherited, and how well they have been groomed to oppose critiques on Whiteness, merit, and other topics that are taught as unfair racial inequities while endorsing individualism and employing racist stereotypes (Tusmith & Reddy, 2002). Professors of ethnic studies, African American studies, and other race-based classes are fighting an honorable and necessary but uphill and stressful battle trying to dismantle a racial ideology reinforced by centuries of racial priming (Anderson, 1994; Feagin, 2000; Jordan, 1968). Many racially primed students express clear messages of opposition toward classes that emphasize racial issues, experiences, and histories through their words (e.g., from strategic silence to open hostility or consistent challenges) or actions (e.g., from subtle uncooperativeness to obvious disruption of the classroom environment to encouraging other students to join in resisting or hijacking the professors' attempts to teach the curriculum). In extreme cases but with increasing frequency, racially primed students have turned to racial harassment and even violence toward people who are seen as the racial other (Blumer, 1958; Federal Bureau of Investigation, 2001; Hurtado, 1992; Rhoads, 1998; U.S. Department of Justice, 2001).

Unfortunately and all too often, White university administrators downplay the race-based stress that African American professors experience at the classroom, department, university, and community level. More specifically, administrators fail to take seriously the level of physiological, psychological, and emotional stress experienced by African American teachers who are assigned classes of predominantly White students who are, usually reluctantly, taking a course that is part of university diversity requirements (e.g., race, racism, sexism, and White supremacy). Certainly, African American studies classes have an unique and even more complicated battle, given the well-developed anti-Black and stereotypical views of African Americans (Jones, 1997; Karenga, 1993; Yancey, 2003; Zubrinsky-Charles 2000). While Black professors in general and African American studies professors in particular may be cognizant of the race-related pressures and battles they face in the classroom, many are unaware of the consequences of racial battle fatigue experienced on a physiological level as they teach contentious African American studies classes semester after semester.

Racial battle fatigue develops in African Americans and other people of color much like combat fatigue in military personnel, even when they are not under direct (racial) attack.[2] Unlike typical occupational stress, racial battle fatigue is a response to the distressing mental/emotional conditions that result from facing racism daily (e.g., racial slights, recurrent indignities and irritations, unfair treatments, including contentious classrooms, and potential threats or dangers under tough to violent and even life-threatening conditions) (Clark, Anderson, Clark, & Williams, 1999; Essed, & Stanfield, 1991; U.S. Department of the Army, 1994; Williams, Yu, Jackson, & Anderson, 1997). A growing body of literature suggests that stress-related diseases result from the fact that African Americans have to keep activated a physiological response, originally evolved for responding to acute physical emergencies, but now "switched on" constantly to cope with chronic racial microaggressions/macroaggression (Clark, Anderson, Clark, & Williams, 1999; Essed & Stanfield, 1991; Sapolsky, 1998; Scaer, 2001; Shay, 2002; Solorzano, Allen, & Carroll, 2002; Williams, Yu, Jackson, & Anderson, 1997).

To extend this metaphor: the college classroom is often a racial theater of contentious, racially primed, White students positioned to unleash their racial weapons (read: discourse and attitudes) of destruction. African American professors and other faculty of color are often on the front lines of race, in the cross-hair focus of racial backlash from uneasy White students semester after semester without appropriate protection and assistance. This backlash adds to the racial battle fatigue that Black professors endure. For example, White students can display their dislike for race-based classes or the professor by inappropriately and uncivilly challenging the lesson, questioning the professor's capabilities, using defiant or disengaged body language, constantly whispering, sending disrespectful and angry e-mails to the professor, having temper tantrums, uttering threats, throwing paper assignments at the professor, plotting a coup d'état for the course, reporting their dislike of the class to the department chairperson or dean, using the course evaluation as a weapon against the subject matter and the teacher, and attempting to defame the professor's reputation as incompetent (Tusmith & Reddy, 2002; such examples are reported in the numerous studies cited in this chapter's references). While some White faculty may argue that they experience similar student reactions, such aggression fails to match the weight of the constant race-based experiences of faculty of color.

Some researchers are certain that White professors face far fewer direct challenges than professors of color: whatever the course context that lower level of hostility and challenge translates into a classroom environment in which it is easier for the [White] professor to work and consequently for students to feel confident in the [White] professor's ability to maintain the class's respectful attention (Reddy, 2002, p. 54). An African American professor's classroom where the focus is on race, racism, and/or White supremacy presents optimal conditions for producing psychological and physiological stress-responses to student expressions of reactionary racism, denial, and resentment (Bowman & Smith, 2002). Consequently, these classroom stimuli would qualify as chronic race-related stressors.

Ultimately, African American professors are prone to develop various psycho-physiological symptoms, including tension headaches and backaches, trembling and jumpiness, chronic pain in healed injuries, a pounding heart beat, rapid breathing in anticipation of conflict, an upset stomach, frequent diarrhea or urination, extreme fatigue, constant anxiety and worrying, increased swearing and complaining, inability to sleep, sleep broken by haunting conflict-specific dreams, loss of confidence in oneself and one's colleagues/department/college/university/community, difficulty in thinking coherently or being able to speak articulately under stressful conditions, rapid mood swings, elevated blood pressure, and emotional/social withdrawal (Clark et al., 1999; Feagin & McKinney, 2003; Feagin & Sikes, 1994; Turner & Myers, 2000; Williams, Yu, Jackson, & Anderson, 1997). Within that framework, a race-related stressor can be defined as anything that throws the body out of allostatic balance (Sapolsky, 1998). A stressor can also be the *anticipation* of a racist event. Thus, the stress-response can be mobilized not only in response to physical or psychological insults, but also in expectation of them (Sapolsky, 1998, p. 8). These symptoms are common in soldiers enduring combat, strengthening the appraisal of the severity of chronic race-related stress that Black people endure (Shay, 2002; U.S. Department of the Army, 1994).

Both the soldier in combat and the Black professor in the racial battlefields of the classroom can respond to their combat conditions, in either low or high intensities, with many of these symptoms. Although it is very rare to experience all of them concurrently, experiencing two or more symptoms simultaneously is very common. However, only about 10–20% of combat soldiers experience combat fatigue (Shay, 2002), while data on the psychological, physiological, emotional, community, and family cost of everyday racism seems to be even higher for African Americans. The cost of racial battle fatigue at one level can be measured by the six or seven years of decreased life expectancy for Blacks, on average, compared to Whites (Feagin & McKinney, 2003; Feagin & Sikes, 1994).

For the African American professor and other professors of color, an additional source of stress is the skepticism and repudiation with which such symptoms are typically greeted. Most White colleagues dismiss the seriousness of those symptoms, asserting that African American faculty are simply personalizing minor to moderate negative experiences too much, being too sensitive, emotional, or paranoid. Such unwillingness to face the hard realities of the racism and racial inequalities that African Americans face by further blaming the victim is not healthy for African Americans, the campus climate, and society as a whole.

In a comprehensive review of the literature on stress, health outcomes, and African Americans, Rodney Clark and his colleagues (1999) noted that Blacks report more exposure to stressors than Whites, thereby increasing the likelihood of both resource strain-behavioral exhaustion and psychological and physiological distress (p. 808). While self-reported measures of stress have been widely acknowledged (e.g., those assessing job strain, life events, and daily struggles), there may be a propensity to ignore reports of racism solely because they involve a subjective component. Such a tendency to discount perceptions of racism as stressful is inconsistent with the stress literature, which highlights the importance of the appraisal process (p. 809). In short, an African American's perception of conditions as stressful is significantly more valuable in initiating stress-responses than objective conditions that may or may not be viewed as stressful by non-Blacks (Burchfield, 1985; Clark et al., 1999).

Consequently, it is far more essential and therapeutic for Blacks to develop adaptive coping strategies to resist or reduce the intensity of racial battle fatigue than it is for them to swallow their anger or remain silent as they endure everyday racism. Almost 20 years of research suggest that racial socialization represents a significant asset for promoting the healthy functioning for African Americans in a racist society (Bowman & Howard, 1985; Boykin & Toms, 1985; Harrison, 1985; Jackson, McCullough, & Gurin, 1988; McAdoo, 1985; Peters, 1985; Spencer, 1983, 1987; Stevenson, Reed, Bodison, & Bishop, 1997; Stevenson & Renard, 1993).

Race-Related Socialization and Adaptive Coping Strategies

As outlined in this chapter, African Americans are products of a long but racist history in the United States, one in which they had to develop successful coping strategies to survive. These strategies have endured into the present day as Blacks still cope psychologically better with stress than Whites but suffer higher rates of disease and death, due to the cumulative effects of stress, especially discrimination (Williams, Yu, Jackson, & Anderson, 1997). On the one hand, frequent and early exposure to racial adversity appears to be the leading explanation for Blacks' better mental health measures. On the other hand, surviving racial adversity takes its toll in physical health problems that apparently result from the persistent and repeated stressors of everyday discrimination rather than from major discrimination, which is episodic and time limited. Williams and colleagues (1997) found that everyday discrimination caused considerable injury to health more, in fact, than major discrimination. These findings agree with more general stress research indicating that day-to-day hassles and frustrations have a greater negative impact than major stressful life experiences. Major discriminatory experiences include inequitable treatment in hiring, firing, or job promotion, and intimidating encounters with police. As previously mentioned, everyday discrimination and racism includes ill-mannered treatment, inadequate services, being made to feel inferior, and being insulted, threatened, or harassed (Williams et al., 1997). This is the historical relationship in the two-ness of being African and American.

W. E. B. DuBois, an eminent intellectual, scholar, and humanitarian, is often cited for his brilliance and his ability to make a very complex situation understandable. His observations on this topic indicate the importance of recognizing the stress-response of racial battle fatigue and also the need for adaptive coping on the part of African Americans:

It is a peculiar sensation, this double-consciousness, this sense of always looking at one's self through the eyes of others, of measuring one's soul by the tape of a world that looks on in amused contempt and pity. One feels his two-ness, an American, a Negro; two souls, two thoughts, two unreconciled strivings; two warring ideals in one dark body, whose dogged strength alone keeps it from being torn asunder. The history of the American Negro is the history of this strife, this longing to attain self-conscious manhood, to merge his double self into a better and truer self. In this merging he wishes neither of the older selves to be lost. He does not wish to African-ize America, for America has too much to teach the world and Africa; he does not wish to bleach his Negro blood in a flood of white Americanism, for he believes-foolishly, perhaps, but fervently—that Negro blood has yet a message for the world. He simply wishes to make it possible for a man to be both a Negro and an American without being cursed and spit upon by his fellows, without losing the opportunity of self-development (1897, pp. 194–195).

It is probably safe to say that every Black person wishes to be respected and validated rather than being cursed and spit upon because of her or his race. The major question to be asked is: How has a people's dogged strength kept them from being torn asunder after centuries of racial torture and discrimination? The most defensible answer is found in proactive and protective cultural strengths that African American parents teach their children the concept of racial socialization.

According to Stevenson and Renard (1993), racial socialization involves the parental instruction to their children or family members about racism in society, educational struggles, extended family relevance, spiritual and religious awareness, African American culture and pride, and transmission of child-rearing values (p. 435). African American cultural patterns and expressions have complexities and nuances that are not always readily apparent or visible, especially, to a mainstream analysis. Racial socialization does not rely on a verbal, didactic, or explicit process alone but can often be transmitted by indirect, tacit, or behavioral methods (Boykin & Toms, 1985; Stevenson & Renard, 1993).

Stevenson (1994) performed a validation study for the Scale of Racial Socialization Attitudes for Adolescents (SORS-A). Unlike previous studies based on the Nigrescence theory of Racial Identity Attitude Scales (RAIS), performed by researchers like William Cross, African American students were asked to respond with their people or community in mind. Stevenson found four major factors with two underlying themes of proactive and protective racial socialization identity beliefs for adolescents. According to Stevenson (1997):

Protective racial socialization beliefs view the world as racially hostile and worthy of distrust, encourage youth to discern supportive or hostile racial intentions, take on a tone of caution, and encourage youth to succeed despite external oppression. Proactive racial socialization beliefs encourage the individual to succeed as a function of internal talent, cultural heritage, and pays [sic] less attention to external oppression. Proactive beliefs are focused more intensively on the respondent's endorsement of parental strategies that instill a sense of cultural empowerment in youth. (p. 40)

Stevenson (1994) identified three main proactive racial socialization beliefs: spiritual and religious coping, cultural pride reinforcement, and extended family caring. In contrast, protective racial socialization beliefs consisted of one factor teaching awareness of racism. Stevenson (1994) suggests:

> A robust racial socialization agenda may require discussions about spirituality and religion and how one's identity is not fully shaped by hostile societal influences. It may suggest that children be reinforced to learn about how their cultural heritage is unique and not solely developed out of socially oppressive experiences. Enslavement is a reality of the history of being Black in America, but it does not solely concretize one's cultural identity. Blood and non-blood extended family members play a crucial role in teaching children about their character and in raising children to be responsive to the inner-community concerns about racism and cultural pride development. . . . Racism awareness teaching may be protective in that it challenges the recipients of the teaching to reject traditional opinions about Black culture that are also influenced by racist, inferior-based rhetoric. (p. 463)

These protective and proactive racial socialization beliefs appear to be successful adaptive coping strategies that mitigate persistent physiological and psychological stress-responses. As a result they can surely help reduce the troubling effects of racism on the health of African Americans.

Implications and Conclusion

African Americans must continue to utilize adaptive coping methods, because racism does not appear to be ending any time soon. To be sure, the full range of African American adaptive coping strategies are extensive. More research must explore other racial and cultural traditions for overcoming racial battle fatigue. One example is to take a second look at the various folktale, folklore, storytelling, aphorisms, and cultural expressions that Blacks use as lessons of endurance (e.g., Br'er Rabbit, Br'er Bear, and Br'er Fox). African American folktales in teaching moral lessons may help explain the endurance of Black men and women and meet the need for answers to apparently unanswerable questions. Black barbershops and beauty salons are filled with these traditions and daily aphorisms. "Big Mamas" and "Papas" are loaded with stories of how we got over. Such resources should never be taken for granted as sources for positive ways to cope. Therefore, tapping the best strategies and sources, given the racial context, is critically important for healthy Black survival. For instance, social drinking or attending a Friday 5:00 club after work may help lessen the racial stress a person has endured during the day or week. However, excessive drinking as a method to suppress racial battle fatigue is a maladaptive approach with physiological fallouts. Employing maladaptive coping strategies or strategies that do not attenuate stress-responses will continue to negatively affect African American health (Clark, et al., 1999). African American parents, grandparents, and other blood and nonblood extended kinships are important role models for dealing with racism effectively.

Unfortunately for African American faculty, as James Anderson has articulated, higher education was and continues to be much more racially exclusive, oppressive, and antagonistic than society at large. African American college and university faculty members are still underrepresented according to their numbers in the U.S. population. Since the fall of 1992, Black faculty numbers continue to plummet, but almost exclusively among African American males. Blacks are approximately 13% of the U.S. population, but are less than 5% of the nation's teaching faculty, while African American students make up less than 10% of their multiethnic cohort (*African American Education Data Book, Vol. 1,* 1997). The future looks less promising for Black males, who continue to represent a declining proportion of the student and faculty numbers in comparison to Black women, Whites, and other people of color. Despite the steady birth rates of Black males, they represent an increasing minority of the Black (and overall racial) proportion of high school and college graduates, graduates with masters, doctoral, and professional degrees, and the numbers of assistant and associate professors recently hired and promoted (*African American Education Data Book, Vol. 1,* 1997; Borden, 2001). In fact, in a rather sexist and racist silence, graduate-level degrees conferred on students of color between 1992–1993 and 1999–2000 have increased markedly among all students of color except for Black males. While recruitment and graduation numbers for Black women can and should always be improved, this group currently represent anywhere from two times to 10 times the numbers of Black males taking degrees in almost every field of graduate-level education in the top hundred programs (Borden, 2001). With the exception of Latina/os, whose representation proportion is similar to that of African Americans, no other racial-gender group manifests such a dramatic pattern. Apparently little public or scholarly attention is dedicated to Black males (or Latinos, for that matter), while the downward trend shows no signs of leveling out or reversing in the near future. This educational dilemma reduces the available pool of potential Black faculty and severely curtails mating selections for Black women who prefer endogamous relationships with men in similar fields.

We know that Black faculty participation has been tenuous throughout the nation's history. Outside historically Black colleges and universities, there has never been a significant Black presence in four-year institutions. Consequently, not having a critical Black mass of professors, deans, and senior level administrators in successive generations on any single campus retards the development of adaptive coping practices created specifically for addressing racism on historically White campuses. Without these available campus socialization networks, racial battle fatigue can have overwhelming physiological, psychological, familial, and community consequences. Moreover, the trickle-down effect is significant: The psychological safety and professional aspirations of both undergraduate and graduate students are jeopardized by the shrinking numbers of racially fatigued, over-committed Black faculty. Racial battle fatigue is a useful framework for analyzing the constant stress from daily racism that people of color face, on and off campus. The research field is wide open for understanding how racism affects folks of color and how they shore up coping strategies. Qualitative inquiry should be our first line of defense.

Notes

1. The Rosenwald Funds list of African American scholars was very impressive even by contemporary research and publication standards. In fact, most of these scholars had higher publication counts than their White contemporaries and they preceded Harvard's publish or perish doctrine. The list included scholars in anthropology, art, biology, creative writing, drama, economics, education, history, home economics, language and literature, law, library science, mathematics, mechanical engineering, medicine, music, philosophy, photography, physics and chemistry, political science, psychology, religion, social service, sociology, and zoology. The main list was continuously updated with new scholars on a monthly basis. The caliber of the individuals, as previously stated, was outstanding. For example, the list included names like W. E. B. DuBois, Merze Tate, Birtill A. Lloyd, Adelaide Cromwell Hill, Percy L. Julian, Mamie Phipps Clark, Henry Aaron Hill, Bonita H. Valien, Nathaniel Oglesby, Estella H. Scott, Abram L. Harris, Mabel Murphy Smythe, Allison Davis, Charles Spurgeon Johnson, John Hope Franklin, E. Franklin Frazier, Ralph J. Bunche, Eric Williams, Benjamin A. Quarles, Sterling A. Brown, Shirley Graham (DuBois), Langston Hughes, Lawrence D. Reddick, Margaret Walker, Richard Wright, Alain L. Locke, Ernest E. Just, and Benjamin E. Mays.
2. I am not equating actual front-line conditions with classroom experiences, not am I minimizing the terror, tensions, fear of injury, physical sufferings, exertions, and death of combat. However, I suggest the metaphor as a useful one in understanding the expressions of stress experienced by Black professors. For Vietnam combat trauma, see Shay (1995, 2002).

References

African American Education Data Book, Volume 1: Higher and Adult Education. (1997). The College FUND/UNCF: A Research Institute on African Americans and Education. Fairfax, VA: Frederick D. Patterson Research Institute.

Anderson, J. D. (1988). *The education of Blacks in the South, 1860–1935.* Chapel Hill: University of North Carolina Press.

Anderson, J. D. (1993). Race, meritocracy, and the American academy during the immediate post–World War II era. *History of Education Quarterly, 33*(2), 151–175.

Anderson, J. D. (2002). Race in American higher education: Historical perspective on current conditions. In W. A. Smith, P. G. Altbach, & K. Lomotey (Eds.), *The racial crisis in American higher education: Continuing challenges to the twenty-first century* (pp. 322). Albany, NY: SUNY Press.

Ani, M. (1994). *Yurugu: An African-centered critique of European cultural thought and behavior.* Trenton, NJ: Africa World Press.

Biddiss, M. D. (1970). (Ed.). *Gobineau: Selected political writings.* New York: Harper & Row.

Blumer, H. (1958). Race prejudice as a sense of group position. *Pacific Sociological Review,* *1*(1), 3–7.

Bobo, L. (2000). Race and beliefs about affirmative action. In D. O. Sears, J. Sidanius, & L. Bobo (Eds.), *Racialized politics: The debate about racism in America* (pp. 137–165). Chicago: University of Chicago Press.

Bobo, L., & Kluegel, J. (1993). Opposition to race-targeting: Self-interest, stratification ideology, or prejudice? *American Sociological Review, 58,* 443–464.

Bonilla-Silva E. (2001). *White supremacy & racism in the post–civil rights era.* Boulder, CO: Lynne Rienner.

Bonilla-Silva, E. & Forman, T. A. (2000). I am not a racist but . . . : Mapping White college students' racial ideology in the U.S.A. *Discourse and Society, 11,* 51–86.

Borden, V. M. H. (2001, July 19). The top 100: Interpreting the data. *Black Issues in Higher Education, 18*(11), 50–116.

Bowman, P. J., & Smith, W. A. (2002). Racial ideology in the campus community: Emerging cross-ethnic differences and challenges. In W. A. Smith, P. G. Altbach, & K. Lomotey (Eds.), *The racial crisis in American higher education: Continuing challenges to the twenty-first century* (pp. 103–120). Albany, NY: SUNY Press.

Boykin, A. W., & Toms, F. D. (1985). Black child socialization: A conceptual framework. In H. P. McAdoo & J. L. McAdoo (Eds.), *Black children: Social, educational, and parental environments.* Newbury Park, CA: Sage.

Brigham, C. C. (1923). *A study of American intelligence.* Princeton, NJ: Princeton University Press.

Burchfield, S. R. (1985). Stress: An integrative framework. In S. R. Burchfield (Ed.), *Stress: Psychological and physiological interactions* (pp. 381–394). New York: Hemisphere.

Clark, R., Anderson, N. B., Clark, V. R., & Williams, D. R. (October 1999). Racism as a stressor for African Americans: A biopsychosocial model. *American Psychologist, 54*(10), 805–816.

DuBois, W. E. B. (1897, August). Strivings of the Negro people. *Atlantic Monthly, 80,* 194–198.

Essed, P., & Stanfield, J. A. (1991). *Understanding everyday racism: An interdisciplinary theory.* New York: Sage.

Feagin, J. R. (2000). *Racist America: Roots, current realities, and future reparations.* New York: Routledge.

Feagin, J. R. (2002). *The continuing significance of racism: U.S. colleges and universities.* Washington, DC: American Council on Education.

Feagin, J. R., & McKinney, K. D. (2003). *The many costs of racism.* Lanham, MD: Rowman & Littlefield.

Feagin, J. R., & Sikes, M. P. (1994). *Living with racism: The Black middle-class experience.* Boston: Beacon Press.

Feagin, J. R., Vera, H., & Batur, P. (2001). *White racism* (2nd ed.). New York: Routledge.

Feagin, J. R., Vera, H., & Imani, N. (1996). *The agony of education: Black students at White colleges and universities.* New York: Routledge.

Feagin, J. R., Vera, H., & Imani, N. (2001). *The agony of education: Black students at White colleges and universities* (2nd ed.). New York: Routledge.

Federal Bureau of Investigation. (2001). *Hate crime statistics, 2000.* Clarksburg, WV: Criminal Justice Information Services Division.

Harrison, A. O. (1985). The Black family's socializing environment: Self-esteem and ethnic attitude among Black children. In H. P. McAdoo & J. L. McAdoo (Eds.), *Black children: Social, educational, and parental environments* (pp. 159–173). Newbury Park, CA: Sage.

Holmes, R. M. (1995). *How young children perceive race*. Thousand Oaks, CA: Sage.

Hurtado, S. (1992). The campus racial climate. *Journal of Higher Education, 63*(5), 539–569.

Jackson, J. S., McCullough, W. R., & Gurin, G. (1988). Family, socialization, environment, and identity development in Black Americans. In H. P. McAdoo (Ed.), *Black families* (2nd ed., pp. 242–256). Newbury Park, CA: Sage.

Jones, J. M. (1997). *Prejudice and racism* (2nd ed.). New York: McGraw-Hill.

Jordan, W. D. (1968). *White over Black: American attitudes toward the Negro, 1550–1812*. New York: W. W. Norton.

Karenga, M. (1993). *Introduction to Black studies* (2nd ed.). Los Angeles: University of Sankore Press.

Kinder, D. R., & Sanders, L. M. (1996). *Divided by color: Racial politics and democratic ideals*. Chicago: University of Chicago Press.

Kinder D. R., & Sears, D. O. (1981). Prejudice and politics: Symbolic racism versus racial threats to the good life. *Journal of Personality and Social Psychology, 40*, 414–431.

King, J. (1991). Dysconscious racism: Ideology, identity and the miseducation of teachers. *Journal of Negro Education, 60*(2), 133–146.

Kluegel, J., & Smith, E. R. (1983). Affirmative action attitudes: Effects of self-interest, racial affect, and stratification beliefs on Whites' view. *Social Forces, 61*(3), 797–824.

Kluegel, J., & Smith, E. R. (1986). *Beliefs about Black inequality: Americans' views of what is and what ought to be*. Hawthorne, NY: Aldine de Gruyter.

McAdoo, H. P. (1985). Racial attitude and self-concept of young black children over time. In H. P. McAdoo & J. L. McAdoo (Eds.), *Black children: Social, educational, and parental environments* (pp. 213–242). Newbury Park, CA: Sage.

McConahay, J. B., Hardee, B. B., & Batts, V. (1981). Has racism declined in America? It depends on who is asking and what is asked. *Journal of Conflict Resolution, 25*, 563–579.

Myrdal, G. (1944). *An American dilemma: The Negro problem and modern democracy*. New York: Harper.

Peters, M. F. (1985). Racial socialization of young Black children. In H. P. McAdoo & J. L. McAdoo (Eds.), *Black children: Social, educational, and parental environments*. Newbury Park, CA: Sage.

Reddy, M. (2002). Smashing the rules of racial standing. In B. TuSmith & M. T. Reddy (Eds.), *Race in the college classroom* (pp. 51–61). New Brunswick, NJ: Rutgers University Press.

Rhoads, R. A. (1998). Student protest and multicultural reform: Making sense of campus unrest in the 1990s. *Journal of Higher Education, 69*(6), 621–646.

Sapolsky, R. M. (1998). *Why zebras don't get ulcers: An updated guide to stress, stress-related disease, and coping*. New York: W. H. Freeman.

Scaer, R. (2001). *The body bears the burden: Trauma, dissociation and disease*. Binghamton, NY: Haworth Press.

Scheurich, J. J., & Young, M. D. (2002). White racism among White faculty: From critical understanding to antiracist activism. In W. A. Smith, P. G. Altbach, & K. Lomotey (Eds.), *The racial crisis in American higher education: Continuing challenges to the twenty-first century* (pp. 221–243). Albany, NY: SUNY Press.

Shay, J. (1995). *Achilles in Vietnam: Combat trauma and the undoing of character*. New York: Touchstone.

Shay, J. (2002). *Odysseus in America: Combat trauma and the trials of homecoming*. New York: Scribner's.

Sleeter, C. (Spring 1994). White racism. *Multicultural Education*, pp. 5–8.

Smedley, A. (1993). *Race in North America: Origin and evolution of a worldview.* Boulder, CO: Westview Press.

Smith, W. A. (1996). Affirmative action attitudes in higher education: A multi-ethnic extension of a three-factor model. *Dissertation Abstracts International, 57*(04), 1557A. (University Microfilms No. AAD96-25196).

Smith, W. A. (1998). Gender and racial/ethnic differences in the affirmative action attitudes of U.S. college students. *Journal of Negro Education, 6*(2), 127–141.

Smith, W. A. (1993–2003). *National African Americans study.* Unpublished interview database. University of Illinois at Chicago and the University of Utah.

Smith, W. A. (2003, April 21). *Battle fatigue on the front lines of race.* Paper presented at the annual meeting of the American Educational Research Association, Chicago.

Smith, W. A., Altbach, P. G., Lomotey, K. (Eds.). (2002). *The racial crisis in American higher education: Continuing challenges to the twenty-first century.* Albany, NY: SUNY Press.

Solorzano, D., Allen, W., & Carroll, G. (2002). "A Case Study of Racial Microaggressions and Campus Racial Climate at the University of California, Berkeley. *UCLA Chicano/Latino Law Review, 23,15–111..*

Spears, M. J. (2003, February 25). Johnson scores another victory for progress. *ESPN.* Retrieved April 22, 2003 from http://espn.go.com/nba/columns/spears_marc/1514129.html.

Spencer, M. B. (1983). Children?s cultural values and parental child rearing strategies. *Developmental Review, 3,* 351–370.

Spencer, M. B. (1987). Black children's ethnic identity formation: Risk and resilience of caste like minorities. In J. S. Phinney & M. J. Rotheram (Eds.), *Children's ethnic socialization: Pluralism and development* (pp. 103–116). Newbury Park, CA: Sage.

Stevenson, H. C. (1994, November). Validation of the scale of racial socialization for African American adolescents: Steps toward multidimensionality. *Journal of Black Psychology, 20*(4), 445–468.

Stevenson, H. C. (1997). Managing anger: Protective, proactive, or adaptive racial socialization identity profiles and African American manhood development. *Journal of Prevention & Intervention in the Community, 16*(1–2), 35–61.

Stevenson, H. C., Reed, J., Bodison, P., & Bishop, A. (1997). Racism stress management: Racial socialization beliefs and the experience of depression and anger in African American youth. *Youth & Society, 29*(2), 197–222.

Stevenson, H. C., & Renard, G. (1993). Trusting wise ole owls: Employing cultural strengths in psychotherapy with African American families. *Professional Psychology: Research and Practice, 24*(4), 433–442.

Sturm, S., & Guinier, L. (1996). The future of affirmative action: Reclaiming the innovative ideal. *California Law Review, 84*(4), 953–1036.

Tuch, S. A., & Martin, J. K. (1997). *Racial attitudes in the 1990s: Continuity and change.* Westport, CT: Praeger.

Turner, C. S. V., & Myers, S. L., Jr. (2000). *Faculty of color in academe: Bittersweet success.* Monograph. Boston: Allyn & Bacon.

TuSmith, B., & Reddy, M. T. (Eds.). (2002). *Race in the college classroom.* New Brunswick, NJ: Rutgers University Press.

U.S. Department of Justice. (2001, October). *Hate crimes on campus: The problem and efforts to confront it.* Washington, DC: Office of Justice programs and Bureau of Justice Assistance.

U.S. Department of the Army (1994, June). *Battle fatigue GTA 21-3-5 warning signs: Leader actions.* Washington, DC: Author.

Van Ausdale, D., & Feagin, J. R. (2000). *The first R: How children learn race and racism.* Lanham, MD: Rowman & Littlefield.

Watkins, W. H. (2001). *The White architects of Black education: Ideology and power in America, 1865–1954.* New York: Teachers College Press.

Williams, D., Yu, Y., Jackson, J. S., & Anderson, N. B. (1997). Racial differences in physical and mental health: Socioeconomic status, stress, and discrimination. *Journal of Health and Psychology* 2(3), 335–351.

Yancey, G. (2003). *Who is White? Latinos, Asians, and the new Black/Nonblack divide.* Boulder, CO: Lynne Rienner Publishers.

Zubrinsky-Charles, C. (2000). Neighborhood racial-composition preferences: Evidence from a multiethnic metropolis. *Social Problems,* 47(3), 379–407.

PART IV

WHERE DO WE STAND? HOW
CAN THE ACADEMY SERVE
AFRICAN AMERICAN STUDENTS
AND FACULTY'S NEEDS

VOICE OF SENIOR AFRICAN AMERICAN FACULTY: UNDERSTANDING THE PURPOSE AND THE PURSUIT OF EXCELLENCE THROUGH TEACHING, RESEARCH, AND SERVICE

Faculty work, productivity, and purpose in American higher education continue to evolve with each new wave of societal change. Working within a dynamic enterprise such as higher education can be exciting, challenging, and frustrating for faculty who want to contribute to a better society and world (Menges & Associates, 1999). Enthusiasm for increasing the number of minorities on campuses has surged beyond experience to assist them in becoming successful faculty and engaged members of the academic guild. With each generation, the seasoned faculty guild is exposed to a new breed of philosophers and thinkers who challenge old ways of knowing, thereby bringing a different way of critiquing and expanding established fields of knowledge.

How do faculty make sense of their lives and places in society in the 21st century? How does one find satisfaction given the multitude of constituents he or she must satisfy? What have we learned about minorities entering the professoriate? What are the characteristics and practices of successful minority faculty, especially Black faculty? Demographic data indicate that most Black faculty are concentrated at less prestigious, two- and four-year colleges and at the lower end of the faculty rank (American Association, 1988; Exum, 1983; National Center, 1989; Olsen, 1994). We need to know more about the institutional factors and the personal and professional proclivities, needs, and interests that influence Black faculty participation in academic life and satisfaction in institutions of higher education.

For Black faculty, these questions are more compounded and more complex. The literature reveals findings, recommendations, and suggestions with regard to

Black faculty over the last three decades. "Although there has been much research on new and junior faculty role performance, limited research has focused exclusively on new and junior faculty of color and their experiences at predominantly White institutions" (Alexander-Snow & Johnson, 1999, p. 88). According to Mor Barak, there is accumulating evidence indicating that, although present in greater numbers, people from diverse backgrounds are more likely to be excluded from information networks and decision-making processes in both formal and informal organizations. In particular, the issues of minority professionals within a predominantly White educational environment has not typically been of interest to the White social scientist.

Furthermore, much of the information available is dated and incomplete. Failure to have comprehensive data may have contributed to the piecemeal way in which we study faculty in general, especially Black faculty (Boice, 1993). Therefore, it is important to discover more salient factors upon which to build recommendations to institutions of higher education for better practices with regards to Black faculty. Why is this "ethno-anthropological dig" so important in higher education? One platform of argument is that an educational organization with multiple perspectives of knowledge is central for a dynamic organization. Second, Black faculty are important to students, especially Black students, and to the true meaning of a university.

Review of Literature

The literature review below is divided into four parts due to the broad scope of the research that is needed to guide this study. The first section presents literature about employee turnover, commitment, and satisfaction from multiple fields and disciplines. The second portion goes into depth about the satisfaction, concerns, and issues related to existing as professionals within institutions of higher education. The third section presents more specific literature on Black faculty concerns and issues. In addition, it also explores in detail both qualitative and quantitative factors and variables to reveal the comprehensiveness needed to support the study. The fourth section presents a list of variables and the rationale used in the theoretical model to be developed for Black faculty.

General Literature on Employee Satisfaction

Naumann (1992) presented a conceptual model of expatriate turnover which identified key contributing factors and intermediate linkages and relationships in U.S. multinational corporations. He built his concept in reaction to Steers and Mowday's (1981) model, and both expand the work of Mobley, Griffeth, Hand, and Meglino (1981) on turnover, suggesting that characteristics of the organization, individuals, and environments shape a person's perceptions and satisfaction, which result in intentions to stay or leave an institution. Steer and Mowday expanded the construct of job to include satisfaction, organizational commitment, and involvement. Hence, Naumann applied these most recent models to international business organizations with the intention of providing a more comprehensive theoretical approach and recognizing the complex interactive and longitudinal effects.

Intent to stay is the individual's perception that he or she will likely continue to participate in the organization. Since intent to stay refers to individual perceptions rather than to individual behavior, it is a social-psychological concept; it refers to the internal orientations of faculty and not to what they do. Intent to stay is often referred to as "commitment" (Price & Mueller, 1981). A sizeable body of literature "supports the idea that commitment has a negative impact on turnover, that is, the stronger the commitment, the less the likelihood of turnover" (Price & Muller, 1981, p. 12).

Tinto's (1975) longitudinal model of institutional departure deals primarily with activities within the institutions. He used Spady's (1970) model which was in turn based on Durkeim's (1961) theorization that suicide is related to an individual's integration into society. This model lends itself to the appropriateness of Black faculty integration into the institution. Tinto's model exhibits how interactions among different individuals within the academic social systems of the institution lead individuals of different characteristics to withdraw from that institution before achieving their goal. For Black faculty, such a goal might be tenure, promotion, retirement, etc. Black faculty are individuals with particular background characteristics who interact with the institution's academic and social domains which have a tremendous impact on their goals.

Job Satisfaction among Faculty

Having established how academicians perceive themselves professionally, we can go on to ask how well their values, abilities, and goals match the values, needs, and goals of the institutions employing them. The concept of integration has been widely applied in organizational settings, defined generally as the congruence between organizational norms and values and the values of persons. A good "fit" or "match" with the institution appears to be useful for various groups such as women and minorities, whose professional values, according to the literature (Patitu & Tack, 1991), are supposed to vary from those of the traditional White male in terms of interests, satisfactions, and relative expenditure of time on work-related activities. A poor fit between a person and the work environment has consistently been associated with lower job satisfaction and higher rates of turnover. Within academe, individual units, departments, colleges, and the overall university should be considered as a context for faculty satisfaction and commitment. Also the portion of support, understanding, and recognition an institution provides is an indicator of fit. Hence, organizations should reward and support interests and activities that are consistent with their own values and goals.

In a study conducted by Olsen, Maple, and Stage (1995) on the effects of professional role interests, satisfaction, and institutional fit for 146 women and minority faculty in three colleges at one research university found no evidence of bias toward service activities nor of less personal commitment to research by gender or race. Second, minority faculty were more likely to demonstrate a greater identification with and satisfaction from teaching than other groups of faculty; however, they did not spend more time on teaching or in service activities. Finally, minority faculty perceived a service load that was burdensome compared with that of both females and White males. Satisfaction from teaching and research proved most predictive of good institutional fit. Their study also revealed that perceived control over one's career and personal satisfaction in academic work directly influenced job satisfaction, while race and gender affected the amount of faculty support received. This study used a LISREL model to analyze the data.

Another study of 265 faculty in eight colleges of education sought to identify predictors of global job satisfaction and their importance in predicting satisfaction. This study used a value appraisal model for gender, rank, and tenure status (Bean & Plascak, 1989). The findings of the study found no main effect or significant interaction differences in job satisfaction by gender, rank, or tenure status.

Pfeffer and Lawler (1980) studied the job satisfaction of more than 4,050 college and university faculty. Their findings revealed that satisfaction with organization and intention to remain in the work setting were positively related to pay, length of time in the organization, and tenure. Pay and tenure were the variables most positively correlated with commitment to the institution.

Some of the variables most commonly used in studies of faculty satisfaction and commitment are time spent in research, teaching, and service; satisfaction with teaching, research, and service; professional role interests; perceived control over career; satisfaction with intrinsic aspects of work; perceptions of role clarity; discrepancies between the real and ideal requirements for tenure; recognition and support; satisfaction with unit, department, or college; job satisfaction; nature of work; fairness and equity; pay and fringe benefits; and opportunities.

African American Faculty

Black faculty satisfaction and commitment to the institution is documented in both qualitative and quantitative studies. This section merges the discussion on the concerns and issues developed by both, highlighting factors that should be considered in developing a theoretical model of satisfaction for Black faculty.

Prior to 1900, faculty positions for Blacks were confined to land-grant colleges rather than to privately supported institutions. Only two Blacks besides W. E. B. DuBois held teaching positions in predominantly White colleges (PWIs) prior to 1900. In 1960, African American faculty represented only 3% of all college and university faculty and were concentrated at historically Black colleges and universities (HBCUs) (Exum, 1983). In 1984 African American faculty numbered only 18,827, down 4.3% from the 1977 total of 19,674. In 1992, 42.1% of the 29,598 Black teaching faculty were employed in the Southeast (*African American Educational Data Book,* 1998). Apparently the number of Black faculty numbers increased throughout the late 1970s and decreased throughout the 1980s. A U.S. Equal Opportunity Commission Report revealed that, in 1985, 90% of the full-time faculty were White, whereas only 4.1% were Black. However, the *Chronicle of Higher Education* reported in that Black faculty represented 4.4% of the senior faculty members at U.S. institutions and 5.4% of the new faculty hires.

Patitu and Tack (1991) report that the main reason for African American faculty decline is their dissatisfaction with salaries, promotion, and tenure processes, and with the racial climate at many predominantly White institutions. Wilson (1987) documented in depth that living in an area with few Blacks and with little appreciation for diversity exposed family members to harassment daily. In addition, families of Black faculty were not included in community activities, whether internal or external to the institution. In a more recent qualitative study, Patitu, Young-Hawkins, Larke, Webb-Jesson, and Sterling (2000) interviewed African American faculty at research institutions and found that racism and working with other African American faculty were very important influences on the interviewees' satisfaction with their work lives. Learning to balance teaching, research, and services is also a challenge for African American because, in addition to personal institutional issues of race, they find themselves advising and mentoring minority students and organizations both formally and informally (Patitu et al., 2000).

While role interests and satisfactions may be important determinants of institutional fit and job satisfaction, the literature suggests two other dimensions as important predictors of the job satisfaction experienced by minority faculty. Both relate to a sense of personal control over one's career. Given higher rates of turnover and lower levels of job satisfaction among minorities, it has been proposed that these groups have a higher need for recognition and support and, inversely, a lower sense of self-efficacy or personal control over their career.

The classroom environment and students strongly influence Black faculty's perceptions of their work life. During a Black faculty research forum, two junior faculty stated that they are very serious about the quality of their preparation for class. Nevertheless, students repeatedly challenge them about the text, the teaching process, and the faculty member's global perspectives. It was very clear that these two faculty demonstrated a very high level of professionalism in making sure that their students got what they need to be successful, yet the students did not appreciate this approach (S. Warner & M. Martin, personal communication, March 27, 2000). To further demonstrate this negative classroom climate, Hendrix (1998) conducted a study of the relationship of the professor's race to student perceptions of the professor's credibility and found that students were more likely to question the competence of Black faculty depending on the subject matter and that Black faculty must work harder to receive the same respect granted to their White counterparts.

Mickelson and Oliver (1991) gave some insight about the route that Black students take to achieve faculty positions, based on a study conducted by the National Study of Black College Students. They found that qualified Ph.D. students are not only in premier institutions, but also in a variety of graduate programs in multiple institutional types, thus indicating that their backgrounds and training are not typical of the traditional middle-class White male route. Therefore, the issue of preparedness for the professorship poses an added challenge for Black junior faculty.

Snow and Johnson (1999) give administrators, faculty, and graduate students specific questions to ponder as a guide to life in the academy:

Questions for administrators about faculty:

1. How many faculty of color have obtained tenure? How many have left the institution prior to review? Why?
2. In what way or ways is your institution or department leading the promotion and tenure of faculty of color?
3. In what ways or ways does your institution or department make it difficulty for faculty of color to advance in the promotion and tenure process?
4. In what departments or disciplines are the majority of the faculty of color at your institution concentrated?
5. Do faculty of color have higher participation rates in service activities than the majority faculty? (p. 113).

Questions for faculty of color:

1. How much are you defined by racial or ethnic identity? In what way or ways does this identity affect your role and place?
2. How many faculty of color are in your department and institution?
3. Throughout the department and institution's history, how many faculty of color and women have obtained tenure? What does this mean for the development of your academic career at this institution?
4. How do administrators represent the institution's culture and racial climate? How do faculty of color perceive the institution's culture and climate?
5. What mentoring programs are in place, and what role or roles do you play in their hindrance or enhancement? Have these programs made a difference in the promotion and tenure of faculty of color? (p. 114).
6. How are faculty of color protected from excessive service burdens?

Questions for graduate students of color:

1. How often do you participate in department or university functions?
2. In what ways are you gaining teaching and research experience? In what area are you most lacking? How can you gain more experience?
3. What are your three greatest strengths and greatest weaknesses? How can you make the weaknesses into strengths?
4. Have you created a strategic plan for your career?
5. Identify a key mentor. How can you better utilize his or her expertise? (p. 114)

Conclusion

Planning from the beginning of one's doctorate degree would be of benefit to future Black faculty members. Given the context of the academy, Black faculty, in addition to surviving in a stressful environment like their counterparts, must also deal with other concerns while trying to secure tenure and promotion. One must understand from the onset that the academy can be an isolated and lonely place for most Black faculty. Hence, one must accept the responsibility to be both an intellectual to the academy and one's field of study and also to the community and the world in order to enhance the process of enlightenment.

Regardless of the stress and pressures that surround the faculty position in institutions of higher education, compared to many other positions that I have had, I am personally far happier and more contented. I also believe that I have found my purpose in life and that nothing will hinder me from achieving my goals as a scholar and Black intellectual during my lifetime, with or without tenure. For those who feel they are called to become a faculty member or Black intellectual, there is no better place or greater rewards than the life in the academy. Rendon (2000) reminds us of her experience in the professoriate:

> How does a woman like me pierce through the seemingly impenetrable walls of the academy? "You are so successful," many tell me. "How did you do it?" An individual from a working-class background normally doesn't aspire to be a professor; there is no strategic plan to go from point A to point Z. Rather, stepping into the academy is serendipitous, almost like destiny or some divine plan put us in these positions. We are at the right place at the right time, with the right credentials. Success, as Oprah Winfrey has put it, comes at the time when preparation meets opportunity. (p. 148)

The important lesson of Rendon's statement is that, for faculty of color, our quest to become a faculty member has elements of being a "calling" or spiritual quest to fulfill our destiny. The dilemma lies in answering the "calling" and surviving the organizational politics and culture so that we can remain a part of the institution over a period of time.

References

Alexander-Snow, M., & Johnson, B. J. (1999). Perspectives from faculty of color. In R. J. Menges & Associates (Eds.), *Faculty in new jobs*. San Francisco: Jossey-Bass.

American Association of State Colleges and Universities. (1998). *Minorities in higher education: At a turning point*. Washington, DC: AASCHE.

Boice, R. (1993). New faculty involvement for women and minorities. *Research in Higher Education, 34,* 291–339.

Chronicle of Higher Education. (1999). *Almanac Issue: 1999–2000, 46*(1).

Collison, M. (1987). Black professors create nationwide organization to promote their interests. *Chronicle of Higher Education,* pp. A19–A23.

Digest of Education Statistics. (1995). Washington, DC: U.S. Department of Education. Office of Educational Research and Improvement.

Exum, W. H. (1983). Climbing the crystal stair: Values, affirmative action, and minority faculty. *Social Problems, 30*, 383–399.

Hendrix, K. G. (1998). Student perceptions of the influence of race on professor credibility. *Journal of Black Studies, 28*(6), 738–763.

Menges, R. J., & Associates (1999). *Faculty in new jobs.* San Francisco: Jossey-Bass.

National Center for Educational Statistics. (1989). *Digest of Education Statistics, 1989.* Washington, DC: Government Printing Office.

Olsen, D. (1994). Women and minority faculty job satisfaction: Examining the effects of professional roles interests, professional satisfactions, and institutional fit. *Journal of Higher Education.*

Patitu, C. L., & Tack, M. W. (1991). *Job satisfaction of African-American faculty in higher education in the South.* Paper presented at the annual meeting of the Association for the Study of Higher Education, Boston, MA (ERIC Document Reproduction Service No. Ed 339 318).

Price, J. L., & Mueller, C. W. (1981). *Professional turnover: The case of nurses.* New York: Spectrum.

Rendon, L. I. (2000). Academics of the heart: Maintaining body, soul, and spirit. In Mildred Garcia (Ed.), *Succeeding in an academic career.* Westport, CT: Greenwood Press.

Tack, M. W., & Patitu, C. L. (1992). Faculty job satisfaction: Women and minorities in peril. *ASHE-ERIC Higher Education Report No. 4.* Washington, DC: George Washington University, School of Education and Human Development.

Tinto, V. (1975). Dropout from higher education: A theoretical synthesis of recent research. *Review of Educational Research, 45*, 89–125.

18

Amiri Yasin Al-Hadid

GRIOTS AND RITES OF PASSAGE: FROM GRADUATE SCHOOL TO PROFESSOR WITH TENURE

Follow in the footsteps of your ancestors, for the mind is trained through knowledge. Behold, their words endure in books. Open and read them and follow their wise counsel. For one who is taught becomes skilled.
THE BOOK OF KHETI, Karenga, 1984, p. 50

Prologue

The journey from graduate school, doctorate degree, tenure track faculty, tenure, and professor is a long and arduous endeavor. It involves a great deal of discipline, personal sacrifice, patience, and a relentless commitment to a long-range goal. On the journey, an internal dialogue with the self might sometimes come to threshold. The impulses for this internal dialogue often originate from anxiety, doubts, stress, and declining confidence and courage. Consequently, perceptions of professors and colleagues constantly change and evolve. The dialectics of friend and foe come onto the stage of reality with dramatic intensity. Each episodic situation demands definition, clarity, and continuity. Indeed, the reality and world of academia has its own culture. It has institutional norms, conflicts, politics, and instrumental rewards. The socialization and assimilation of African American graduate students and faculty into this alien western culture are encumbered with alienation, cognitive dissonance, isolation, and loneliness. Navigating this illusory and treacherous academic landscape requires sharp cognitive skills, political astuteness, confidence, courage, discipline, focus, patience, and self-control.

Higher education originated in the Nile Valley among the ancient Kemites or Egyptians (James, 1954; Hilliard, 1986a, 1986b). Therefore, peoples of African descent should never view education as an alien experience appropriated by Europeans. Africans must claim education as their historical property and reappropriate its culture, knowledge, skills, and wisdom. Indeed, in this sense "knowledge is power." Individual and collective empowerment comes from culture or the collective memory. Culture defines the intellectual paradigm that determines the philosophy, worldview, mission statement, and curriculum of the educational system.

In African cultures and societies, education is essentially the intergenerational transmission of culture. The process by which each generation is initiated into the culture is known as rites of passage. It is the duty of elders, chiefs, griots, healers, marabouts, babalawos, and sages to transmit the traditional knowledge, skills, and wisdom of the ancestors to the living. The stages of development in the rites of passage process are libations, initiation, matriculation, ceremonies, and rituals. These activities follow a prescribed and highly structured curriculum. For the traditional African, education is both secular and sacred, material and spiritual. It bridges the spatial and temporal gaps between the living-dead and the unborn. In a word, cosmology and epistemology are not mutually exclusive.

Once an African American has completed graduate school, the next task is seeking lucrative employment at a university that offers good career opportunities, fringe benefits, a good retirement plan, and a good location. A married person needs to take his or her spouse and children into account, selecting a city that has employment and educational opportunities for the spouse and good schools for the children. The quality of life for the family should be a major factor in any employment considerations and decisions. Other major factors to be considered are rank at the time of employment, promotion and tenure requirements, health insurance, retirement programs, travel expenses, library resources, and research facilities.

A career as a university professor is a challenging and exciting profession. It offers the instrumental rewards of promotion, tenure, sabbaticals, and recognition as a scholar and educator. Additionally, the intrinsic rewards of educating and mentoring students, achieving research and publication goals and objectives, and receiving recognition and respect from one's colleagues and eminent scholars in the field are stimulating and exhilarating experiences. In fact, these accomplishments can be defining moments and mountain-top plateaus in one's career trajectory. While most professors do not earn the same salaries as their counterparts in government and the private sector, the creative and intellectual freedom, vacations, travel to conferences, and participation in the cultural and intellectual mode of production offer both instrumental and intrinsic rewards that more than compensate for the salary differentials.

The uninitiated sometimes suggest that the academic world of learning, teaching, research, and public service is not the real world—that it is an abstract and idyllic world of concepts, debates, ideas, notions, opinions, paradigms, theories, and arcane canons. However, I beg to differ with this assessment. The academic world is as real as one's paradigm, theory, and praxis (method of study and work). If one's epistemology is predicated on the abstract rather than the concrete, then one's teaching, research, and publications will reflect this orientation. Likewise, if one's teaching, research, and publications are based on concrete reality, then the finished products will be practical and relevant to the human condition. Some scholars pursue knowledge for the sake of knowledge and others pursue knowledge in order to reinforce the status quo or bring about social transformation. All three pursuits are valid enterprises in the academy. After all, this is truly what academic freedom is all about.

In the past half century (1950–2002), the university has been undergoing a rapid paradigm shift. Computer technology has inducted the university into the Information Revolution and the Digital Divide (Huntington, 1996; Toffler, 1980, 1990; Wiener, 1954). With the arrival of African Americans (students, faculty, and administrators) on the campuses of predominantly White institutions (PWIs), the cultural and intellectual discourse shifted from a WASP (White Anglo-Saxon Protestant) monologue to a multicultural dialogue (Aldridge, 1994; Hall, 2000; Karenga, 1988). The avant garde of this cultural and intellectual paradigm shift was the creation and establishment of Africana Studies as a legitimate discipline within the academy. The ensuing great debate has exploded with profound magnitude and velocity in the traditional arts, education, humanities, and the behavioral and social sciences. Counter-revolutionary publications have emerged in an effort to stem the tide of this movement (Schlesinger, 1991; Lefkowitz, 1996). However, these reactionary efforts by Euro-American and African American scholars have only intensified the resolve and determination of the African-centered scholars.

Finally, the university by definition is a cultural and intellectual community in which its members (teachers, students, and administrators) are relentlessly engaged in a great debate to dispel the slavery of ignorance, myths, prejudice, superstition, false paradigms, and incorrect theories. The university seeks to engage its members in universal and international discourse. It further seeks to improve the quality of life of its members, alumni, the contiguous community, the society, nation, and the world. At the same time, the university strongly encourages its member to live in harmony, peace, and unity with the human family, nature, the world, and the universe. Moreover, the true and authentic university has an enduring commitment to academic excellence with social responsibility.

In Graduate School

Boards that grant admission to graduate and professional schools suggest that standardized aptitude tests are good predictors of success in post-baccalaureate education. Therefore, they place a strong emphasis on GRE, MCAT, and LSAT scores. Historically, African Americans have not scored as well on these tests as other ethnic and racial groups. Critics of these tests have argued that the tests have class, cultural, gender, and racial biases. The same arguments have been presented against the ACT and SAT, which are aptitude tests for undergraduate admissions. These arguments have their foundation in structural inequalities in society due to social patterns of class, culture, ethnic, gender, and racial stratification. In spite of these artificial barriers to vertical social mobility and higher education attainment, African Americans have met the challenges of graduate and professional education in significant numbers.

The upsurge of these significant numbers of African Americans in graduate and professional schools can be traced back to the 1960s. It occurred when the vestiges of Jim Crow (1865–1965) or American apartheid were being confronted by the civil rights movement in the South and the Nation of Islam in the North. These two movements, specifically the great debate between Dr. Martin Luther King Jr. and El-Hajj Malik El-Shabazz (Malcolm X), "complemented and corrected each other" (Baldwin & Al-Hadid, 2002; X, 1990). The dialectical tensions in the American society produced by these movements hit the PWIs like a tidal wave. Colleges in the North, Midwest, and on the West Coast made the greatest concessions to admitting African American students. Southern colleges resisted the changes with the passion of a second Civil War.

Where did the first wave of African American students, faculty, and administrators come from? They emerged from the historically Black colleges and universities (HBCUs), working- and middle-class families, and from those already at the PWIs. Ironically, HBCUs were being challenged as academically inferior even while PWI headhunters were raiding them for faculty, students, athletes, and administrators. The recruitment campaign had a devastating impact on the demographics of these institutions. In 1950, more than 90% of African American students were enrolled in HBCUs. Today HBCUs enroll about 16–18% of African American students. The good news is that they award 29% of the baccalaureate degrees earned by African American students (Al-Hadid, 2000, p. 94).

Matters have become precipitously worse due to the so-called desegregation of public institutions and the so-called cultural diversification of the private institutions. HBCUs are currently in a life or death struggle for the dignity of their cultural identity and the integrity of their economic survival. As such, most HBCUs are primarily undergraduate teaching institutions (Humphries, 2002). They are dependent on PWIs to provide graduate and professional education opportunities for their graduates. In this regard, HBCUs still remain a fertile ground for recruiting African American graduates.

Graduate school by definition is an intense and rigorous intellectual experience. The competition for scholarships, fellowships, and graduate/research/teaching assistantships is political and subjective. Graduates and professional schools are very expensive. Most African Americans are not able to attend graduate and professional schools without some type of financial support. This is the major factor that limits the number of African Americans in the pipeline for faculty positions. Some institutions have a commitment to admit African Americans to their programs but fall short when it comes to providing the financial support that is absolutely necessary for them to matriculate at these institutions.

Graduate seminars are designed to give students mastery of a highly specialized body of knowledge within a chosen field of study. These seminars seek to examine the depth and breath of the knowledge, canons, paradigms, and theories within the discipline. It is not unusual for a graduate student to read more than two hundred pages per week for each class. Performances on quizzes, examinations, and research papers must clearly demonstrate subject mastery and deep thought. Yet at the same time, the evaluation and grading of these performances by professors can sometimes be subjective and disappointing. Indeed the drama and trauma of graduate school can be furious rites of passage.

Douglas Davidson (1973) wrote a graphic and painful account of his experiences as an African American graduate student in the 1960s. He saw his graduate experience as just such a "furious passage" through a colonial situation of institutionalized racism. The anger and hostility felt by many African American graduate students was rooted in the fact that the African American community was an internal colony, yet college-educated African Americans were expected to assimilate into a Euro-centrist mentality and be willing to serve as go-betweens in the indirect rule and exploitation of the African American community. Davidson and other students flipped the script and rebelled against this paradigm and racist social expectation. They refused to become tools of the colonial domination of the African American community. Many valuable historical lessons can be learned from these pioneering graduate students during the 1960s and their predecessors from decades before the 1960s, especially since, from all indications, the plight and struggle of African American graduate students has not fundamentally changed since the 1960s.

Given the level of cultural and intellectual warfare and the emotional trauma that accompanies this level of struggle, African American graduate students and faculty must always stay in good health mentally, physically, and spiritually—mind, body and soul. Eating a healthy diet, daily exercise, meditation, and prayer are absolutely essential elements in the daily routines of the African American graduate student and faculty member. Stress, obesity, smoking, drinking, drugs, and other self-destructive vices all conspire against the mind, body, and soul. One cannot come to grips with the internal dialogue occasioned by anxiety, fear, declining courage, and diminishing self-confidence unless love, peace, and harmony reign supreme in the mind, body, and soul. The music of John Coltrane can be very therapeutic; especially the composition "Love Supreme" which was inspired by his personal recovery from drugs and the advent of his spiritual journey. It is important to learn to depend on one's faith, spirituality, or philosophy of life. Oftentimes even close friends and loved ones fail to understand the dimensions of the struggle occasioned by commitment to higher education. Nevertheless, their encouragement and love can work miracles in boosting one's confidence and self-esteem.

As a Faculty Member

The student who finishes course work to become ABD (all but dissertation) or even the next step—achieving the doctoral degree, must now move to the challenging stage of landing a faculty position at a prestigious university or at least one that will support one's teaching and research goals and objectives. A usual first step in response to a successful application is a face-to-face interview, at which the aspirant has the opportunity to make a decisively favorable impression on an succession of administrators, committees, faculty, and students. This step, often called show time or selling oneself, is the big moment that all of the years of study, prayer, and effort have been aiming toward. The rewards for the successful are a contract and tenure-track position.

Candidates who have been hip-hop with locks, in other words, authentic Black in graduate school in order to protect their dignity and sanity, must now make a soul-searching decision: to cut the locks and tone down the Blackness, or stay true to the game? Those who compromise and sell out on the front end might end up being a hypocrite to the culture and a permanent sell-out. Of course, these are personal decisions; and as history has recorded, conservatives and moderates have their place in the academy. However, African American faculty cannot afford the luxury of individualism; they must not allow the powers that be to manipulate them by employing the classic strategy of divide and conquer.

Once candidates have been employed as either junior or senior tenure-track faculty, they must decide on the stance and style they will assume in the academy. It frequently provides needed objectivity to consider academia as a game with winners and losers. By analogy, the game is checkers, dominoes, and chess operating at various levels in the food chain hierarchy. On the faculty level, instructors and assistant professors play checkers, associate professors play dominoes, and professors play chess. On the administrative level, department chairs and directors play checkers, deans play dominoes, and vice presidents and presidents play chess. Furthermore, the promotion and tenure dialectics is a zero-sum game of winners and losers, driven by the Darwinian principle of publish or perish, feast or famine. Moreover, these structurally induced conflicts set the stage for mad drama which can rise to the insane level of Wagnerian opera, driven by Machiavellian machinations. Consequently, Black faculty who sell their souls for silver and gold can expect only Faustian outcomes.

To avoid the agony of defeat and enjoy the thrill of victory, I suggest the consideration of a few realities. At all times, one must be aware that African Americans (faculty, administrators, and students) in the academy are engaged in protracted cultural and intellectual warfare (Carruthers, 1999). This is the major predicate. Given this dialectic, Africans must be purposive, strategic, patient, and mindful of details and changing circumstances and situations. The unity of African Americans on campus is the key to victory. Unfortunately, this dialectic also holds true for Black faculty, students, and administrators at HBCUs. The mad drama differs, not in kind, but only in degree, somewhat moderated by a shared culture and historical experience.

However, as early as 1933, Carter G. Woodson defined HBCUs as "white colleges for Negroes." The analogy has not fundamentally changed in the 21st century because of White control of boards of regents and trustees and the willingness of some administrators to genuflect to the tyranny of the White ruling class. Beyond the parameters of White power, some African American administrators actually want to assimilate into the pernicious culture of the White ruling class, resulting in the Black bourgeoisie's insatiable desire for White acceptance, approval, and permission (Frazier, 1957; Hare, 1965).

Promotion and Tenure

The rites of passage up the food chain of promotion and tenure are the ultimate contest of cultural and intellectual warfare. In this ordeal, the tenure applicant's scholarly productivity, pedagogical skills, and public services to campus and community are evaluated. Allegedly, the process is objective, devoid of such biases as prejudice, discrimination, and punitive behaviors. Of course, this is the academic ideal. In reality, the process is subjective and can be highly political and racist, especially in the case of African Americans. The data are replete with cases of blatant racial and gender discrimination and prejudice against African American faculty (*Journal*, 1999/2000; *Black Issues*, 2000). Some of the cases have been adjudicated through grievance procedures on campus, while others have required external legal remedies. Thus, navigating one's career through the political and subjective contradictions in the academic bureaucracy requires that the candidate produce unimpeachable evidence of scholarly productivity, excellent teaching skills, and outstanding public service to the campus and community. Although these qualifications are necessary, however, they are not sufficient. Academic excellence gets you in the game; it does not mean that you are going to hit a home run.

The winning edge demands that one must be politically astute and not naive. Promotion and tenure considerations are very competitive and political. Ostensibly, the process is designed to reward those who have been devoted and diligent in their rigorous pursuit of academic excellence, scholarly productivity, and research discoveries, while underachievers are eliminated through the Darwinian process of natural selection. In the academic arena, compassion and prejudice are both viewed as subjective variables. Hence, the scholar-warrior must master the art of intellectual warfare.

Cultural and intellectual warfare is a contest of intellect, instinct, and the will to win. It is imperative to have a realistic knowledge of one's own strengths and weaknesses as well as knowing those that stand in an adversarial relationship to one's interests. The laws of Newtonian physics maintain that, for every action, there is an equal and opposite reaction. In this context, the dialectics of the situation and its attendant circumstances and reactions must be taken into full account at all times. The theater of the absurd is constantly changing in character, form, motives, and power relationships. Carlene Young (2000) has suggested the following propositions about the academic bureaucracy:

1. They are set up to protect themselves and promote themselves. They are not structured to facilitate what you as an individual may want to do. In fact, the structure, function, and goals of the institution may be directly contradictory or at cross-purposes with the desires or goals of an individual or group.
2. They relate to their members in hierarchical fashion or restrict contact except through the chain of command. Rules are applied about who can be approached.
3. They use rules, regulations, and procedures to achieve goals, maintain order, administer rewards, and inflict punishments. They allow exception to the rules for in-group members.
4. They maintain a façade of impartiality while practicing subjectivity as necessary to attain a particular goal or to reward in-group members.

These propositions are invaluable principles for translating the grammar of power in the academic marketplace. Scholar-warriors must maintain a certain degree of detachment to be able to observe the theater of the absurd in its full manifestations.

Epilogue

In conclusion, the scholar-warrior must keep "life, liberty and the pursuit of happiness" in proper perspective. Cultural identity, family, history, and community are extremely important values in the cultural and intellectual exchange between the Euro-centered academy and the vested interest of African Americans. In some instances, the vested interest of the two entities coincide, but in most instances they are in a state of conflict and dissonance. Staying in tune with culture and history and maintaining balance and harmony between family and career is an enormous struggle. Therefore the scholar-warrior must be "fit" in this Darwinian "survival of the fittest" environment. The dialectics between the Diopian (1981) Northern and Southern Cradle paradigm is played out with remarkable exactness in the Europe-centered academy whether it is an HBCU or a PWI. The administrative apparatus of both institutions operate on the same instrumentality and value system. The HBCU is a carbon copy or clone of the PWI. Its paradigm, leadership, curriculum, epistemology, and pedagogy converge in the mainstream of American higher education. Mainstream American higher education is not the issue. Rather, the critical issue for the HBCU is the difference between external and internal locus of control within the constraints of institutional authority, power, and resources.

African American faculty, scholars and students should be inspired by the words of El-Hajj Malik El-Shabazz: "Education is an important element in the struggle for Human Rights. It is the means to help our children and people rediscover their identity and thereby increase self-respect. Education is our passport to the future, for tomorrow belongs to the people who prepare for it today" (X, 1990, p. 337). Dr. Martin Luther King Jr. taught us: "We must remember that intelligence is not enough. Intelligence plus character—that is the goal of true education. The complete education gives one not only powers of concentration, but worthy objectives upon which to concentrate. The broad education will, therefore, transmit to one not only the accumulated knowledge of the race but also the accumulated experience of social living" (1992, p. 124).

As African American faculty, scholars and students, we stand on the shoulders of the ancestors. Our ancestors laid the foundation for knowledge, law, medicine, science, and technology. Higher education is the lost property of all Africans. Therefore, we must stake our claim to this cultural and intellectual enterprise and move passionately to become owners and controllers of the cultural and intellectual mode of production.

References

Aldridge, D. (1994). *Leadership for diversity: The role of African American studies in a multicultural world*. Atlanta: Southern Education Foundation.

Al-Hadid, A. (2000). Africana studies at Tennessee State University: Traditions and diversity. In D. Aldridge and C. Young (Eds.), *Out of the revolution: The development of Africana studies* (pp. 93–114). New York: Lexington Books.

Baldwin, L., & A. Al-Hadid (2002). *Between cross and crescent: Christian and Muslim perspectives on Malcolm and Martin*. Gainesville: University Press of Florida.

Black Issues in Higher Education. (2002). Low number of Black faculty, student draws concern, 18(23), 18.

Carruthers, J. H. (1999). *Intellectual warfare*. Chicago: Third World Press.

Davidson, D. (1973). The furious passage of the Black graduate student. In J. A. Ladner (Ed.), *The death of White sociology* (pp. 23–51). New York: Random House.

Diop, C. A. (1981). *Civilization or barbarism: An authentic anthropology*. New York: Lawrence Hill Books.

Frazier, E. F. (1957). *Black bourgeoisie: The rise of a new middle class*. New York: Free Press.

Hall, P. (2000). Paradigms in Black studies. In D. Aldridge & C. Young (Eds.), *Out of the revolution: The development of Africana studies* (pp. 25–37). New York: Lexington Books.

Hare, N. (1965). *The Black Anglo-Saxons*. New York: Marzani and Munsell.

Hilliard, A. (1986a). Kemetic concepts in education. In I. Van Sertima (Ed.), *Nile Valley civilizations: Proceedings of the Nile Valley Conference* (pp. 153–162). New Brunswick, NJ: Journal of African Civilizations.

Hilliard, A. (1986b). Pedagogy in ancient Kemet. In M. Karenga & J. Carruthers (Eds.), *Kemet and the African Worldview: Research, Rescue and Restoration* (pp. 131–148). Los Angeles: University of Sankore Press.

Humphries, F. S. (2002, October 18.) *Keynote Address at Ninth National HBCU Faculty Development Symposium, Nashville, TN.*

Huntington, S. P. (1996). *The clash of civilizations and the remaking of world order.* New York: Touchstone.

James, G. (1954). *Stolen legacy: Greek philosophy is stolen Egyptian philosophy.* New York: Philosophical Library.

Journal of Blacks in Higher Education. (1999/2000, Winter). A JBHE report card on the progress of Black faculty at the nation's leading universities. *Journal of Blacks in Higher Education, 26,* 6–8.

Karenga, M. (1984). *Selections from* The Husia: *Sacred wisdom of ancient Egypt, selected and re-translated.* Los Angeles: Kawaida Publications.

Karenga, M. (1988, June). Black studies and the problematics of paradigm: The philosophical dimension in *Journal of Black Studies. Journal of Black Studies, 18,* 395–414.

King, M. L., Jr. (1992). The purpose of education. In C. Carson, R. Luker, & P. Russell (Eds.), *The Papers of Martin Luther King, Jr., January 1929–June 1951, Vol. 1.* Berkeley: University of California Press.

Lefkowitz, M. (1996). *Not out of Africa: How Afrocentrism became an excuse to teach myth as history.* New York: Basic Books.

Schlesinger, A., Jr. (1992). *The disuniting of America: Reflections on a multicultural society.* New York: W. W. Norton.

Toffler, A. (1980). *The Third Wave.* New York: William Morrow.

Toffler, A. (1990). *Power shift: Knowledge, wealth, and violence at the edge of the 21st century.* New York: Bantam Books.

Wiener, N. (1954). *The human use of human beings: Cybernetics and society.* New York: Avon Books.

Woodson, C. G. (1933). *The mis-education of the Negro.* Washington, DC: Associated Publishers.

X, Malcolm. (1990). *Malcolm X: The Man and His Times.* John Henrik Clarke (Ed.). Trenton, NJ: Africa World Press.

Young, C. (2000). The academy as an institution: Bureaucracy and African-American studies. In D. Aldridge & C. Young (Eds.), *Out of the revolution: The development of Africana studies* (pp. 133–146). New York: Lexington Books.

19

Jerlando F. L. Jackson

AN EMERGING ENGAGEMENT, RETENTION, AND ADVANCEMENT (ERA) MODEL FOR AFRICAN AMERICAN ADMINISTRATORS AT PREDOMINANTLY WHITE INSTITUTIONS

Although many individual colleges and universities are giving attention to retaining African Americans, key stakeholders remain concerned with institutional commitment to diversity (Cabrera et al., 1999; Holmes et al., 2000; Jackson & Rosas, 1999). Indeed, these institutions have focused on retention for African Americans, especially of students and faculty (Jackson, 2001). Some institutions concerned about increasing the overall diversity of their campuses have taken a three-tiered approach—students, faculty, and administrators. For example, the Board of Regents for the University of Wisconsin System has committed to increase the number of faculty, staff, and administrators of color in addition to increasing the numbers of students of color (University of Wisconsin System Plan 2008, 1998). The reporters who monitor higher and postsecondary education have tagged access, retention, and advancement for African Americans in predominantly White institutions (PWIs) as an area of concern and a hot topic for debate (Bennefield, 1999; Black Issues in Higher Education, 1999). Further, research-based responses to these questions of access, retention, and advancement have redirected attention toward considering the retention for African American administrators as a benchmark for institutional commitment to diversity (Davis, 1994; Jackson, 2001).

Higher and postsecondary education literature abounds with recommendations for retaining African American students and faculty; however, little empirical or practice-based knowledge is provided for retaining African American administrators (Jackson & Flowers, 2003). A major challenge for colleges and universities in engaging, retaining, and advancing (ERA) African American administrators is knowing how to use past research to build a conceptual framework, while at the same time producing useful knowledge for policy implementation. This research problem is significant because in 1997 African Americans represented 8.9% of the full-time administrators in higher education, while their White counterparts constituted 85.9% (Harvey, 2001).

This chapter establishes the foundation for such a framework by integrating the results of two Delphi studies into actionable strategies. It presents four phases, each of which addresses retention factors internal or external to the position: (a) preengagement, (b) engagement, (c) advancement, and (d) outcomes. The long-term purpose of this inquiry focuses on the question: Under what conditions are African American administrators most likely to remain and develop professionally in administrative careers in higher and postsecondary education institutions?

This chapter represents the initial step toward developing an ERA model for African American administrators at PWIs in higher and postsecondary education. The first section provides a rationale for retaining African American administrators at PWIs as an important measure for diversity. The next section describes the two Delphi studies that provided the data used in this chapter. The third defines the four phases of the model and describes how each component works. The concluding section outlines implications for the model and prefaces a research agenda for further development of this model.

The Representation of African American Administrators: A Diversity Measure

Retention of African Americans in higher and postsecondary education has received increased attention within the last decade (Cabrera et al., 1999). As noted earlier, the majority of this literature focused on students and faculty of color. Thus, information about the access and retention of these two groups has been used to inform conversations of representation and diversity (Crase, 1994; Loo & Rolison, 1986). Nonetheless, there has been one glaring omission in these conversations—the representation of African American administrators (Davis, 1994; Jackson, 2001). The focus on African American administrators stems from two interests, one empirical and the other practical. As noted above, the empirical reason is a desire to help develop an ERA model for African American administrators at PWIs. To achieve this goal, I merged the results of two Delphi studies with the outcome of retention and advancement based on variables that have produced the greatest explanatory connections.

Empirically, most studies have focused on the retention of students and faculty. This research has produced a greater sensitivity toward diversity as it relates to representation, but it has not produced a complete explanation, which may have led some researchers and policymakers to assume that these outcomes are the most important to attain. Retention for students of color in higher and postsecondary education consists of a rich body of knowledge. This body of knowledge can be divided into three strands: (a) the involvement of students; (b) the institution's validation of students; and (c) the integration of students into the university. Astin's (1984, 1996) theory of student involvement sets the stage for this line of research based on the concept that the more involved students are in college, the more likely they are to graduate. Emphasizing the institution's validation of students is based on the premise that success for students of color is a function of experiences both in and out of class (Rendon, 1994). Tinto's (1993) theory of integration is based on the concept that the student's level and extent of interaction with the educational environment directly affects how and whether he or she persists.

The research on faculty of color has generally focused on reasons for staying in academe. Results, for the most part, have been professional development factors, which are strategies that could be used to increase the effectiveness of the working environment for faculty of color (Turner & Meyers, 2000). Another element of diversity by representation is to focus on the group that links policy and implementation—administrators. Davis (1994) provided the groundwork for this line of thinking:

> The litmus test for institutional commitment to diversity is the number of senior-level administrators of color remaining at the institution with a tenure of four or more years. Certainly, five years or more reflect an excellent benchmark for institutional commitment to diversity. (p. 3)

Further, Jackson (2001, 2002) explored environmental and professional growth factors necessary to engage, retain, and advance African American administrators at PWIs. Although little conceptual and empirical work has been done on this topic, institutions are beginning to view it as useful (Bennefield, 1999). A conceptual model focused on engaging, retaining, and advancing administrators not only holds the potential for moving beyond static progress for retaining this group, but it also embeds concepts that could help to recruit and retain the two other populations (students and faculty).

The second, more practical, reason for pursuing this line of inquiry arises from a concern that past research has done little to expand knowledge about retaining African American administrators in the form of concepts or models for colleges and universities. Key stakeholders on college campuses often lack information about the full range of options available for them in retaining African American administrators. Many times, imposing new programs seems to be the most feasible, because of apparent convenience and appropriateness. However, new programs may not be the most beneficial approaches for the targeted individuals themselves.

Although these programs may sometimes be used together or in combination with other approaches, key stakeholders rarely have sufficient information about how such strategies can most effectively be integrated with one another for maximum benefit. Key stakeholders also lack systematic knowledge about the relative effectiveness of alternative programs in addressing retention for African American administrators. Additionally, there is little information about how well these programs fit with the overall retention efforts at the respective campuses. As a result, the link between research and practice is not as strong as it might be, due to the lack of information about engaging, retaining, and advancing African American administrators.

Consequently, the primary purpose of this chapter is to expand and integrate previous work into a model that can be implemented in practice. These two approaches are not dichotomous (empirical and practice), but rather represent two ends of a continuum. At one end lies a set of theoretical constructs, at the other, instrumental or applied concepts. However, both are linked. Because the analysis for this chapter was designed both to advance theory and produce useful information for decision makers, an attempt is made herein to draw on the strength of both approaches in negotiating their conventional boundaries.

The Two Delphi Studies

Data for this chapter were derived from two Delphi studies that explored concepts for retaining African American administrators at PWIs (Jackson, 2001, 2002). Both studies were guided by the motivation-hygiene theory, and similar research methodologies. Motivation-hygiene theory was chosen because it provided a connection to job satisfaction, and the bifurcated nature of the theory addressed both professional growth factors and environmental factors (Herzberg, Mausner, & Syndermen, 1964; Herzberg, 1979; Herzberg, Mathapo, & Wiener, 1974). I selected the Delphi technique because the literature provided little guidance on studying this topic, and this technique provided the opportunity to explore the topic by using a panel of experts (Clayton, 1997).

The initial study asked the panel to suggest practical steps that PWIs could implement to retain African American administrators at PWIs (Jackson, 2001). After analyzing these data and comparing them with motivation-hygiene theory, I found that only two of the 10 steps loosely addressed motivation. Therefore, the second study focused specifically on professional growth factors. I asked another panel of experts to suggest professional growth strategies that PWIs could use to help retain African American administrators (Jackson, 2002). An abridged version of the methodology section follows. (For a fuller treatment please see Jackson, 2001, 2002).

Both studies used a panel of 10 African American administrators employed at public four-year PWIs. They were located at public four-year institutions throughout the United States with a student of color population of 10% or less. I selected the panelists based on the tenets of purposeful sampling that included finding typical cases where the African American administrator satisfied the criterion of a senior administrator (dean level or above). I used a modified, two-round Delphi method to collect data for each study (Delbecq, Van de Ven, & Gustafsun, 1975). The first round used an open-ended question to obtain opinions from the panel of experts. In Jackson (2001) This question was: "Please list practical steps predominantly White institutions could implement to retain African American administrators?" In Jackson (2002), the question was: "What professional growth factors could predominantly White institutions implement to help retain African American administrators?" (Murry & Hammons, 1995). In the second round, panelists were asked to rank, edit, and comment on the retention strategies generated from the first round. I analyzed the data using traditional methods of qualitative research (Keeves, 1988).

The ERA Model

The following phases and properties for engagement, retention, and advancement emerged from the two Delphi studies and provided a preliminary grounding for the resulting ERA model. This model represents an initial attempt to consolidate previous research to develop a heuristic tool for colleges and universities vested in engaging, retaining, and advancing African American administrators at PWIs. Further, the model will undoubtedly be reshaped as I and others interested in the topic conduct future research. This work is concerned about the range of options available for addressing the research problem, the underlying theoretical premises of those options, the fit between the problem and options, and the implementation problems associated with the task of ERA African American administrators at PWIs. The concerns of retention can be captured by four phases: preengagement, engagement, advancement, and outcomes. (See Figure 1.)

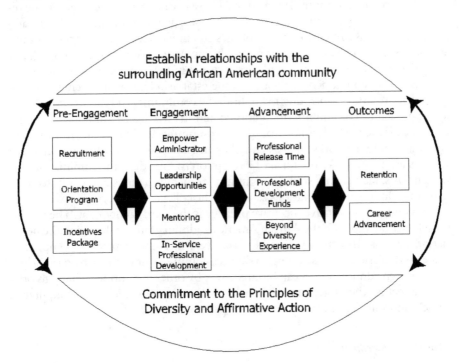

FIGURE 1. An Emerging Model for Engaging, Retaining, and Advancing African American Administrators at Predominantly White Institutions

The components of the four phases are grounded by two foundational concepts that are critical to the implementation of this model. First, colleges and universities should establish relationships with the surrounding African American community. Participation in local community organizations, businesses, and industries could assist in forming a sense of connection between the administrator and the community. This connection could serve dual purposes: (a) provide a community for the administrator to interact with, particularly if a concentration of African Americans does not exist on campus; and (b) develop positive rapport between the college or university and the African American community. Second, colleges and universities should commit to the principles of diversity and affirmative action. One gesture could be simply to add a diversity educational component to all institutional training programs for its personnel. Such an innovation would send a message that the institution truly wishes its members to understand and appreciate differences. But more importantly, it shows that the institution values the African American experience and perspective.

Phase 1: Preengagement

In the preengagement phase, the institution interacts with the candidate prior to his or her arrival on campus. It is a critical phase because it sets the stage for the remaining phases. The first component in Phase 1 is recruitment, which can and should be used as a retention tool. Colleges and universities with well thought out and published practices for recruiting and hiring African Americans are more likely to send a positive, welcoming, and supportive message to potential colleagues.

The second component in Phase 1 is the establishment of an orientation program that provides an introduction to both the community and the campus. A logical approach to community orientation could involve leaders in the community introducing the new administrator to that community and providing information about available networks such as churches and social groups. Orientation at the campus level could take the form of a reception to introduce the administrator to the students, faculty, and staff. It might further include a series of sessions to acclimate the administrator to various aspects of the college or university.

Providing a competitive incentive package is the third component. The professional relationship with the African American administrator is shaped in the negotiation process. Institutions should make every attempt to provide competitive wages and salaries, because doing so shows a commitment to the person in the position. Often administrators can be lured away by other institutions willing to offer more benefits; therefore, financial packages have to be sufficient and equitable. Timely and sufficient increases are also important aspects.

Phase 2: Engagement

Engagement occurs when the African American administrator assumes the official responsibilities of his or her position. During this phase, the administrator becomes engaged with the campus community and comes to understand his or her assigned roles and responsibilities. Further, the administrator engages the community and becomes a member with full rights and privileges. The first key component of this phase is the empowerment of the administrator, or providing him or her with the power and authority to give direction and leadership to the operating unit. More basically, this gesture shows that the institution has confidence in the African American administrator and permits him or her to carry out the responsibilities of the job.

The second component is leadership opportunities. An appealing aspect for recruiting and retaining any administrator is the possibility of engaging in the full range of leadership opportunities available at the institution. Such opportunities groom the African American administrator for job advancement within the institution. One cautionary note is to make these leadership opportunities available at an appropriate pace while the administrator is becoming familiar with the university and his or her job. The goal is to prevent the administrator from being overwhelmed and placed in a position where he or she would not be able to take advantage of the leadership opportunities provided.

Mentoring is the third component within the engagement phase. Institutions that develop mentoring programs focused on career and academic development for African American administrators provide a critical opportunity both for professional development and for successful retention. The African American administrator should be partnered with one or more seasoned administrators for guidance and advice. Formal and informal mentors ideally would play strong roles in the administrator's pursuit of his or her career aspirations. Moreover, these mentors could provide local knowledge about the political environment, helpful hints about understanding campus culture, and other forms of in-depth knowledge that would enable the African American administrator to perform his or her job successfully.

The last component of the engagement phase is in-service professional development. Such development can be quite helpful in supplementing the skills that the African American administrator brought to the job with context-specific information. Furthermore, these sessions could serve as an excellent cross-campus networking opportunity. For such professional development to be useful, it should be in alignment with the administrator's position and it should be developed specifically for African Americans.

Phase 3: Advancement

Advancement is very important in providing growth for, and ultimately retaining, African American administrators. Opportunities for and the possibility of advancement at one's institution minimize the need to move solely for professional advancement. The first component of the advancement phase deals with providing two forms of professional release time for the African American administrator. The first is release time to pursue research and professional development activities (e.g., mini-sabbaticals). This aspect is especially important for administrators who would like to remain actively engaged with their scholarship and professional organizations. The second is monthly release time as a substitute for additional hours worked (e.g., advising) with underrepresented student populations. Such time adjustments will encourage African American administrators to connect with African American students.

Providing professional development funding is the second component of this phase. Institutions should support and endorse professional development for their African American administrators. For example, joining national organizations and attending their meetings let these administrators maintain affiliations with multicultural subgroups within these organizations. Further, such opportunities could enhance skills that may or may not be utilized on campus.

The final component of this phase is providing professional experiences beyond the diversity mission of the institution—a factor that can be quite critical in future professional advancement. More often than not, African American administrators get locked into positions in which they must devote a significant portion of their time on diversity-related issues. Moving beyond diversity experiences will help the administrator gain a better understanding of operations on the whole campus. Insights into the challenges encountered by other aspects of the campus are helpful when advancing to higher-level positions.

Phase 4: Outcomes

The proposed outcomes for this model are twofold: (a) retention, and (b) career advancement for African American administrators at PWIs. Retention in this model refers to maintaining African American administrators in their positions equally when compared to their White counterparts at the same institution. Even though retention at the same institution is an isolated outcome, career advancement benefits higher and postsecondary education generally. Career advancement entails promotion within or outside the home institution with the ultimate goal of retention in the field of administration. These two outcomes conjointly seek to improve the status of African American participation in the administration of higher and postsecondary institutions in the United States.

Components of this model not only address issues germane to creating an environment conducive for African American administrators but also explore professional development and growth factors as aspects for engagement, retention, and advancement. Approaching engagement, retention, and advancement in such a dualistic manner highlights variables both internal and external to the job. The model is based on the concept that, if more positive linkages exist between these components, the African American administrator is more likely to stay and grow in administration in higher and postsecondary education.

Figure 2 represents the relationship between the three targeted groups (students, faculty, and administrators), if all three are included in the representation and retention process. African American students represent the bottom of the pyr-

FIGURE 2. Three-Tiered Approach to Diversity

amid for two reasons. First, this group should ideally be the largest represented on campus. Second, students are the foundation for any represented measure of diversity. Faculty are in the middle of the pyramid because research suggests that the presence of African American faculty can enhance the representation of students (Turner & Myers, 2000). Not only does the representation of African American faculty attract more students, but it may also attract African American administrators. African American administrators are at the top of the pyramid because they generally represent the smallest group at PWIs.

Additionally, administrators are at the top because they are involved in policy development and implementation that can shape the representation of the other two groups. This research argues that not only should engagement, retention, and advancement for African American administrators be included in the overall efforts of the college or university, but they should also be offered as another test of institutional diversity. The number of African Americans elevated to key decision-making positions is a good indicator of an institution's commitment to diversity.

Conclusion and Implications

A major challenge for this chapter was to apply findings from past studies (Jackson, 2001, 2002; Jackson & Flowers, in press) to build a model and, at the same time, produce actionable strategies for colleges and universities. As a result, I concentrated on identifying model components that translated theory into practice. Further, the four phases capture the major dimensions of engagement, retention, and advancement, in both internal and external relation to the position. I was drawn to this topic because of the increasing interest of college and university leaders in achieving diversity through engagement, retention, and advancement. Most of the extant literature emphasizes students and faculty, with little attention placed on the administrators who develop and implement policy. Thus, this work was designed not only to produce useful information about engaging, retaining, and advancing African American administrators but also to show how the ERA model may help increase the representation of students and faculty.

This chapter is the first step in a long process of refining the properties of this model and empirically testing hypotheses about their interactions. The next step will consist of empirical research that attempts to further classify a diverse set of strategies, operating in different institutional contexts, according to the four phases of this model. The goal is to make certain that the properties of the model can be implemented at most, if not all colleges and universities. One empirical test for this model will be the degree to which the proposed properties can fit the variation of institutional types in academe.

The initial approach to this research was a multi-year examination of strategies for engaging, retaining, and advancing African American administrators at predominantly White institutions. Consequently, this focus provides a unique opportunity to explore concepts of engagement, retention, and advancement. To the extent that this initial research was productive, it applies to other people of color as well as to various institutional settings.

Another component of the empirical research will develop fine distinctions within and across components of this model based on how they actually operate. I conceptualized single properties for this model to make the distinctions among them clearer. However, when choosing from varied options, key stakeholders often use a combination of strategies to achieve a particular goal. Although the model is designed to encourage stakeholders to select a dominant approach, other approaches may be used to supplement or follow it. This line of research will not only identify the different ways that these properties can be used with one another but also various options for use within each phase.

Despite the number of unanswered questions and the size of the future research agenda, the focus on engaging, retaining, and advancing African American administrators at PWIs is a productive one. Because it seeks to develop a predictive framework that links the major properties of previous research, the ERA model holds the potential for producing a theory-rich body of knowledge on engagement, retention, and advancement. Yet the ability to provide the higher and postsecondary education community with new insight beyond that gained from other theories or analytical frameworks may be the strongest test of whether this model constitutes a valid depiction of engagement, retention, and advancement for African American administrators and its effects.

References

Astin, A. W. (1984). Student involvement: A developmental theory for higher education. *Journal of College Student Personnel, 25*, 297–308.

Astin, A. W. (1996). Involvement in learning revisited: Lessons we have learned. *Journal of College Student Development, 37,* 123–134.

Bennefield, R. M. (1999). Trench warriors: On the front lines. *Black Issues in Higher Education, 16,* 69–71.

Black Issues in Higher Education. (1999). Vital signs. *Black Issues in Higher Education, 25,* 85–93.

Cabrera, A. F., Nora, A., Terenzini, P. T., Pascarella, E. T., & Hagedorn, L. S. (1999). Campus racial climate and adjustment of students to college. *Journal of College Student Development, 35,* 98–102.

Clayton, M. J. (1997). Delphi: A technique to harness expert opinion for critical decision-making tasks in education. *Educational Psychology, 17,* 373–386.

Crase, D. (1994). The minority connection: African Americans in administrative/leadership positions. *Physical Educator, 51,* 15–20.

Davis, J. D. (Ed.). (1994). *Coloring the halls of ivy: Leadership & diversity in the academy.* Bolton, MA: Anker Publishing.

Delbecq, A. L., Van de Ven, A. H., & Gustafson, G. H. (1975). *Group techniques for program planning.* Glenview, IL: Scott Foresman.

Harvey, W. B. (2001). *Minorities in Higher Education: 2000–2001.* 18th Annual Status Report. Washington, DC: American Council on Education.

Herzberg, F. (1979). New perspectives in the will to work. *Personnel Administrator, 24,* 72–76.

Herzberg, F., Mausner, B., & Snydermen, B. B. (1964). *The motivation to work* (2nd ed.). New York: John Wiley & Sons.

Herzberg, F., Mathapo, J., Wiener, Y., & Wiesen, L. E. (1974). Motivation-hygiene correlates of mental health: An examination of motivation and inversion in a clinical population. *Journal of Consulting and Clinical Psychology, 42,* 411–419.

Holmes, S. L., Ebbers, L. H., Robinson, D. C., & Mugenda, A. G. (2000). Validating African American students at predominantly White institutions. *Journal of College Student Retention: Research, Theory, & Practice, 2,* 41–58.

Jackson, J. F. L. (2001). A new test for diversity: Retaining African American administrators at Predominantly White Institutions. In L. Jones (Ed.), *Retaining African Americans in higher education: Challenging paradigms for retaining Black students, faculty, and administrators* (pp. 93–109). Sterling, VA: Stylus Publications.

Jackson, J. F. L. (2002). Retention of African American administrators at predominantly White institutions: Using professional growth factors to inform the discussion. *College and University, 78*(2), 11–16.

Jackson, J. F. L., & Flowers, L. A. (in press). Retaining African American student affairs administrators: Voices from the field. *College Student Affairs Journal.*

Jackson, J. F. L., & Rosas, M. (1999). *Scholars of color: Are universities derailing their scholarship?* Keeping our Faculties Conference Proceedings, Minneapolis, Minnesota, 86–107.

Keeves, J. P. (Ed.). (1988). *Educational research methodology, and measurement: An international handbook.* Elmsford, NY: Pergamon Press.

Loo, C., & Rolison, G. (1986). Alienation of ethnic minority students at a predominantly White university. *Journal of Higher Education, 57,* 58–77.

Murry, J. W., & Hammons, J. O. (1995). Delphi: A versatile methodology for conducting qualitative research. *Review of Higher Education, 18,* 423–436.

Rendon, L. I. (1994). Validating culturally diverse students: Toward a new model of learning and student development. *Innovative Higher Education, 19,* 33–51.

Tinto, V. (1993). *Leaving college: Rethinking the causes and cures of student attrition* (2nd ed.). Chicago: University of Chicago Press.

Turner, C. S. V., & Myers, S. L. (2000). *Faculty of color in academe: Bittersweet success.* Needham Heights, MA: Allyn & Bacon.

University of Wisconsin System. (1998). *University of Wisconsin System Plan 2008.* Madison, WI: Author.

20

Ella Forbes

20/20 HINDSIGHT

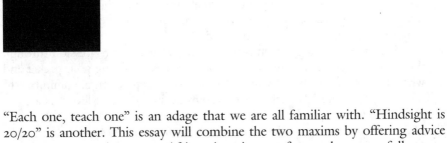

"Each one, teach one" is an adage that we are all familiar with. "Hindsight is 20/20" is another. This essay will combine the two maxims by offering advice based on my experience as an African American professor who successfully negotiated the tenure system in a White institution. My experience was somewhat unusual, however, because my department is an African American Studies unit and it was there that I had the most trouble.

I had worked previously at a historically Black college and university (HBCU). As a result, I looked at my African American Studies Department in a predominantly White institution (PWI) as a microcosm of a typical HBCU because many of their issues also plagued the department in which I received tenure. The problems of ego, lack of resources, and limited support that can cripple HCBUs also greatly impacted my tenure path.

The tenure process is usually not easy; mine was tough. It was made more difficult because I had had personal problems with the former department chairperson who appointed the departmental tenure committee before a new chairperson was selected. That committee was my first hurdle. Another problem was that I was also a product of that department, having received my Ph.D. there. I have decided that it is probably not a good idea to accept a faculty position in one's own department immediately after completing a graduate program in it. There are advantages to putting some distance between yourself and the department before working there. For instance, the other faculty members might find it too difficult to relinquish their view of you as a student. Obviously, I did not follow my own advice—an excellent example of 20/20 hindsight.

However, rather than detailing these problems, I would like to give practical recommendations based on what I learned from the experience, phrased informally, as though in a personal letter or conversation with you, the reader.

1. First, and most important, know your institution's tenure requirements. Get a copy of your tenure policy and read it. Do this as soon as you are hired. It gives you a roadmap of where you will eventually need to be so that you can immediately start working toward it. You will also know when the procedure is not operating properly and what to do about it. The tenure policy will tell you how and when to appeal a negative decision.

   Understand what material you will have to provide, what information you will have access to, and whether or not you will receive copies of evaluations, letters, and other materials generated by the tenure committees. Some schools allow you access to everything produced at every level; others are more secretive and allow you access only to certain items. Some allow you to have copies only after the entire process is completed.

2. Another important suggestion is to monitor your own progression through the tenure system. Know when each committee is reviewing your packet and what they are reviewing. If you depend on your departmental committee to forward your materials to the next level, make sure the next level has a complete packet.

3. Make sure your tenure packet is complete, professional-looking, and on time. Other professionals are looking at it so it should not be sloppy, late, or incomplete. Even if your tenure procedure policy does not direct you to include a table of contents with your packet, do it anyway. This step enables you to monitor your own progress because you can send it to the next committee level in case your departmental committee forwards, deliberately or otherwise, an incomplete packet. Without a table of contents, the receiving committee will not know what is supposed to be in your packet and will review only what they receive.

   Also, keep your curriculum vitae up-to-date. Record every lecture, book review, article, course taught, independent studies, recommendations, and other relevant information. This listing will help when you need to pull your packet together. Beware! Not only will you have to provide a copy of the curriculum vitae, but you will also have to document what it cites.

4. Know who is on your tenure committee at the departmental, college, and university levels. Each institution has its own unique tenure system; but in most, faculty play some role in the selection process. In my university, most tenure committee members serve for at least two years, and the membership is staggered. Find out who makes the decisions, how the committees are structured, and something about the history of tenure at your school. How many people were refused tenure and why? What did the tenure committee stress most? Do

they seem political or friendly with one or another faction? You can sometimes get a feel for how things are going in your own tenure process by interacting informally with committee members. Attend conferences or lectures that their departments sponsor. Do this long before you come up for tenure; otherwise, it will be too obvious what you are doing.

5. You must have contacts outside of your department. Make yourself known to the academic community by attending events, lectures, and conferences before you have to stand for tenure. Many of these contacts will be on one of the tenure committees, or you can ask them for recommendations to include in your packet.

6. Join associations connected with your discipline. These organizations give you valuable contacts, publishing venues, and possible recommendations from established scholars. The tenure procedure policy at my school allows the tenure seeker to submit names of scholars to serve as external examiners. Scholarly associations are good sources also for such examiners. Again, you can sometimes find out informally how your own tenure process is going through these contacts. For example, it was from two external examiners that I discovered that my tenure committee was sending out only a fraction of my work for review; thanks to their information, I was able to challenge and correct this unfair procedure. I have subsequently been asked to serve as an external examiner. Not only did I feel honored to be asked but I really looked forward to reading and evaluating the work of people who will make major contributions to my discipline. In other words, do not be shy about asking established academicians to serve as external examiners. You are paying tribute to their scholarship.

7. Ask other faculty members about their tenure experience and note what was most difficult for them. That way you will know what is stressed most and least. For instance, it was a White female professor in another department who took me aside and gave me valuable counsel about the tenure process. She explained the criteria that the Tenure and Promotions Committee at my institution used in assessing research/publications, teaching, and service. At a research university, research/publications rank the highest, with solely authored books counting more, much more, than edited volumes or coauthored volumes. Creative writing generally counts less than a scholarly volume, unless the piece has received major critical acclaim. A certain number of articles published in refereed scholarly journals is usually equal to a solely authored book. It is, therefore, essential that you publish.

The easiest thing to publish is your dissertation. It has to be reworked, of course, but you will have already done the research for it. Submit a manuscript or a book proposal to a reputable publisher. Ask colleagues whom they recommend or contact the publishers of books written by other faculty members. Submit articles to scholarly journals. Another route is to publish short articles or commentaries in local journals. While these do not count nearly as much books or scholarly articles, they will provide some quantity and give you practice. Also, many scholarly conferences publish their proceedings, so submit papers when requested. It usually takes quite a while for the proceedings to be published but you will receive correspondence that you can include in your tenure packet, along with the paper itself.

Tenure committees will assess the quality and quantity of your research and publications. Committee members who have expertise in your area are likely to be the most critical because they have the most background. This means that the samples of your work must be first-rate. At my university, committee members made specific comments about the content of my work, showing that they had read it very closely. In addition, committees often assess the publishers. Are they reputable academic publishers? Clearly, self-published books carry less weight so it is important that you have a well-known publisher or that you include information, such as brochures and catalogs, about the publisher in your packet. Being African-centered, I made a commitment to myself that I would primarily use African American publishers. I found, and still have, an excellent publisher who understands the African-centered perspective and who produces quality academic texts. I included samples of the publisher's work in my packet.

8. Teaching is usually the next highest ranked, although it might have primary ranking if you work at an institution whose top mission is teaching rather than research. Your tenure guidelines will let you know that. Develop a teaching portfolio with samples of your syllabi, exams, evaluations, teaching philosophy, notes from students, and other teaching information. Highlight innovations and unique tools you have developed or used.

9. Have a peer whom you trust evaluate your teaching. This person should be tenured and well-respected in the university. You should have the evaluation/observation done early. Some schools offer college or university-wide teaching evaluations; take advantage of them. Note any suggestions for improvement, implement them, and ask for a reevaluation. Often, the departmental tenure committee will observe and evaluate your classes. Being proactive by getting your own evaluations might offset a negative evaluation from a hostile member of your tenure committee. And, if you are lucky, the person who evaluated your teaching might be on the tenure committee and can speak about your commitment to teaching, discipline, dedication, and other aspects of your worth.

You should also respond in writing to negative evaluations. Explain misinterpretations, unusual circumstances, class culture, history with class, or whatever it takes to moderate what the observer noted. Make sure such responses go in your packet. Speak to the points raised by the evaluator. Don't attack the reviewer or allude to politics in the department. The committee usually knows about the internal politics and issues but dislikes having to deal with personality or grievance issues. A sometimes unspoken requirement is that the tenure candidate must fit with the department. In cases of obvious personality conflict, the committee may decide it is easier to refuse tenure than deal with the wrath of a tenured professor.

10. Get copies of your student evaluations for your own files. Do not wait until the year of your tenure review to do this, and do not depend upon the secretary to provide you with what you need. Obtain copies from your first semester of teaching and continue to steadily build your file.

11. Attend teaching improvement seminars and other in-service training, if offered by your college. Not only will these development opportunities improve your teaching, but they will also let you make other useful contacts. Often, the directors of teaching improvement programs serve on tenure committees or will be tapped by tenure committees to give unbiased evaluations. You should include such seminars on your curriculum vitae.

12. Service counts for very little at my institution, although you should check the tenure requirements at yours. My department gave untenured faculty assignments that could not be counted toward merit or tenure—the grunt work, in other words. It is not easy to refuse to serve when requested, especially in an area of personal competence, but it is important to know your own limitations. Some service is, of course, necessary; but when service impacts negatively on your research, you should make your priorities clear and limit the amount of service.

13. Maximize the amount of benefit from your service. It is also helpful to get a written statement from your chairperson about the worth for tenure of the service that you perform. You may also put your concerns in writing to your chair so that you can demonstrate later, if necessary, that you were aware of priority conflicts early and tried to resolve them. However, it is important to serve on selected committees outside your department, if only to develop important contacts beyond the confines of your department.

In conclusion, my perception of the tenure process is that it is highly politicized. It is not appropriate to detail in print the problems that I experienced. I still work with many of the people involved in the process; and although many of those relationships were so severely damaged that it is difficult to envision a pleasant outcome, many others have been repaired. Even though the tenure process can have political and emotional tensions that can, in bad-case scenarios, make it very unpleasant, it is important to realize that you are more than the process or the evaluation. Don't get so wrapped up in the tensions that you lose perspective or jettison your peace of mind. Otherwise, even if you achieve tenure, you may feel that it wasn't worth it.

Good luck. Asé.

21

Sibby Anderson-Thompkins,
Marybeth Gasman, Cynthia Gerstl-Pepin,
Karry Lane Hathaway, and Lisa Rasheed[1]

"CASUALTIES OF WAR": SUGGESTIONS FOR HELPING AFRICAN AMERICAN GRADUATE STUDENTS SUCCEED IN THE ACADEMY

Nothing that I learned . . . lessened my feelings of pain and confusion and bitterness as related to my origins: my street, my family, and my friends. Nothing showed me how I might try to alter the political and economic realities underlying our Black condition in White America.

JORDAN, 1989, p. 58

June Jordan made this comment in a lecture on her experience in 1975 as a student at Barnard College. While the words were written over two decades ago, they reflect many of the concerns expressed by African American graduate students today. In response to their research interests, students like June Jordan often hear, "That issue is not really valid . . ." "You may be labeled a feminist if you pursue that topic . . ." "You know, you may be ghettoized for choosing to study that [African American issue] research agenda . . ." Many students in doctoral programs across the country receive these messages from faculty. What is their result? To what extent are qualified and interested African American graduate students discouraged from participation in the academy or confined in their pursuit of research topics? To what extent do they feel that they are casualties of an invisible war? In this article, we seek to amplify the voices of African American graduate students.

This article emerged from a series of conversations among the authors about race and ethnicity in the academy. We realized how important these issues were and how rarely the traditional structures of an academic department offered any forum in which to explore them. Our conversations quickly evolved into a collaborative research project aimed at understanding graduate student experiences and what faculty could do to support them in and outside of the classroom.

Throughout this article, we quote faculty and graduate students who reflect upon environments in which alternative viewpoints are marginalized and contrast them with environments in which these viewpoints are valued and encouraged. Our intent is to promote an awareness of salient issues, and to provoke discussion toward action. We will address two central questions: "How do we create a nurturing learning environment that empowers students?" and "How do we support African American students as they find their voices as researchers and scholars?"

Issues Facing African Americans in the Academy

Recent researchers have explored the issues faced by African American graduate students (Carter-Obayuwana, 1995; Cheatham & Phelps, 1995; Chism & Pruitt, 1995; Davidson & Foster-Johnson, 2001; Ellis, 1997; Morris, 1993; Steele, 1999; Willie, Grady & Hope, 1991), yet much remains unknown. To better understand these struggles, we uncovered three key themes in the literature: the lack of faculty mentors and professional opportunities, the devaluation of African Americans as scholars, and the exclusion of African Americans as intellectuals.

Several studies have focused on the lack of faculty mentors and professional opportunities for African American graduate students (Cheatham & Phelps, 1995, Davidson & Foster-Johnson, 2001; Ellis, 1997; Robertson & Frier, 1994). Many researchers connect the issue of mentoring to the "dry pipeline" blamed for the shortage of faculty of color in colleges and universities across the country (Blanchett & Clarke-Yapi, 1999; Hood & Freeman, 1995; Linthicum, 1989). However, as Linthicum (1989) found, the lack of prospective faculty of color is not the sole problem. Instead, she argues, it is symptomatic of what may be wrong in graduate education: Faculty of color "do not simply emerge with doctorates in their hands, ready to assume professorships in academy. They evolve as a result of a deliberate academic course" (p. 1). In essence, both graduate students and graduate faculty are products of "the academic pipeline." They proceed from undergraduate studies to graduate school and, upon completion of their terminal degrees, are eligible to assume faculty positions. Thus, the pool of available faculty mentors of color depends on an available pool of minority doctoral students to fill the pipeline. However, Steele (1991) stresses that, although it is important to have faculty of color as role models, the act of mentoring is not contingent upon race.

Steele (1991) also offers several strategies for developing Linthicum's "deliberate academic course," such as offering apprenticeships, providing counseling and support, introducing graduate students to key people in the academic field, advocating on behalf of students, and recommending or sponsoring students for grants, fellowships, and research opportunities. Likewise, Davidson and Foster-Johnson (2001) suggest that faculty "(a) integrate students into the fabric of the department,

(b) cultivate essential professional and social networks, (c) aid students in acquiring core research competencies, and (d) pave the way for placement in the work force upon matriculation for graduate school" (p. 550).

Though mentoring and the availability of professional opportunities have had a positive impact on the success of many African American graduate students, researchers suggest that faculty must examine the pedagogy and practices that often leave these students feeling isolated within or disconnected from the learning setting (Cheatham & Phelps, 1995; Steele, 1999). A growing number of studies explores the impact of cultural differences among learners, specifically looking at the varying experiences of African American graduate students in the classroom (Blanchett & Clarke-Yapi, 1999; Ellis, 1997; Turner & Thompson, 1993). These studies confirm that students' gender and racial background have a significant effect on their experiences in graduate school and suggest that African American graduate students are more likely than their White counterparts to experience alienating instances of discrimination, stereotyping, and other attitudes and behaviors that impede their educational success (Cheatham & Phelps, 1995; Steele, 1995).

According to Chism and Pruitt (1995), African American graduate students encounter a "chilly climate" in the classroom due to faculty's interpersonal and pedagological practices. Oftentimes, issues of interest to African American graduate students or materials related to their experiences may be absent or excluded from the formal curriculum (Chism & Pruitt, 1995; Jiwani & Regan, 1998). Among the few studies that have focused on voicing the perspective of graduate students, Dowdy et al. (2000) document how graduate students of color "counter" mainstream ideology and assumptions made about them. The researchers/participants discovered that they were perceived as "noises in the attic" and were considered rebellious by their faculty. Thus, it is no surprise that many African American graduate students report feeling socially and academically isolated within their own departments (Ellis, 1997; Steele, 1999). However, Lupton (1999) found that "culturally responsive instruction" could have a positive impact on the interactions between teachers and their students. Most recently, Davidson and Foster-Johnson (2001) urged faculty at colleges and universities to "ensure that diversity objectives are embedded in the curriculum, where appropriate" and to "employ a variety of teaching approaches to address diversity issues in class content" (p. 567).

Overall, much of the current literature about the challenges facing African American graduate students has been written by researchers removed from the experience or by graduate students engaged in the experience. However, little has been written from the perspective of graduate students and faculty working in collaboration. The absence of these collaborative voices tells us that there is a pressing need to better understand the complexities of how race, gender, and class collude to create challenging learning situations for African American students and their faculty.

Transgressive Pedagogy as a Framework for Reflection

In *Teaching to Transgress: Education as the Practice of Freedom,* hooks (1994) recalls her own experience in graduate school to explain how faculty teaching styles can harm faculty of color: "The vast majority of our professors often used the classroom to enact rituals of control that were about domination and the unjust exercise of power" (p. 5). hooks provides a way of conceptualizing the classroom as a site of political and personal struggle over knowledge. Her work highlights how the structure of classes—such as the readings selected, how the topic is treated, and how the faculty member sets up classroom interactions—all impact how students experience the class and how they construct knowledge of the topic.

hooks evolved her work from feminist, postcolonial, and critical theory, her own identity as an African American woman, and her experiences as both a student and teacher in the academy. She draws heavily upon the work of Paulo Freire, specifically his *Pedagogy of the Oppressed* (2000), and Thich Nhat Hanh's philosophy of engaged Buddhism to conceptualize "a way of thinking about pedagogy which emphasized wholeness, a union of mind, body, and spirit" (hooks, 1994, 14). This form of pedagogy is aimed at the pursuit of freedom and social justice through praxis—the intentional joining of theory and practice to strive, "not just for knowledge in books, but [also] knowledge about how to live in the world" (pp. 14–15). As Freire notes, the aim of a praxis-based pedagogy is to liberate students in order to transform society: "Liberation is a praxis: the action and reflection of men and women upon their world in order to transform it" (Freire, 2000, p. 60).

bell hooks (1994) challenges academics to create supportive learning environments by developing a pedagogy that transgresses boundaries and functions more as communities than dictatorships. Building on hooks's (1994) work, we examined some possibilities for creating classroom environments in which all students are valued and in which students and students' perspectives are valued.

Autobiographical Methods in Qualitative Collaboration

We designed our research project as a collaborative qualitative study using autobiographical methods. Kemmis and McTaggart (2000) state that collaborative research has emerged as a form of resistance to more conventional research practices that have historically been viewed by the oppressed "as acts of colonization—that is, as means of normalizing or domesticating people to research and policy agendas" (p. 572). Unlike more traditional research practices, this type of research has the capacity "to bring together broad social analyses: the self-reflective collective self-study of practice, the way language is used, organization and power in a local situation, and [social or political] action" (p. 568). Thus, social transformation is accomplished through critical self-reflection on the part of the participants/researchers regarding the language, values, and intentions associated with educational praxis.[2]

To that end, we employed autobiographical methods including personal narratives, subject journaling, participant observations, and casual chatting (Creswell, 1998). Creswell suggests that these methods facilitate "the study of groups of individuals participating in an event, activity, or an organization" such as graduate education (p. 134). Also, autobiographical methods provide participants with an opportunity to theorize or make sense of their experiences through critical self-examination or self-reflection. Furthermore, women and people of color have historically experienced powerlessness, exclusion, and silence within the academy. Denzin and Lincoln (1998) contend that autobiographical methods kindle a sense of power and agency for those long denied a voice (p. 187).

Our article began as casual conversations—conversations among faculty members, conversations between students and faculty members, and conversations among students. These conversations took place in many different settings over the course of a year. They were at times enjoyable, but sometimes frustrating, and always probing. These casual chats among colleagues began to hold much meaning. As a result, we decided to make them more formal for the purpose of a conference presentation and this article.

To begin our formal discussion, we had a meeting to set some parameters for our project. We each committed to contributing to our project a minimum of once per week—more if we were able and felt inspired. We decided that a weekly e-mail journal would be the most successful way to gather regular data, given our hectic schedules. For six weeks, we contributed to the journal, sometimes writing independently but often responding to each other and to the events and conversations around us. Our writings were honest, often intense, and sometimes emotional. We agreed that some things would not be shared publicly, but overall, we felt comfortable voicing our opinions for this article.

After six weeks, we met as a group (over good food, of course), chatted about our previous journal "conversations," and began new discussions. We organized the data which resulted from our journal entries according to themes: (a) devalued as a scholar, (b) excluded as an intellectual, (c) seeking mentors and professional opportunities, (d) taking risks, and (e) confronting injustice. We presented these themes in the body of this article using our voices. However, we chose to remain anonymous, not attributing specific comments to specific individuals.

We used our journal and conversational data and the literature on experiences of African American graduate students to make recommendations for faculty regarding their pedagogy and practice, inside and outside of the classroom.

Narratives of Personal Experience as Graduate Students

Seeking Mentors and Professional Opportunities

> I searched for faculty within my department who would value my research and more importantly my contribution as a Black woman.

Finding faculty who attempt to understand the perspectives of African American graduate students and who respect the contributions of those outside the White male canon can have a positive influence on one's graduate school experience. But do such faculty have to be of the same ethnicity or race? Can African American students, for example, benefit from mentoring relationships with White professors? Does race matter? Or, is acceptance and openness in a faculty member the key to a better graduate experience?

> Though I wish I had more opportunities to interact and be mentored by Black professors, I must acknowledge that race may not be the most significant factor in determining a professor's ability to mentor or direct graduate students of color.

> I gravitate to faculty who "model" different ways of thinking, who seek to facilitate my own thinking, my intellectual development (as opposed to expecting me to mimic theirs), and who try to create inclusive classrooms.

> We have so few African American faculty within the academy that we graduate students have expectations that Black faculty who are here will extend themselves to us. And sometimes they don't.

Devalued as Scholars

The graduate student experiences in our group are both representative of the literature and revealing in terms of the ways we interact as students and faculty. Much like the experiences described by Cheatham and Phelps (1995), Steele (1999), and Ellis (1992), we have felt at times "devalued as scholars." Rather than feeling embraced and treated as worthwhile and valuable contributors to the Ph.D. program, we have sometimes felt excluded—occasionally even hazed by some of our faculty members.

> I can't recall how many conversations I had last week where a Black female doctoral student in education shared that, at some point, she had considered quitting. What is it about the academic socialization process that leaves so many of us feeling less like "valued colleagues" and more like "casualties of war?"

> It's tough. We met last week for the first time Black males in this program. We just talked about different issues that were going on in our lives and the program. The stories we have are amazing. Really what I heard was how each of us saw ourselves as Black men in this program. . . . What spoke the loudest was that we don't feel connected or a part of this program. We talked about how we wish we had more Black faculty mentors.

Our ideas have also been challenged, not based on their content or the arguments used to define and support them, but on their subject matter—race, gender, and class.

> "You could do more than race." That was the response given by my advisor, a White female professor, when I shared with her my tentative research plans. I was perplexed,

in part, because my area of concentration at the time was cultural studies. Wouldn't a Black woman's perspective on educational issues be of use to the academy?

Although their work is often minimized by advisors or other faculty, African American graduate students make important contributions within the academy. By offering diverse viewpoints and experiences, providing new ways of looking at issues or problems, and challenging mainstream ideologies, the scholarly work and classroom participation of African American graduate students contribute to the educational experience of all students.

Excluded as Intellectuals

At times, we have thought that the above-mentioned experiences were based on the ignorance of faculty who chose to remain oblivious to others or their surroundings. But we believe that, more often, efforts to exclude African American graduate students from intellectual discourse and academic success are purposeful.

> I would argue that there is a very conscious intention to exclude. I don't think it is as simplistic as race or gender. It is much more complex. I do think, though, there are characteristics other than talent that make some of us more desirable than others.

> [A woman commented:] While in pursuit of doctoral study, I think I have experienced the convergence of race, gender, and regional biases in both covert and overt demonstrations. I can think of a recent incident where my advisor made consistent and repetitive reference to a male advisee despite the fact that I have been his advisee for a longer period of time. It was as though I was invisible or had not merited equal consideration. When I commented on the observation, it was seemingly dismissed in a patronizing way. I couldn't help but wonder if this was solely because of gender since the other student is also African American and from the South.

What characteristics make some students more attractive intellectually to faculty? In the classroom, students sometimes felt slighted or offended because faculty members were indifferent or disinterested in race, often avoiding racial issues. Being recognized as an intellectual in the academy has specific conditions that are both spoken and unspoken.

> Whenever my classmates, professors, and I talk about race in class, it is because I [raised] the topic. This is a problem for many of them because they feel I am too aggressive, too outspoken, or too opinionated. But I never gave their responses much thought until a few years ago. I realized after taking classes that dealt with race, class, and gender, [those] classmates' and faculty's responses reflected their resistance. They, including the professors, were not willing to talk about African American perspectives in the classroom, in research, or anywhere else because of their unwillingness to understand my experience as it related to my Blackness, but they were interested in my experiences as they related to my Americanness—a context [about] which they felt less afraid, less threatened, but more understandable, only because my Americanness was more identifiable to them and aligned with their White ideology.

Many African American graduate students have been socialized to believe that we should avoid "ethnic topics," "ethnic ways of dressing," or "ethnic ways of approaching our topics," if we want to receive the "right" kind of attention. Instead we are encouraged to censor ourselves, to "White wash" our experiences. Steele (1999) contends that traditionally White ways of acting may be privileged within the academy. When we as African American students draw upon our personal experience and express ourselves in ways that are typically attributed to "our culture," we are criticized for engaging in stereotypic behavior. This is particularly the case for many African American males:

> Aggression is a characteristic that has been attached to Black males for many years. To others, we are acting like typical Blacks, when really we are fighting the same uphill battle [that] many before us have fought.

> In the classroom, Black male Ph.D. students are not just learning; they are fighting to become serious scholars, fighting to prove their academic abilities, and fighting to write about issues they are passionate about, specifically those that reference Black topics of interest. The complexity of this [situation] for Black male students is that, once they speak up for their topics of interest, they are labeled as a problem or not deemed serious scholars because their topics pertain to Black issues. It is tough when you walk through the door and you are already looked upon as "not serious" or "a problem."

Another researcher/participant discussed feeling pressured to conform to someone else's notions of scholarship:

> I thought it was nice that he [my faculty advisor] was making an effort. But what is clear is that I would still have to align myself to his perception of what scholarship is.

Many times Black graduate students feel alienated in the classroom because the texts used and subjects discussed do not speak to their experiences:

> My interest in this project started when I was a graduate student. During a class in which we were studying social theory, a Black graduate student from Trinidad expressed her concerns that the class readings did not represent her "family pictures." She wondered why we had to look at the canon of White, male, European theorists.

The experiences of the researchers/participants point to the multiple ways in which African American graduate students struggle in the academy. They suggest that there is an urgent need for faculty to address these issues.

Personal Experiences as Faculty Members

Taking Risks

What is different about faculty members who actively create comfortable spaces for African American graduate students? How do they do it? What are their motivations? And how do other faculty members respond?

It is difficult to admit your biases and [admit] that you don't know it all—especially within the academy, an academy in which you are judged by your peers. It is hard to confront your prejudices and your assumptions. And when you decide to act and try to counteract these negative forces in the lives of students, sometimes your "other" students and your colleagues decide you "use too many African American or female authors in a class that is not supposed to be about race and gender" or "you only like a faculty candidate because they are Black."

I feel very strongly that in my own teaching I try to support the concerns of all graduate students (as long as they are not intended to be hurtful to another student). I constantly struggle with these issues and how to deal with them in my classes. My personal belief is that race, class, gender, and other issues around discrimination should be threaded throughout all classes. I see linkages with research, leadership, policy, foundations, and higher education.

Electing to take these issues on, especially as an untenured faculty member, can feel risky. It can also *be* risky. In our case, it felt less threatening when we decided not to do it alone. Finding students and other faculty who are willing to address and confront these issues is an important step. By working with others, concerned faculty can create an important support network to sustain their work.

Confronting Injustice

How do we, as faculty, avoid falling into the norms and assumptions of the academy? The academy is based on assumptions of meritocracy. Pay raises, tenure, job appointments, and awards are offered based on a belief that those who reap the benefits of academia do so because of their superiority to the competition. Top-tier schools are more prestigious because we believe that they are. Their tenured faculty members receive the largest grants and often are published in the more exclusive journals. Graduate school, then, becomes a site where faculty must weed out undesirable students to ensure the health and strength of the field. Moving beyond these meritocratic assumptions and recognizing the potential of each student is a crucial step. This means seeing the faculty member's role as nurturing and guiding students.

It is also the purpose of our colleagues to determine who the "best" faculty are. This creates a competitive environment rather than a supportive environment and is more patriarchal. Notions of caring and community are more of a feminine approach. In a caring environment, if a student or faculty member fails, then the faculty need to ask themselves if they did everything to support them and provide them with formative feedback. I think we constantly struggle with these issues because it is difficult to determine the criteria we establish for deciding who is the "best" and whether it might be entangled with issues such as politics, race, class, gender, and sexual orientation.

My goal as a teacher is to try and remember that in my classroom you do not need to be tough to survive. I believe a classroom space should be a space were students feel free to express their opinions and where they can feel intellectually nurtured.

Recognizing that the academy can produce a "chilly climate" for anyone—but especially for faculty and students of color—is important. Creating a supportive environment in the classroom and among students is a way to counteract merito-cratic assumptions. This attitude assumes that all students have a right to be in graduate school and that all students have potential, but this view may be in direct conflict with tacit cultural assumptions of the academy.

Recommendations: How Can Faculty Be Supportive?

This study provides important insights into how graduate faculty can create suppor-tive and nurturing learning environments for African American students. Faculty can encourage students, regardless of their backgrounds, to pursue issues relevant to them personally and, in cases where sensitive topics will be covered, set classroom expectations for discussing issues. Faculty can also acknowledge and value students' cultural experiences even if they diverge from their own. More importantly, faculty can support students as they find their own voices as researchers and scholars.

As a result of our analysis, we identified three primary avenues through which faculty can be attentive to issues affecting African American graduate students and support their research interests: personal reflection, creating a nurturing environ-ment in their classroom, and mentoring.

Personal Reflection

In the endeavor of providing greater support to African American graduate stu-dents, we think that self-reflection is critically important. The first thing a faculty member can do is acknowledge that the academy is rife with unequal power rela-tionships and sowed with cultural landmines of embedded discrimination and op-pression (Carty, 1991; Collins, 1998). Being aware of these issues and recognizing one's role and subjectivity (positionality) in this process as both a teacher and re-searcher is an important step.

Personal reflection provides space for acknowledging the complexity of oppres-sion and issues of power embedded within the academy, departments, and class-rooms. In itself, self-definition means disowning labels, categories, and groupings assigned by society in order to embrace a liberated consciousness of self. For exam-ple, Steele (1999) speaks of the "stereotype threat," how students of color fear that many faculty members will assume that they are less intellectually able than White students. Many will assume that they were admitted to graduate school or hired because of the color of their skin rather then merit.

Creating a Supportive Classroom Environment

Building on the critical pedagogy literature, we acknowledge that the classroom is often a site of political struggle (Banks, 1996; Freire, 2000; hooks, 1994). While classes as benign as research methods or educational finance may seem free from these issues, we would argue that no class is actually free. Power inequities pervade all aspects of our culture. Consequently, all faculty need to be sensitive to these issues. That is why we suggest integrating social justice issues in the classroom regardless of the topic. It is important that faculty model engage pedagogy and be willing to share power with students. This is not an easy task and can actually evoke anxiety, fear, and resentment. Giving up power is a complex task, requiring the faculty member to maintain a balance between an open and free exchange of ideas, sharing content information, and meeting the needs of each student.

As our narratives have shown, we believe that it is critically important for faculty to support students as they find their voice. This support requires nurturing their agency by valuing their experience and helping them recognize their own power. In this endeavor, we found transgressive critical pedagogy a helpful approach (hooks, 1994; Freire, 2000).

Mentoring Outside the Classroom

Our experiences have taught us that students need supportive mentoring. We have found that students need to be treated as equal colleagues rather than as "casualties of war." This critical difference implies that students need to be treated as professionals and intellectual equals where treatment is commensurate with opportunities to experience and reinforce collegiality. A faculty member may have more experience in scholarship, teaching, and service; but it does not mean that students deserve to be treated as deficient or less than equal. As graduate students progress, letting them know of conference presentations and publishing opportunities is a way to help them make the transition into academic expectations. Offering to work with them on research projects and conference presentations is an additional way to be supportive. Keeping up on the opportunities available for special graduate students' seminars and fellowships is also useful.

Students confronted with racism, classism, or sexism in their graduate programs often need someone to talk to regarding these issues. A faculty member who is very supportive of students is also a faculty member who is often advising a large number of students and who may find it difficult to always be there when a student is in need. Nurturing collegiality among students is one way to create an additional support network for students. By sharing stories, students will know that they are not alone in their experience and can form an invaluable support network for each other.

Our process for writing the article, which was egalitarian and collaborative, is an example of what we suggest faculty members do to enhance the experiences of African American graduate students.[3] As faculty and students, we worked together to understand the academic process, to gain conference presentation experience, to write this article, and to explore issues of transgressive pedagogy. We have engaged in this project to encourage faculty to have similar conversations with their students and with each other in an effort to prevent African Americans graduate students from feeling like "casualties of war."

Notes

1. Each of us contributed equally to this article; our names are in alphabetical order. Punctuation and spelling in our quotations has been standardized.
2. This type of research has its limitations. Kemmis and McTaggart (2000) note that engaging in collaborative research can privilege subjectivity and confuse social action with social research.
3. But reducing these issues to race is also problematic. While we are focusing here on African American graduate students, we also want to acknowledge that these issues are not reducible to race alone. We have found that issues such as class, gender, ethnicity, religion, sexual orientation, and ableism are deeply intertwined.

References

Banks, J. (Ed.). (1996). *Multicultural education, transformative knowledge, and action: Historical and contemporary perspectives*. New York: Teacher's College Press.

Blanchett, W., & Clarke-Yapi, M. (Fall 1999). Cross-cultural mentoring of ethnic minority students: Implications for increasing minority faculty. *Professional Educator, 22*(1): 49–62.

Carter-Obayuwana, A. (1995, Fall). A model of hope and caring for African American women in higher education. *The Black Scholar, 25*(4): 72–76.

Carty, L. (1991). Black women in academia: A statement from the periphery. In H. Bennerji, L. Carty, K. Dehli, S. Heald, & K. McKenna (Eds.), *Unsettling relations: The university as a site of feminist struggle* (pp. 13–44). Boston, MA: South End Press.

Cheatham, H., & Phelps, C. (1995). Promoting the development of graduate students of color. In A. Pruitt & P. Isaac (Eds)., *Student services for the changing graduate student population, 72*(4), 91–99.

Chism, N., & Pruitt, A. (1995). Promoting inclusiveness in college teaching. In W. Wright (Ed). *Teaching improvement practices: Successful strategies for higher education*. Bolton, MA: Anker.

Collins, P. H. (1998). *Fighting words: Black women and the search for justice*. Minneapolis: University of Minnesota Press.

Creswell, J. W. (1998). *Qualitative inquiry and research design: Choosing among five traditions*. Thousand Oaks, CA: Sage Publications.

Davidson, M. N., & Foster-Johnson, L. (2001). Mentoring in the preparation of graduate researchers of color. *Review of Educational Research, 71*(4): 549–574.

Denzin, N. K., & Lincoln, Y.S. (Eds.). (1998). *Strategies of qualitative inquiry*. Thousand Oaks, CA: Sage Publications.

Dowdy, J., Givens, G., Murillo, E., Shenoy, D., & Villenas, S. (2000). Noises in the attic: The legacy of expectations in the academy. *International Journal of Qualitative Studies, 13*(5), 429–446.

Ellis, E. M. (1997). *The impact of race and gender on graduate school socialization, satisfaction with graduate study and commitment to completion of the degree among Black and White doctoral students*. Unpublished dissertation. College Park: Pennsylvania State University.

Freire, P. (2000). *Pedagogy of the oppressed*. Trans. Myra Bergman Ramos. New York: Continuum. Originally published in 1970.

Hood, S., & Freeman, D. (1995). Where do students of color earn doctorates in education? The top 25 colleges and schools of education. *Journal of Negro Education, 64*(4), 423–436.

hooks, b. (1994). *Teaching to transgress: Education as the practice of freedom.* New York: Routledge.

Jiwani, A., & Regan, T. (1998). Race, culture, and the curriculum. In T. Modood & T. Acland (Eds.), *Race and higher education.* London: Policy Studies Institute.

Jordan, J. (1989). *Moving towards home: Political essays.* London: Virago Press.

Kemmis, S., & McTaggart, R. (2000). Participatory action research. In N. K. Denzin & Y. S. Lincoln (Eds.), *Handbook of qualitative research* (2nd ed.), Thousand Oaks, CA: Sage Publications.

Linthicum, D. S (1989). *The dry pipeline: Increasing the flow of minority faculty.* Annapolis, MD.: National Council of State Directors of Community and Junior Colleges.

Lupton, D. (Ed.). (1999). *Risk and sociocultural theory: New directions and perspectives.* Cambridge, UK: Cambridge University Press.

Morris, F. L. (1993). Doctoral opportunities in the United States: The denial of equal treatment for Black students. *Urban League Review, 16*(1), 9–16.

Robertson, P. F., & Frier, T. (1994, Fall). Recruitment and retention of minority faculty. *New Directions for Community Colleges, 22*(3), 65–71.

Steele, C. (1999). A threat in the air: How stereotypes shape intellectual identity. In E. Lowe (Ed.), *Promise and dilemma: Perspectives on racial diversity and higher education.* Princeton, NJ: Princeton University.

Steele, R. (1991). *Mentoring: An effective tool for retention of minorities.* Opinion paper. Missouri. Eric Document Reproduction Service (ED 342 841).

Turner, C. S., & Thompson, J. R. (1993). Socializing women doctoral students: Minority and majority experiences. *Review of Higher Education 16*(3), 355–370.

Willie, C. V., Grady, M. K., & Hope, R. O. (1991). *African Americans and the doctoral experience: Implications for policy.* New York: Teacher's College Press.

22   *Mark A. Williams*

"I GOT MINE, NOW YOU GET YOURS": DERAILING THE UNDERGROUND RAILROAD

The completion of doctoral studies is never a solo project or accomplishment. Rather it involves the dedication and active involvement of many people. Their individual expertise and experiences collectively create the framework upon which the doctoral research/studies are built. At a minimum, the graduate student, the dissertation advisor, and the dissertation committee are involved in a concerted effort; but additionally the dissertation often requires the committed participation of a mentor or predecessors who serve as a continued source of encouragement and inspiration for the student. This network is particularly important for the student of color.

One sentiment echoed by many minority faculty and students who have either completed or are completing their doctoral degree requirements is that the graduate school environment, particularly at primarily White institutions, is covertly and/or overtly hostile. Most students and faculty who have successfully navigated through the many obstacles placed before them by academe have done so with the help of conductors who formed an underground railroad of sorts—a network of collaborators who direct other students of color through hostile territories along a path to academic success and attainment of the doctorate.

Institutional ineptness and unwillingness to embrace cultural diversity mandates the creation of this "underground railroad." Cultural norms and behaviors that stress cooperation and altruism keep it operational. However, definite forces and philosophies endanger its continued existence. This essay discusses cultural norms that influence minority student and faculty collaboration, thus facilitating the success of other minority students and faculty. It also discusses philosophies and actions of the dominant culture of academe that seemingly aim to annihilate these intrinsic cultural ideals.

The Collectivist Mindset and Its Benefits

What motivates a student to continue graduate education through completion of the doctoral program? Davidson (2001) suggests that mentoring relationships play a critical role, a finding reinforced by several other investigations (Adams, 1992; Phillip, 1993). According to Davidson, mentoring relationships (a) integrate a student into the fabric of the department (b) cultivate essential professional and social networks (c) aid students in acquiring core research competencies, and (d) pave the way for placement in the workforce after achieving the degree.

Many students of color do not have the benefit of adequate mentoring. One study indicated that a third of the African American graduate students surveyed reported that they had received no mentoring support or guidance in their programs (Smith & Davidson, 1992). In another study of 12 prominent business schools, only 7% of the African American students agreed that they had adequate opportunities to work with professors of color (Catalyst, 2000). The lack of adequate and culturally appropriate mentoring for minority students represents a significant threat to graduate student success. Davidson (2001) reported that this scarcity places students of color and women at greater risk of (a) not receiving sufficient training in research and specialized content areas (b) not completing their degree programs, and (c) not being well positioned to succeed in their postdoctoral careers.

As a mechanism for survival in graduate school, many African American students opt to venture outside their departmental and hierarchical boundaries to develop relationships with other African Americans (Thomas, 1990). In some cases the only culturally appropriate mentor available is another student, who may be further advanced in his or her training. Whether mentoring is provided by a faculty or another student, the desire to seek out same-race mentoring relationships can be partly explained by cultural behaviors and values. The construct of individualism vs. collectivism provides an interesting framework in which to explore this dynamic.

Individualism is a societal pattern in which individuals view themselves independent of any collective. The individual's goals are given higher priority than those of the group or community (Triandis, 1995). By contrast, within the construct of collectivism, individuals emphasize their connection to other members of the communal. They are motivated by norms, duties, and obligations associated with the collective (Triandis, 1995). Anglo- and European-based cultures tend to find the individualistic construct more appealing while African- and South American-based cultures are more collectivist (Gaines et al., 1997; Hofstede, 1980). Accordingly, Whites tend to focus on activities that emphasize individual skills. Ethnic groups that are more collectivist, like African Americans, typically tend to be more cooperative. When given tasks in which participants can choose to compete or cooperate, African Americans usually opt for collaboration (Cox, Lobel, & McLeod, 1991).

Whites and members of other cultures with individualistic social patterns often view self-promotion as an indication of self-confidence and leadership potential. Cultures with more collectivist social patterns typically view self-promotion as deplorable and consequently will often avoid drawing attention to themselves or to their individual accomplishments (Brookhiser, 1991; Cervantes, 1992). Because so many faculty members are of Anglo-European descent and institutions are based on these individualistic cultural norms, reluctance to self-promote is often seen as unwillingness or inability to take on a strong leadership role (Carnevale & Stone, 1995), when in fact it simply represents a desire to esteem the welfare of the collective more highly than that of the individual.

The collectivist mindset of African Americans can be evidenced by walking into a classroom at any primarily White institution; if there is more than one African American, you will usually find them sitting together. This tribal or communal behavior, which is almost instinctive, communicates an allegiance that ensures mutual success. If one student has access to beneficial resources, he or she openly shares them with the others. If one student struggles or fails, the whole group grieves for that individual and sometimes feels that it reflects on them as a whole. Consequently, there is often an unspoken accountability among the members of the group. Just as Harriet Tubman, brandishing her pistol, insisted: "You will be free or you will die," these alliances are like the barrel of a firearm aimed squarely at the student who requires a little motivation along the way. In this setting, there is a consistent, unwavering commitment to the success of the group.

Because minority students are grossly underrepresented in graduate school, opportunities to form such alliances within one's own department may be scarce. For this reason, minority students will often formally organize to provide the social and academic networks that are vital to the success of the communal. Through these alliances, minority students learn how other cultural differences influence student success in doctoral programs and academic careers. Many times such learning occurs through the sharing of personal experience; the communal learns from the encounters of one.

Take, for example, the experience of one African American graduate student who was nearing the completion of his research. In preparation for the meeting of his dissertation committee during which he planned to propose the termination of further experimentation and moving on to writing, he was thoroughly prepared to address any question or concern that was brought up by committee members. Indeed, he had anticipated and formulated an answer or rebuttal to each question that was posed. Unbeknownst to him, this confident preparation gave the impression that he was insulting the intelligence of the committee members, an egregious offense by any graduate student.

After what he assessed as a flawless presentation and defense of his data, the student was asked to wait outside the room while the committee discussed his progress. Forty minutes later, he was invited back into the room. He was confident that they would agree that he had given a stellar presentation and that he was finished with the experiments. He sat at the end of an enormously long conference table opposite the committee members. The intense look of trepidation on their faces told him, before anyone spoke, that bad news was pending. This student felt that they viewed him as a vicious junkyard dog waiting for their disapproval, which would serve as a command to attack.

The committee proceeded to express their desire to see additional experimentation. This statement was followed by a short hush in the room. An eternity seemed to pass; they shrank back in their seats, uncertain of his response. Fortunately, the student detected their uneasiness, rapidly evaluated possible causes for it, and couched his response in a way that fit within the parameters of what they deemed appropriate. The student's White, Jewish advisor later confided that he was certain the student would flip the table over in protest of their decision—acting like the "typical angry Black man." He later added that the student's responses to the committee's inquiries were too "forceful" and, consequently, were perceived as aggressive posturing. What I've since learned and now share with other graduate students of color is that cultural differences mandate that the tone of dialogue and debate between me and my White colleagues in academe be distinctly different from those that would otherwise occur within the communal setting.

Kochman (1981) reported that Whites typically communicate in a low-key, detached, and reserved manner, manifesting very little affect, while African Americans are often frank, freely giving and taking strong criticism. This communication style, while common and culturally appropriate, is often viewed by White mentors, other faculty, and students as being aggressive and irascible. Even though a White audience may not be able to articulate what makes them uncomfortable, a Black student or faculty member must be consciously aware of this personal/cultural style and its potential impact on his or her ability to succeed in academe. Unfortunately, most African American faculty members and students have to learn how these differences influence perceptions and promotion through trial and error. For this reason, a venue for the open exchange of information and experiences such as these greatly facilitates the success of upcoming African American students. In this way, members of the collective (i.e., faculty and students) who are able and willing to freely contribute serve as conductors, ensuring the safe passage of African Americans along the railway to completion of the doctorate and "academic freedom."

Slaves, after entering into free territories, quickly learned that the freedom they experienced was still not equality. So are the experiences of African Americans who remain in academe after completing their doctorates. Forces that limit or prevent academic freedom, are discussed elsewhere in this book. These same forces also derail vehicles that aid minorities in the completion of their doctoral training. Some forces are deliberate and directly work toward this end, while others are indirect. This essay discusses two: (a) the desire of the institution to have students and faculty of color assimilate into the dominant culture, and (b) the underrepresentation and overextension of minority faculty.

Assimilation: Abandoning Cultural Uniqueness and Identity

There is a clear distinction between freedom by geographical location and true emancipation. After being freed, slaves faced the unfortunate reality that life for them in the free world was still unfair and unequal. Racism and segregation still prevented or at least hindered their acquisition of the resources required for success and even survival. Though their geographic location granted them freedom, they fully understood that, if they stepped outside certain boundaries, they were reenslaved.

Although African Americans have been permitted to attend graduate school and gain academic appointments, and a few are allowed to hold positions where they are given a small measure of administrative authority, few if any are truly emancipated. They frequently do not enjoy the support of their departments, much less that of the institution. Insensitivity to cultural differences and the devaluation of research efforts that focus primarily on minority issues remain serious problems within academe. Perhaps the single most important factor that keeps minority students and faculty from complete emancipation is the requirement that they assimilate into the individualistic framework of Anglo-European academe.

Many White faculty expect that, when students of color matriculate in graduate school, they will quickly assimilate into the dominant culture. Such assimilation often requires that the student or faculty member of color learn the behaviors of the dominant culture and modify his or her own style to conform. When this does not occur, the student or faculty member is viewed as a loose cannon, a nonconformist, and a rebel. Immediately, additional barriers go up, and the assistance that the student or faculty member needs to succeed within that environment becomes unattainable. The student is often unaware of the dynamics that have occurred and frequently has no effective remedy. All he or she recognizes is that the climate is unfriendly and not conducive to success.

Under these circumstances, the faint-hearted student or faculty member will abandon or modify certain aspects of his or her cultural identity and behaviors rather than run the risk of being ostracized and not enjoying access to resources. He or she then assimilates, as expected of him by White faculty members and other students. Academic life, though still fraught with obstacles, is less challenging in that he or she has now acquired a portion of the institutional resources. He or she often experiences less consternation from other faculty members, and opportunities for advancement seem more likely. At this point, addressing minority issues may have become too risky for this individual; he or she abandons key aspects of racial identity. Like many fair-skinned African Americans during times of great oppression and segregation, these faculty members "pass" for White. They have successfully assimilated into the individualistic framework within which the dominant culture of the academy functions, thus relating with the apparent goal of an institution that will not accommodate cultural diversity.

It is lamentable that one who has experienced the injustices inflicted upon minorities within academe would deliberately adopt a self-preservationist philosophy. The sentiment of the collectivist philosophy denies any minority faculty who has gained entry to academe the right to leave it without leaving behind greater opportunities for success for other students of color than he or she was afforded. Although accomplishing this goal may be costly, we don't have the luxury of resting on our laurels because so many have struggled to provide opportunities for us, while others are still struggling to attain the same opportunities we enjoy. With this charge, "passing" or assimilating should not be a consideration for the minority student or faculty member. Rather, faculty and students alike should be strong proponents for the institutional adoption of the concept of cultural pluralism.

In cultural pluralism, cultural differences are identified, understood, and appreciated. This philosophy enables the student or faculty to maintain his or her racial identity without fear of castigation. Furthermore, it enriches our collective understanding and interpretations of data. Heisenberg (1958) astutely noted, "What we observe is not nature itself, but nature exposed to our method of questioning" (p. 58). Cultural norms and values prejudice our methods of questioning positively and negatively. Indeed, if the questions asked dictate discovery, then broadening the perspective of scientific inquiry by the inclusion of the diversity in cultural pluralism broadens our collective ability to discover. Thus, cultural diversity contains the ability to enrich the academic production of publishable scholarship, which is the vaunted mission of institutions of higher learning. To this end, it behooves the institution to change to embrace our cultural differences rather than forcing assimilation to create a uniform culture.

The Few, the Proud, the Minority Faculty

In their current state of underrepresentation, minority faculty who are committed to academe and the training of future scholars find themselves overextended. Many fully accept the cultural construct of collectivism and accordingly find themselves duty-bound to meet the developmental needs, not only of their own protégés, but also those of nonminorities who retreat to them in a desperate attempt to acclimate without assimilating. Additionally, the collectivist mindset compels the individual to meet his or her social obligations to the minority community at large. The unique privilege and the responsibility of minority faculty are that they are obliged in many instances to serve as role models not only in the workplace but also within the community. These dedicated faculty live on the underground railroad of academe. While it is time consuming to mentor one or two students, it is even more challenging to mentor a community of students and nonstudents.

Many departments and institutions capitalize on and even exploit the collectivist mindset of minority faculty. Although they have given the individual apparent academic freedom in granting him or her professorship, they frequently have not provided adequate resources to accomplish all of the goals now expected of this new faculty member. Many of these institutions are fully aware that their one African American professor is being sought out by ten minority students from different departments but continue to appeal to the collectivist nature of the good professor to accept still more burdens. Certainly, the faculty member still has his or her obligations to the department and institution and is justifiably expected to produce research, publish, and perform the other tasks necessary to obtain tenure. But there sometimes seems to be an almost eager anticipation of failure which would herald the return of the freed slave to the plantation to become an indentured sharecropper.

The mentor then finds himself faced with an ethical dilemma. On one hand he or she is culturally bound to fulfill his societal obligation. On the other, his or her departmental and institutional duties are unrelenting. Many, when faced with this dilemma, may opt to neglect their cultural duties. They then adopt the mentality, "I got mine. Now you get yours the best way you can." This indentured sharecropper works, unknowingly, to ensure that minorities never become the plantation owners. If cultural diversity is ever to be embraced and work conditions for minorities in academe are ever to be improved, then minorities must be placed in policy-making positions. This will never occur if the shortage persists of minority faculty and students who are willing to act as conductors, aiding other minority students and faculty in their academic and postdoctoral career pursuits.

As grievous a situation it is for minority faculty and students to adopt the "I got mine, now you get yours" mentality, it is equally deplorable that he or she should be compelled to make such choices. Forces that compel such decisions can be traced to the institution's unwillingness to hire additional minority faculty and train nonminority faculty to be culturally sensitive and thereby become effective in their mentoring strategies. This situation derives from an institutional philosophy that race doesn't matter. Certainly, it may not be a major factor for success with the students from the dominant culture; but for those who must reconcile the conflict between their own cultural indoctrination and that of the dominant population, it is a tremendous hurdle to overcome. In this manner, the graduate department culpably neglects to provide the tools and resources necessary for minority students and young faculty to achieve success. The burden then falls upon the shoulders of "the few, the proud," the minority faculty. And if they, too, fail to meet this mandate, students and young faculty are left to perish.

Over a period of ten years, Harriet Tubman made at least nineteen trips from the North to the South to free slaves. With a $40,000 bounty on her head, she faced the threat of being captured or killed with each trip she made. Her selfless commitment to ensuring freedom for slaves compelled her to conduct over 300 Blacks to freedom along the Underground Railroad (Bradford, 1886). How many will you help?

It is prudent for every person of color who has completed doctoral training to re-examine the course of his or her study and recognize that there were conductors—some White, some Black, and some of other races—who guided them along the path to academic success. The successful doctorate of color owes them a debt for their efforts and sacrifices. This debt of gratitude is most appropriately repaid in making an unselfish commitment toward ensuring that our successors are better placed to succeed than we were. Rather than insisting that others struggle alone to "get theirs," we should more altruistically say, "I got mine. Now let me help you get yours."

References

Adams, H. G. (1992). *Mentoring: An essential factor in the doctoral process for minority students.* South Bend, IN: National Consortium for Graduate Degrees for Minorities in Engineering.

Bradford, S. (1886). *Harriet, the Moses of her people.* New York: for the author by G. R. Lockwood & Son.

Brookhiser, R. (1991). *The way of the WASP: How it made America, and how it can save it, so to speak.* New York: Free Press.

Carnevale, A. P., & Stone, S. C. (1995). *The American mosaic: An in-depth report on the future of diversity at work.* New York: McGraw-Hill.

Catalyst. (2000). *Women and the MBA: Gateway to opportunity.* New York: Author.

Cervantes, R. C. (1992). Occupational and economic stressors among immigrant and United States-born Hispanics. In S. B. Knouse, P. Rosenfeld, & A. L. Culbertson (Eds.), *Hispanics in the work-place* (pp. 120–133). Newbury Park, CA: Sage Publications.

Cox, T., Jr., Lobel, S. A., & McLeod, P. L. (1991). Effects of ethnic group cultural differences on cooperative and competitive behavior on a group task. *Academy of Management Journal, 34*(4), 827–847.

Davidson, M. N., & Foster-Johnson, L. (2001). Mentoring in the preparation of graduate researchers of color. *Review of Educational Research, 71*(4), 549–574.

Gaines, S. O., Jr., Marelich, W. D., Bledsoe, K. L., Steers, W. N., Henderson, M. C., Granrose, C. S., et al. (1997). Links between race/ethnicity and cultural values as mediated by racial/ethnic identity and moderated by gender. *Journal of Personality & Social Psychology, 72*(6), 1460–1476.

Heisenberg, W. (1958). *Physics and philosophy: The revolution in modern science.* New York: Harper & Brothers.

Hofstede, G. (1980). *Culture's consequences: International differences in work-related values.* Newbury Park, CA: Sage.

Kochman, T. (1981). *Black and White styles in conflict.* Chicago: University of Chicago Press.

Phillip, M. C. (1993). Enhancing the presence of minorities in graduate schools: What works for some institutions. *Black Issues in Higher Education, 10*(10), 33–35.

Smith, E. P., & Davidson, W. S. (1992). Mentoring and the development of African American graduate students. *Journal of College Student Development, 33*(6), 531–539.

Thomas, D. A. (1990). The impact of race on managers' experiences of developmental relationships (mentoring and sponsorship): An intra-organizational study. *Journal of Organizational Behavior, 11*(6), 479–492.

Triandis, H. C. (1995). *Individualism and collectivism.* Boulder, CO: Westview Press.

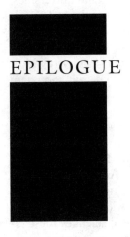

Etta R. Hollins

EPILOGUE

The dramatic transformation in the composition of the student population of America's colleges and universities over the past generation is unparalleled in the history of Western higher education institutions. In the early 1960s, with the exception of those attending historically black colleges and universities, only a relative handful of Americans of color went to college in the United States; today, upwards of one in five undergraduates at four-year schools is a minority. That this revolution has led the way to the social and economic integration of millions of minority individuals into the mainstream of American life is remarkable, if unsurprising, because in the past 30 years, a college education has become almost prerequisite to advancement in our society. Equally remarkable, though less often recognized, are the contributions these individuals make not only to American society, economic, and cultural vitality, but also to the academic, intellectual, and educational vigor of the college and university communities of which they are members. Nevertheless, the nation's march to full equality of educational opportunity for all its citizens is not over.
AMERICAN COUNCIL ON EDUCATION, 2000

Demographic shifts in the nation's population significantly increasing the percentage of people of color, the increase in the enrollment of students of color in undergraduate and graduate programs in colleges and universities, and the increase in the percentage of students of color in the nation's public elementary and secondary schools have not led to dramatic increases in the percentage of these groups among university faculty. Recruiting and retaining a diverse faculty continues to be a challenge for many predominantly White public and private colleges and universities. According to Carter and Wilson (1997) people of color comprise approximately 12% of university faculty. The *Chronicle of Higher Education* (2002) reported that African Americans comprise approximately 4.5% of the professorate. The majority are employed in historically Black colleges and universities. Explanations for the shortage of faculty of color include limited numbers of people of color earning the doctorate and job opportunities outside academe that offer higher pay. An environment on many campuses characterized by exclusion, isolation, alienation, and racism has also made it difficult to retain faculty of color. Many White faculty perceive reverse discrimination in efforts to recruit and retain faculty of color, assuming that faculty of color are inherently less qualified than their White peers (Phillips, 2002).

The response of faculty of color to what many experience as a hostile work environment is most often documented in qualitative studies or surveys. These studies have been helpful in bringing forth the voice of faculty of color. However, this volume is unique in presenting the authentic voices of African American faculty in their own words and framed by their own perceptions portraying their experiences from graduate school preparation through employment in academe. This provides the reader a first-hand opportunity to better understand the challenges these faculty members have faced and many have overcome. The recommendations proffered by these authors are important for those who follow and for those seeking to diversify the faculty in colleges and universities.

It is important to point out that many of these young people have, in fact, already demonstrated superior strength of character, determination, and academic competence before entering college or earning a degree by extracting for themselves a high quality education from urban elementary and secondary schools in the absence of qualified teachers, adequate resources, and a comfortable and supportive classroom learning context. Remarkably, many of these young people of color from urban settings are able to outperform their more advantaged peers who attended schools with well-qualified teachers, an abundance of resources and materials, and a comfortable and supportive classroom learning context. This is not to suggest that all people of color, or all African Americans, come from low-income urban settings. Certainly, some African Americans come from advantaged backgrounds just like other people of color. However, it is often the case that this advantaged background does not provide the same connections within academe as it does for White students.

The three parts of this book address the preparation, experiences, teaching about race, and the standing of African American graduate students and faculty on predominantly White university campuses.

In Part I, Joy Gaston reflects on her own graduate school experience to make suggestions for other graduate students preparing for the professorate. She contends that African American graduate students are required to assume more responsibility for their own preparation than their White peers, are less likely to have a mentor relationship with a faculty member, and are less likely to receive an assistantship. Also, she points out the need for African American graduate students to prepare for the professorate by doing their own research concerning tenure, promotion, and different standards set by different types of institutions. She emphasizes the need for African American graduate students to identify their own mentors as they transition to academe.

Cyrus Ellis, in Part III, extends Gaston's argument that African American graduate students are required to assume more responsibility for their preparation than their White peers as do African American faculty teaching about race on a predominantly White university campus. He points out that, while addressing the issue of race is central to changing the social and academic context of the university, African American faculty face great risks in doing so. African American faculty in this context have their academic freedom challenged by White students and faculty. In spite of these challenges, Ellis posits that those who teach about race should do so "with a passion but without fear and without assigning blame." He argues that African American faculty who teach about race must assume responsibility by preparing themselves with the basic credentials for expertise in the field, by acquiring experience as a teacher and scholar, and by establishing a clear purpose for their work. He recommends using the "four points of a circle" icon that includes respect, listening, equity, and healing.

In Part IV of this book Lemuel Watson concludes:

> For faculty of color our quest to become a faculty member is more of a "calling" or spiritual quest in nature to fulfill our destiny. The dilemma lies in answering the "calling" and surviving the organizational politics and culture so that we can remain a part of the institution over a period of time.

A most important contribution of this book is evidence of the commitment, dedication, persistence, and sense of personal purpose found among many African American faculty in predominantly White colleges and universities. Additionally, this book serves multiple purposes: For African American faculty it is a simultaneous catharsis, healing, and validation. For all of us, it is a call to action for improving the social and academic context within predominantly White colleges and universities.

References

Carter, D. J., & Wilson, R. (1997). *Minorities in higher education*. Washington, DC: American Council on Education.

Chronicle of Higher Education. (2002, September). *Almanac: Characteristics of faculty members with teaching duties by type of institution*. Available at: http://chronicle.com/weekly/almanac/2002/nation/0103102.htm.

American Council on Education and American Association of University Professors. (2000). *Does diversity make a difference? Three research studies on diversity in college classrooms*. Washington, DC: Author.

Phillips, R. (2002). Recruiting and retaining a diverse faculty. *Planning for Higher Education, 30*(4), 32–39.

CONTRIBUTORS

AMIRI YASIN AL-HADID is Chair and Professor with Tenure of Africana Studies at Tennessee State University. He is Founder and Emir of the Great Debate Honor Society, Inc., which is based on the philosophies of El-Hajj Malik El-Shabazz (Malcolm X) and Dr. Martin Luther King Jr. Dr. Al-Hadid earned his B.A. degree in sociology and psychology from Alabama State University (HBCU) and his Ph.D. in sociology from the University of California—Santa Barbara. His most recent book, *Between Cross and Crescent: Christian and Muslim Perspectives on Malcolm and Martin,* is coauthored with Lewis V. Baldwin of Vanderbilt University (Gainesville: University Press of Florida, 2002). Dr. Al-Hadid is currently working on a new book: *El-Hajj Malik El-Shabazz: Muslim and Pan-African Statesman.*

SIBBY ANDERSON-THOMPKINS is a third-year doctoral student in Educational Policy Studies at Georgia State University with a concentration on qualitative research methodologies. She has earned a B.A. and an M.A. from the University of North Carolina at Chapel Hill. In addition, she holds a master of science from Georgia State University in educational research with a concentration in ethnography. Prior to graduate school, Anderson-Thompkins spent several years in college administration serving as an assistant dean of students and academic affairs at Chapel Hill and as an associate dean of student affairs at Hampshire College in Amherst, Massachusetts. Her research interests include critical race theory, feminist activist research, and arts-based research.

DENISE TALIAFERRO BASZILE is an Assistant Professor of Educational Leadership at Miami University, Oxford, Ohio. She received her M.Ed. in secondary English education and her Ph.D. in curriculum theory at Louisiana State University. Her research interests are in the historical, political, and philosophical foundations of race and its relationship to curriculum studies.

THEODOREA REGINA BERRY is a teacher-educator, researcher, community activist, poet, and singer who writes, teaches, and researches about teacher-educator development, teacher preparation, autobiography, multiculturalism, and diversity from a critical race feminist perspective. Her work with the Department of Defense Dependent Schools—Europe, Department of Defense Children and Youth Services Division in Germany, the Center for Urban School Policy at Northwestern University, and the Teachers' Academy for Mathematics and Science in Chicago has broadened her experiences in preparing teachers for diverse student populations. Dr. Berry completed her dissertation *Songs and Stories: Lyrical Movements in Teaching and Learning of an African American Woman* and received her doctor of education degree at National-Louis University, Evanston, Illinois, in April 2002 while serving as Visiting Assistant Professor at North Carolina Central University in Durham, where she taught classes in educational research, educational foundations, and cultural diversity, among others. She is an AERA/OERI Post-Doctoral Fellow at the University of Illinois at Chicago, conducting research based on her proposal entitled *To Teach, To Learn, To Teach: Educational Autobiographies for Critical Reflection of Teaching Practice*.

PAUL F. BITTING, who is an Associate Professor in the College of Education at North Carolina State University, began his professional service as a classroom teacher, counselor, and administrator in New York City's public schools. He holds master's degrees from the City University of New York (educational administration), St. John's College (liberal education), and the University of North Carolina at Chapel Hill (philosophy). He received his Ph.D. from the University of North Carolina at Chapel Hill in the social foundations of education specializing in the philosophy of education. He has published on critical thinking, philosophy for children, and multicultural philosophy and the schools.

FRED A. BONNER II earned his B.A. in chemistry from the University of North Texas, an M.S. Ed in curriculum and instruction from Baylor University, and an Ed.D. in higher education and administration and college teaching, also from Baylor. He was the recipient of the American Association for Higher Education (AAHE) Black Caucus Dissertation Award and the Educational Leadership, Counseling, and Foundations Dissertation of the Year Award from the University of Arkansas College of Education for "The Cultivation of Academic Giftedness in the Historically Black College and University and the Traditionally White Institution: Case Studies Involving the Perceptions of Two Academically Gifted American-American Male Undergraduates." He has served as editor for the *National Association of Student Affairs Professionals Journal* and has completed two summers in residency as a research fellow with the Yale University PACE Center, focusing on issues that impact academically gifted African American male college students. Among recent works are his "Liberty and Justice . . . Just Not for All," a review published in *Contemporary Psychology* (December 2002) and "To Be Young, Gifted, African-American, and Male," forthcoming from *Gifted Child Today*.

DARRELL CLEVELAND earned his Ph.D. in Culture, Curriculum, and Change in the School of Education at The University of North Carolina at Chapel Hill, an Ms.Ed. in elementary education from St. Joseph's University in Philadelphia, and a bachelor's degree in African American Studies from Temple University, also in Philadelphia. He has taught in

Philadelphia middle schools and also worked with at-risk youth, individuals with mental illness, and the drug and alcohol population. Dr. Cleveland's areas of research interest include beginning teachers, out-of-field teaching, alternative certification, teacher shortages, teacher attrition, the state of Black education, diversity and inclusion, high-stakes testing, charter schools, multicultural education, and minorities in higher education. He has presented and published on many of these topics. Through his teaching and research, Dr. Cleveland aims to address the problems associated with ignorance as it relates to difference. His professional and scholarly affiliations include membership in the American Educational Studies Association, the American Educational Research Association, The National Alliance for Black School Educators, and Brothers of the Academy Institute. *A Long Way to Go: Conversations about Race by African American Faculty and Graduate Students* is his first edited book.

CYRUS MARCELLUS ELLIS is currently a University Professor of Counseling at Governors State University in University Park, Illinois, and is the North Central Region Chair for the Adoption of Multicultural Counseling Competencies for the Association of Counselor Educators and Supervisors (ACES). His research interests involve family functioning affecting adolescent self-concept and socio-racial conditions of disadvantaged youths. Dr. Ellis earned his B.A. in psychology and M.A. in counseling from Rider University in Lawrenceville, New Jersey, and his Ph.D. in counselor education through the Curry School of Education at the University of Virginia. Dr. Ellis is the recipient of the Lincoln Scott Walter Award in Counseling from Rider University and the William Van Hoose Memorial Award from the Curry School of Education Foundation at the University of Virginia. Dr. Ellis has a dual career path as an academician and as a Captain in the U.S. Army Reserve. His citations and decorations include the Army Commendation Medal (awarded twice), the Army Achievement Medal (awarded three times), the Army Good Conduct Medal, the National Defense Service Medal, and the Army Green to Gold Scholarship. Dr. Ellis has presented at numerous state and national conferences, including the American Counseling Association, the Virginia Counselors Association, the Association for Counselor Educators and Supervisors, and the Association for the Advancement of Educational Research. He publishes on socio-racial issues, diversity, addiction, and health interventions. Among his current publications are "Examining the Pitfalls Facing African American Males," in Lee Jones (Ed.), *Making It on Broken Promises: African American Male Scholars Confront the Culture of Higher Education* (Sterling, VA: Stylus Publishing, 2002), and two chapters,"Conducting a Structured Observation" and "Helping Students with HIV and Other Health Problems" in Bradley Erford (Ed.), *Professional School Counselor's Handbook* (Alexandria, VA: American School Counselors Association, in press). Dr. Ellis is married to the former Deirdre Marie Waiters and has one daughter, Courtney Lynn Ellis.

MARCHETA P. EVANS is an Assistant Professor in the Counseling, Educational Psychology, and Adult and Higher Education Department at the University of Texas, San Antonio, and is currently the university's Counseling Program Coordinator. This program has one of the largest and fastest growing graduate programs at the university. She earned her B.S. in Psychology and her M.A. in Rehabilitation Counseling from the University of Alabama—Tuscaloosa, her M.Ed. in Elementary education from the University of Alabama—Birmingham, and her Ph.D. in Counselor Education from the University of Alabama—Tuscaloosa. She has served in numerous leadership positions at the national, regional, and state level of the American Counseling Association. Her research interests include diversity, multiculturalism, leadership, organizational commitment, and job satisfaction. Among recent publications are "Losses and Gains," in L. Golden (Ed.), *Case Studies in Marriage and Family therapy* (pp. 47–54) (Upper Saddle River, NJ: Merrill/Prentice Hall, 2000), and with Fred Bonner and S. Burns, "Triple Jeopardy: The Nontraditional African American Female Undergraduate," *NASAP Journal*, 5(1), 82–89.

ELLA FORBES is an Associate Professor and the Director of Graduate Studies in the Department of African American Studies at Temple University. She received her Ph.D. in African American Studies from Temple in 1991 which at that time had the only Ph.D. program in the discipline in the country. Her areas of interest include African resistance movements (especially during the antebellum period), mass media and the African American community, African women, and public policy and its impact on the African American and global communities. Dr. Forbes is the author of *African American Women During the Civil War* (New York: Garland Publishing, 1998) and *"But We Have No Country": the 1851 Christiana, Pennsylvania Resistance* (Africana Homestead Legacy Publishers, 1998). She is the co-author with Edward Wonkeryor, James Guseh, and George Kieh of *American Democracy in Africa in the Twenty-First Century* (Cherry Hill, NJ: Africana Homestead Legacy Publishers, 2000). She has also contributed several articles to scholarly journals and acted as a consultant to many institutions and projects. She was a member of the Black History Advisory Committee of the Pennsylvania Historical and Museum Commission, and is a member of the Association for the Study of African American Life and History, the National Council for Black Studies and the Association of Black Women Historians. In addition, she was a Commonwealth Speaker for the Pennsylvania Council for the Humanities and is a co-founder of a grassroots organization, Mothers Organized Against Police Terror. Dr. Forbes has been a paid consultant for such projects and organizations as the Detroit Museum of African American History, the Philadelphia and Baltimore School systems, Scribe Video (Philadelphia) and the Robert M. Hughes Academy Charter School in Springfield, Massachusetts.

MARYBETH GASMAN is an Assistant Professor of Higher Education in the Department of Higher Education Management in the Graduate School of Education at the University of Pennsylvania with a Ph.D. in higher education from Indiana University. A historian of higher education, she explores issues of philanthropy and historically Black colleges, Black leadership, contemporary fund-raising issues at Black colleges, and African American giving. Among Dr. Gasman's recent works are *Charles S. Johnson: Leadership beyond the Veil in the Age of Jim Crow* (Albany: SUNY Press, 2003) and *Supporting Alma Mater: Successful Strategies for Securing Funds from Black College Alumni* (Washington, DC: CASE Books, 2004). She is currently researching the United Negro College Fund (UNCF), examining the fund-raising rhetoric used by both UNCF's African American leaders and the White philanthropists who responded. Dr. Gasman has also published on philanthropic issues in *Educational Researcher*, the *American Educational Research Journal*, the *History of Education Quarterly*, the *International CASE Journal*, and the *History of Higher Education Annual*.

JOY L. GASTON is an Assistant Professor in the Higher Education program at Florida State University. Her research interests include the intersection of intercollegiate athletics and higher education, Blacks in higher and postsecondary education, and student affairs administration. She completed her doctoral studies in higher education administration at Ohio State University where she also worked as an academic counselor and coordinator of student athlete advising for the Undergraduate Student Academic Services Office. Dr.

Gaston earned a B.S. in adapted physical education from Shaw University and received a post-graduate scholarship from the National Collegiate Athletic Association (NCAA) for her talent in softball and superior academic performance as an undergraduate. She completed an M.S. in higher education at Auburn University. Dr. Gaston has received numerous awards and honors for her work and dedication to the field of education, including the Holmes Scholar Award, Providing Research Opportunities for Future Scholars (PROFS) Fellow, and first place in the 2002 graduate student research forum at Ohio State. In addition to her scholarly pursuits, Dr. Gaston serves her community through membership in Alpha Kappa Alpha Sorority, Inc.

CYNTHIA GERSTL-PEPIN is an Assistant Professor of Educational Studies and Educational Leadership at the University of Vermont. In her research she seeks to bridge the gap between theory and practice by exposing submerged social justice issues in education, examining the role of researchers in the process, and learning from practitioners, advocacy groups, and reformers engaged in the process of improving schools. She is currently working on a book about advocacy policy analysis and has published in such journals as *Educational Policy, Educational Foundations,* and the *International Journal of Qualitative Studies in Education.*

LISA D. HOBSON-HORTON is Assistant Professor of Science and Math Education in the Department of Curriculum and Instruction at Mississippi State University. She earned her doctorate from the University of Wisconsin—Madison with a major in educational administration and a minor in curriculum and instruction. As a doctoral student, she mentored education students, conducted educational seminars, supervised preservice teachers, and conducted research in the areas of educational careers, affirmative action, the principalship, and women in education. Dr. Horton has taught in the Jackson Public School District in Jackson, Mississippi, Verona Area School District in Fitchburg, Wisconsin, and Madison Metropolitan School District in Madison, Wisconsin. She has also held administrative internships in the Wisconsin districts. Dr. Horton has received grants for research at the K–12 and university levels on teacher recruitment and retention, mathematics, language arts, science, technology, and behavioral management. During the spring of 2002, she received a grant to study teacher attrition and retention in Mississippi. During the summer of 2000, she was awarded a grant from the Mississippi Institutions of Higher Learning to instruct secondary teachers on the integration of language arts and technology in the teaching of math. Recently she received a grant to provide professional development to teachers regarding science, math, engineering, and technology. Her current research interests include the retention and recruitment of K–12 teachers, women in educational leadership, technology usage in K–12 schools, and the recruitment and retention of students/faculty at the university.

KARRY LANE HATHAWAY is an Assistant Professor of English at Georgia Perimeter College, Assistant Chair of its Humanities Department, and a third-year Ph.D. candidate at Georgia State University in Atlanta, majoring in higher education with an emphasis in educational policy studies and a concentration in African American literature. Mr. Hathaway earned a B.A. and M.A. in English from the University of Georgia, in Athens. His research interests include Black male identity, Black male mentoring in institutions of higher education, and perceptions of Black male culture. He is also interested in research on race, class, and gender, and has done extensive studies and papers on race and gender in higher education.

ETTA RUTH HOLLINS, former Associate Dean and Professor of Teacher Education at Wright State University, joined the Rossier School in fall 2000 as Chair of its Teacher Education Program. The focus of her scholarship is preparing teachers for culturally diverse populations. She is the author of *Culture in School Learning* (Hillsdale, NJ: Lawrence Earlbaum, 1996), editor of *Transforming Curriculum for a Culturally Diverse Society* (Hillsdale, NJ: Lawrence Earlbaum, 1996), senior editor with Joyce E. King and Warren C. Hayman of *Teaching Diverse Populations* (Hillsdale, NJ: Lawrence Earlbaum, 1994), editor with Eileen Oliver of *Preparing Teachers for Cultural Diversity* (Hillsdale, NJ: Lawrence Earlbaum, 1999), and editor with Rosa Sheets, *Ethnic and Racial Identity in School Practices* (Hillsdale, NJ: Lawrence Earlbaum, 1999). She was the coprincipal investigator on a study of teacher development for literacy acquisition among African American children in collaboration with the Oakland Unified School District and California State University, Hayward. She recently served AERA as Vice President for Division G and as a member of the Executive Board; as a member of the Editorial Advisory Board for the American Educational Research Journal; and on the Early Career Awards Committee.

ROBIN HUGHES is an Assistant Professor in the Department of Educational Leadership and Higher Education at Oklahoma State University. She holds a B.A. in chemistry from the University of North Texas, and an M.S. in educational administration and Ph.D., both from Texas A&M University. Her research focus, in general, is the critical examination of the everyday struggles over difference and inequality for students and faculty of color, particularly the retention and recruitment of African American students (especially men), and their experiences, development, and perceptions of the campus climate. She has recently completed *The African American: College Student Experience: How Students of Color Choose College,* a three-year ethnographic research project exploring how African American students choose a college and their experiences during their student years. To date, most of her research on faculty of color has been autoethnographical. At UTEP, she teaches courses in qualitative research methodologies, student affairs, and higher education.

SHERICK HUGHES is an assistant professor of Educational Theory and Social Foundations in the School of Education at the University of Toledo in Ohio. His work explores the relationships between home, community, and school cultures and studies the construction of educational struggle and hope during the aftermath of *Brown* as southern schools and universities move from desegregation to re-segregation. He also investigates messages about the post-*Brown* trials and triumphs of students and educational hope, because he views those messages as opening navigable avenues toward positive change in Black student outcomes. He earned his B.A. from the University of North Carolina—Wilmington, his M.A. from Wake Forest University, and his MPA from UNC—Chapel Hill. As a former research associate for the North Carolina Education Research Council (NCERC), Hughes was one of the authors of the first annual *NC Schools First in America 2010* report. This report introduced the elimination of the "minority achievement gap" as one key goal of the governor and the state (2000, p. 18). Hughes was also credited for contributing ideas and material used in drafts of the NCERC's *Eliminating the Black-White Achievement Gap* report. Among his recent publications are "The MSEN Pre-College Program: What Are the Costs and Benefits Based on Estimates of Its Impact on Black High School Graduates?" *High School Journal* (February–March 2002) and "Where Identity Meets Knowledge," co-authored with George Noblit and Beth Hatt-Echeverria, editors of *The Future of Educational Studies* (New York: Peter Lang, 2003).

Acknowledgments: "I wish to thank Tawannah Allen for helping to transform her field experiences with the African American women graduate student into interview data. Her patience and collaboration were invaluable in attaining a higher degree of authenticity as we translated the woman's narrative."

JERLANDO F. L. JACKSON is an Assistant Professor of Higher and Postsecondary Education in the Department of Educational Administration and Faculty Associate for the Wisconsin Center for the Advancement of Postsecondary Education at the University of Wisconsin—Madison. In addition, he serves as a Research Associate for the Center for the Study of Academic Leadership, which is developing and publishing a new generation of research on academic administrators. Dr. Jackson's central interest has been the study of administrative diversity, executive behavior, and the nexus between administrative work and student outcomes in higher and postsecondary education. Recent publications include studies of factors associated with the engagement, retention, and advancement for administrators of color and the nature of administrative work in higher and postsecondary education. He previously presented this paper at the annual conference of the American Educational Research Association, New Orleans, April 1–5, 2002.

LEE JONES is Associate Dean for Academic Affairs and Instruction and Associate Professor of Educational Leadership and Policy Studies, Florida State University, Tallahassee, where he is responsible for coordinating the college's Offices of Clinical Partnerships, Academic Services, Learning Resource Center, Curriculum Resource Center, Living Learning Center, and Student Access, Recruitment, and Retention. He also produces and hosts a TV talk show that reaches over a million viewers in Florida and southern Alabama and Georgia. He received his B.A. from Delaware State University in drama, speech, communication, and theater, his M.A. in higher education administration, a second M.A. in business and administration, and a Ph.D. in organizational development, all from The Ohio State University. He is the editor of *Making It on Broken Promises: African American Male Scholars Confront the Culture of Higher Education* (Sterling, VA: Stylus Publishing, 2002). His motto is: "The bottom line is results. Anything else is rhetoric."

GLORIA KERSEY-MATUSIAK is a registered nurse and nurse educator, an Associate Professor of Nursing at Holy Family College, and the college's first Coordinator for Diversity. She holds an MSN and a doctorate in psycho-educational processes and an advanced certificate in culturally competent human services from Temple University where she is also an adjunct faculty member in the Multicultural Training and Research Institute. During more than 25 years of clinical practice in ethnically diverse settings, Dr. Matusiak has developed a strong interest in multiculturalism and diversity. In addition to teaching pathophysiology and medical-surgical nursing courses, Dr Matusiak has developed and teaches classes in culture and health care for nurses and multicultural counseling for counseling psychology majors at Holy Family College. Among her recent publications is "An Action Plan for Nurses: Building Cultural Competency," *Nursing Spectrum,* *10*(7) (2001), 22–24, and has conducted numerous workshops and presentations for a variety of educational, health care, and business institutions.

KIMBERLY LENEASE KING completed her B.A. in sociology from Grinnell College, her M.S. in higher education administration from Indiana University—Bloomington, and her Ph.D. in history, philosophy, and policy studies from the same institution. She has held dissertation fellowships from Indiana University and Grinnell College. She is currently an Associate Professor in Educational Foundations, Leadership, and Technology in the College of Education at Auburn University, Auburn, Alabama. Her research interests focus on the impact of race, class, and gender on educational equity both in the United States and abroad. Her dissertation was "From Exclusion to Inclusion: A Case Study of Black South Africans at the University of Witwatersrand." She is coeditor of and a contributor to *Apartheid No More: Case Studies of Southern African Universities in the Process of Transformation* (Westport, CT: Greenwood Press, 2000), and coauthor of *Moving Beyond the Numbers: Implementing a Strategic Plan for Comprehensive Racial Inclusion* (working title), forthcoming from Greenwood Press. In addition, she has authored or coauthored a number of book chapters and articles on equity in education.

H. RICHARD MILNER IV is Assistant Professor in the Department of Teaching and Learning at Peabody College of Vanderbilt University. Dr. Milner began his career teaching high school English at Lower Richland High School and Keenan High School both in Columbia, South Carolina. He has also taught developmental English at Columbus State Community College in Columbus, Ohio. Dr. Milner earned his Ph.D. in curriculum foundations at Ohio State University. He had earlier earned an M.A. in educational policy and leadership from the same school and, from South Carolina State University, his B.A. in English (cum laude) and his M.A. in teaching in English education. Among other awards and recognitions, he received the South Carolina State University Outstanding Graduate Assistant Award (1996), the Alpha Phi Alpha Outstanding Service Award (1996), the Student Tribute to Education Professors Award and Scholarship (2000), the Ohio State Exceptional Teaching Recognition Award (2000), the Holmes Scholar Award (1999–2001), the Project PROFS Fellowship (1998–2001), the Ohio State Mentor Team Award (1999), the Ohio State College of Education Student Service Award (2001), the Ohio State College of Education Alumni Society Award and Scholarship (2001), and the New Salem Baptist Church Academic Award and Scholarship (2000–2001). His research interests concern teacher thinking, teacher reflection, and teacher self-efficacy beliefs in cultural contexts as well as multicultural education. Dr. Milner has presented his research at numerous local, national, and international conferences, including the American Educational Research Association, and the Lancaster, England, Graduate Student Symposium. His work has appeared or is forthcoming in *Teaching and Teacher Education; Race, Ethnicity and Education;* the *Journal of Curriculum and Supervision; Urban Education; Action in Teacher Education; Teachers and Teaching: Theory and Practice;* and the *Journal of Critical Inquiry into Curriculum and Instruction.* Dr. Milner's life's credo is: "But they that wait upon the Lord shall renew their strength; they shall mount up with wings as eagles; they shall run, and not be weary; and they shall walk, and not faint" (Isaiah 40:31).

JAMES E. OSLER II completed a baccalaureate in fine art from North Carolina Central University. Always interested in teaching and the methodology of instruction, he next pursued a master's degree in educational technology at his alma mater, then earned a doctorate in technology education in which he developed strategies to meet the needs of students in a variety of formats. Currently, he is coordinator of the Graduate Program in Educational Technology and an associate professor at North Carolina Central University, in Durham. His interests and pursuits include exhibiting his work as a fine artist, developing a graphic art company, developing a telecommunications company, interacting and advising students, personal training consultation, teaching, and writing poetry.

LISA RASHEED received a B.S. degree in communications from Berry College and an M.S. in social work from Clark Atlanta University. She is currently a fourth-year doctoral student at Georgia State University, Atlanta, pursuing a degree in educational policy studies with a concentration in higher education. Her research interests include African American women in higher education and issues of race, gender, and social equity. Commensurate with this agenda is her interest in social welfare and policy pertaining to the health and mental health of African Americans.

DIA SEKAYI has worked in education for the past 12 years. She began her career in education as a teacher of math, science, and Spanish to children from preschool through Grade 4 at Nile Valley Shule, an independent African-centered school in Buffalo, New York. Here her interest in culturally grounded teaching and learning had its beginnings. Dr. Sekayi spent five years on the faculty of Cleveland State University in the Department of Curriculum and Foundations before joining Howard University's School of Education. She holds a B.S. in business administration, and a master's and a Ph.D. in the sociology of education from the State University of New York at Buffalo.

CASSANDRA SLIGH DEWALT has a Ph.D. and M.Ed. in Rehabilitation Counseling and has held several positions in academia, other educational agencies, or counseling agencies, including: Assistant Professor, Assistant Coordinator of the National Accreditation on Teacher Education, Assistant Director of Internship, Distance Education Course Developer, and Distance Education Course Instructor. Dr. Sligh DeWalt has also been employed at ACT as an extern in the Minority Student Development Office, as a case management supervisor, and as a mental health counselor/social worker at a psychiatric hospital. She is certified in the North Carolina area as a Qualified Mental Health Professional and a Qualified Developmental Disabilities Professional. Dr. Sligh DeWalt's research concentrates on the value of mentoring in graduate programs, e.g., teacher education programs, counselor education programs, and elementary/secondary programs. Dr. Sligh DeWalt's dissertation, "Black and White Graduate and Professional Students' Perceptions of Mentoring in Higher Education," has generated other publications including an article on mentoring students in rehabilitation counseling, forthcoming in *Annals Journal*. She has written several grants in minority student issues and quality in teaching. Dr. Slight DeWalt also has published *My Soul Is Not Broken; I Am Stronger Than Ever.*

WILLIAM A. SMITH is an Assistant Professor at the University of Utah, Salt Lake City, in the Department of Education, Culture, and Society and the Ethnic Studies Program. He received his Ph.D. from the Educational Policy Studies Department at the University of Illinois at Urbana—Champaign in 1996. After teaching in the African American Studies Program and Sociology Department at Western Illinois University, he was awarded a two-year postdoctoral research fellowship at the Center for Urban Educational Research and Development at the University of Illinois at Chicago. With Philip G. Altbach and Kofi Lamotey, he edited a revised edition of *The Racial Crisis in American Higher Education: Continuing Challenges to the 21st Century,* rev. ed. (Albany: SUNY Press, 2002). Dr. Smith's current research focuses on interethnic relations, racial attitudes, racial identity, academic colonialism, affirmative action attitudes, and the impact of student diversity on university and college campuses. With Bryan Brayboy and Octavio Villalpando, he founded the Center for the Study of Race and Diversity in Higher Education at the University of Utah in 2002, and serves as its associate director.

MARK A. WILLIAMS is a recent graduate of the Physician-Scientist Training Program at the University of Cincinnati College of Medicine (UCCOM); he also earned his Ph.D. in pharmacology and cell biophysics at the University of Cincinnati, studying the regulation of neutrophil function in inflammation. He then obtained his medical doctorate and is currently training in otolaryngology—head and neck surgery at the UCCOM. He aspires to specialize in laryngology and professional voice disorders.

IVAN E. WATTS completed his B.A. in criminal justice from Ohio State University, an M.S. in policy studies from the State University of New York at Buffalo, and an Ed.D. in social foundations from the University of Cincinnati. He is currently an Assistant Professor in Educational Foundations, Leadership, and Technology, at Auburn University, Auburn, Alabama, where he teaches courses in philosophy, history, sociology, and cultural foundations of education. His research examines the impact of educational and school policies on student behavior in a context of structural and institutional violence, with particular attention to the hypothesis that institutional policies may create, enhance, and perpetuate school violence. An analysis of race, class, and gender is critical to this inquiry. He is coauthor of "Desegregation," in *Knowledge and Power in the Global Economy,* edited by David Gabbard (Mahwah, NJ: Lawrence Earlbaum, 2000), pp. 131–140; "Project NIA: Mentoring Students of Color," in *Examining the Organizational and Human Dimensions of Mentoring in Diverse Settings,* edited by Frances K. Kochan (Greenwich, CT: Information Age Publishing, 2002); and "Diversity among Families," in *Home-School Relations: Working Successfully with Teachers and Parents,* edited by Mary Lou Fuller and Glenn W. Olsen (Boston, MA: Allyn & Bacon, 2003), pp. 44–70.

LEMUEL W. WATSON is Full Professor and Chair in the department of Counseling, Adult and Higher Education at Northern Illinois University, a native of South Carolina, with a B.S. in business from the University of South Carolina, an M.A. from Ball State University, and his doctorate of education from Indiana University. He is a certified training consultant and certified systems engineer. His career spans various divisions in higher education, both as faculty and as an administrator, and his institutional experience is equally broad, including both two-year and four-year institutions, both public and private. His research agenda focuses on educational outcomes; faculty development; and social and political issues that affect schools, community, and families with regards to advancement in a capitalist society. He has recently been asked to conduct research on the South Carolina Reading Recovery program outcomes. He is also Senior Research Fellow for the Charles Hamilton Houston Center at Clemson University and a Research Fellow for the Institute of Southern Studies at the University of South Carolina. He is the author, editor, and coeditor of many articles and books.

INDEX

Questions about the
Purpose(s) of Colleges
and Universities

Norm Denzin,
Joe L. Kincheloe,
Shirley R. Steinberg
General Editors

What are the purposes of higher education? When undergraduates "declare their majors," they agree to enter into a world defined by the parameters of a particular academic discourse—a discipline. But who decides those parameters? How do they come about? What are the discussions and proposed outcomes of disciplined inquiry? What should an undergraduate know to be considered educated in a discipline? How does the disciplinary knowledge base inform its pedagogy? Why are there different disciplines? When has a discipline "run its course"? Where do new disciplines come from? Where do old ones go? How does a discipline produce its knowledge? What are the meanings and purposes of disciplinary research and teaching? What are the key questions of disciplined inquiry? What questions are taboo within a discipline? What can the disciplines learn from one another? What might they not want to learn and why?

Once we begin asking these kinds of questions, positionality becomes a key issue. One reason why there aren't many books on the meaning and purpose of higher education is that once such questions are opened for discussion, one's subjectivity becomes an issue with respect to the presumed objective stances of Western higher education. Academics don't have positions because positions are "biased," "subjective," "slanted," and therefore somehow invalid. So the first thing to do is to provide a sense—however broad and general—of what kinds of positionalities will inform the books and chapters on the above questions. Certainly the questions themselves, and any others we might ask, are already suggesting a particular "bent," but as the series takes shape, the authors we engage will no doubt have positions on these questions.

From the stance of interdisciplinary, multidisciplinary, or transdisciplinary practitioners, will the chapters and books we solicit solidify disciplinary discourses, or liquefy them? Depending on who is asked, interdisciplinary inquiry is either a polite collaboration among scholars firmly situated in their own particular discourses, or it is a blurring of the restrictive parameters that define the very notion of disciplinary discourse. So will the series have a stance on the meaning and purpose of interdisciplinary inquiry and teaching? This can possibly be finessed by attracting thinkers from disciplines that are already multidisciplinary, for example, the various kinds of "studies" programs (women's, Islamic, American, cultural, etc.), or the hybrid disciplines like ethnomusicology (musicology, folklore, anthropology). But by including people from these fields (areas? disciplines?) in our series, we are already taking a stand on disciplined inquiry. A question on the comprehensive exam for the Columbia University Ethnomusicology Program was to defend ethnomusicology as a "field" or a "discipline." One's answer determined one's future, at least to the extent that the gatekeepers had a say in such matters. So, in the end, what we are proposing will no doubt involve political struggles.

For additional information about this series or for the submission of manuscripts, please contact Joe L. Kincheloe, 1 Sand Piper Drive, South Amboy, NJ 08879. To order other books in this series, please contact our Customer Service Department at: (800) 770-LANG (within the U.S.), (212) 647-7706 (outside the U.S.), (212) 647-7707 FAX, or browse online by series at: www.peterlangusa.com.